Other**Wise**

The Wisdom You Need to Succeed in a Diverse and Divisive World

Dick Martin

AMACOM

American Management Association

New York · Atlanta · Brussels · Chicago · Mexico City
San Francisco · Shanghai · Tokyo · Toronto · Washington, D.C.

Bulk discounts available. For details visit:
www.amacombooks.org/go/specialsales
Or contact special sales:
Phone: 800-250-5308
E-mail: specialsls@amanet.org
View all the AMACOM titles at: www.amacombooks.org

This publication is designed to provide accurate and authoritative information in regard to the subject matter covered. It is sold with the understanding that the publisher is not engaged in rendering legal, accounting, or other professional service. If legal advice or other expert assistance is required, the services of a competent professional person should be sought.

Library of Congress Cataloging-in-Publication Data

Martin, Dick, 1946–
    OtherWise : the wisdom you need to succeed in a diverse and divisive world / Dick Martin.
      p. cm.
    Includes bibliographical references and index.
    ISBN 978-0-8144-1752-2 (hbk.)
    1. Management--Social aspects. 2. Management--Cross-cultural studies. 3. Cultural pluralism. 4. Cultural relations. 5. Intercultural communication. 6. Diversity in the workplace. 7. Social responsibility of business. I. Title.
    HD30.19.M23 2012
    658.4'09--dc23

                                                2012005588

About AMA
American Management Association (www.amanet.org) is a world leader in talent development, advancing the skills of individuals to drive business success. Our mission is to support the goals of individuals and organizations through a complete range of products and services, including classroom and virtual seminars, webcasts, webinars, podcasts, conferences, corporate and government solutions, business books, and research. AMA's approach to improving performance combines experiential learning—learning through doing—with opportunities for ongoing professional growth at every step of one's career journey.

Printing number

10 9 8 7 6 5 4 3 2 1

In remembrance of
Marilyn Laurie
April 1939–July 2010

———

*Colleague, mentor,
friend, and inspiration.*

Contents

Introduction: How This Book
Came to Be   vii

1 Who Is "Other"?   1

Part One   Strangers at Home

2 Strangers Climbing in the Window   11

3 Strangers Making Themselves at Home   14

4 Bouillabaisse or Consommé?   19

5 A New America   26

6 It's the Culture, Stupid!   34

7 Race Matters   42

8 The Cost of Diversity   52

9 Queerness   61

10 Strangers with a Strange God   69

11 World Values   78

12 Gut Values   84

13 Second That Emotion   89

14 Feeling What Others Feel   92

Part Two   Strangers Abroad

15 Strange Places   101

16 Roots, Not Branches   107

17 Political Attunement   114

18   Management Across Borders   121

19   Organizational Culture   128

20   We Are What We Speak   133

21   Horizontal Empathy   141

22   Practical Empathy   146

Part Three   Strange Times

23   Me, Us, and Them   153

24   Sisyphus Had It Easy   161

25   Lost in a Loop   168

26   Voting with Your Feet   176

27   Free-Floating Anger   181

28   Mind the Gap   185

29   The Chicken Soup of Social Life   191

30   People Are Crazy   197

31   Fluent Listening   204

32   Presence   209

33   Congruence   212

Conclusion: How to Be OtherWise   217

Acknowledgments   223

Notes   227

Index   265

Introduction

How This Book Came to Be

This book explores a perennial, but increasingly consequential, mystery of business and personal life—how to relate to people unlike ourselves.

Indeed, these days, the gap between different groups sometimes seems to run so deep as to be unbridgeable, particularly on hot-button political, social, and cultural issues. At their most extreme, people facing off across the deepest chasms of difference think of those on the opposite side as "Other" with a capital O. Not just different, but inferior and dangerous. Even a little scary. This process of "other-izing"—seeing the world as camps of "us" and "them"—may be the defining issue of our time.

Originally, I was supposed to have a copilot in exploring that issue. My interest sprang from a speech that my friend Marilyn Laurie gave in 2006 when she received a lifetime achievement award. The achievement was in public relations and, for some reason, the award was named after Alexander Hamilton, who was a Founding Father, economist, lawyer, and political philosopher, but as far as I know, never did PR. In any case, by that point of her life, Marilyn was used to getting awards. As one of the cofounders of Earth Day when she was a stay-at-home mom in the late 1960s, and later as the first woman promoted into the most senior ranks of AT&T, she was used to being trotted out as a role model for smart young women who aspired to business careers.

I'm ashamed to admit that when I climbed the corporate ladder at AT&T, if you saw a woman on the rung above you, you were likely to think it was either because the company had a quota to fill or she had used her "feminine charms" to get ahead. Well, AT&T *was* under pressure to promote women at that time, and Marilyn was not without feminine charms, but few of us seriously thought any of that had much to do with her rapid rise in the company. She was so tough, so creative, and so hardworking it was obvious why she was getting ahead. Her story made it a little easier for other women. And it gave those of us with a Y chromosome a model to emulate, too.

Many of us walk around with pockets full of good intentions we never tap. Marilyn spent hers. She didn't let her bulging inbox define her; she thought more expansively about her role and responsibilities. Her acceptance speech for the Hamilton Award was a good example. She wasn't the main speaker on the agenda. She was allotted about five minutes for acceptance remarks. And she could have easily spoken off the cuff, said "thank you," and sat down to finish her dessert. One past award winner had literally phoned in his acceptance.

But that wasn't Marilyn. With a remarkable economy of words, she put the award in a historical context, referencing both Hamilton's time, when "the colonies struggled with new ideas about liberty, security, and nationhood," and our own, "when America the superpower is dealing with these same ideas—under the pressures of globalization." And then she teed up the challenge facing our political and business leaders at the dawn of a new century:

> As a result of our immense political, military, and economic power, we have inherited enormous responsibilities for global leadership. A tough challenge for exercising that leadership is to grow our capacity to deal with the "Other"—the immigrant at home, the stranger abroad.

I don't know about you, but I've become obsessed with the concern that if we don't educate ourselves in a hurry about the rest of the world—and understand how they see issues that are critical to us—we will keep stumbling into the kind of messes that our self-centered attitudes got us into the last few years.

Maybe you can sit in some countries and be totally absorbed in your own concerns, your own culture, your religion, your clan. Not in America. Not anymore.

It wasn't all high-altitude philosophy. Marilyn ended by suggesting that the times call for a new approach to the management function for which she was being recognized. "When we talk about what we do in PR," she said, "the focus is usually on advocacy." But maybe it's time, she suggested, to put more emphasis on "the other side of what we do—the listening and analysis that helps put decisions into a sound context." Then she listed four specific things she had resolved to do, from reading more international media to contributing to organizations here and abroad that teach tolerance and conflict resolution to young people.

The fellow who organized the evening later told me he felt bad "for the guy who had to follow her." He meant the next speaker. But I had to smile because he had also described me, since I followed Marilyn as executive vice president of public relations and brand management at AT&T. She was indeed a tough act to follow. She was also a generous sounding board and an endless source of intellectual stimulation. After my AT&T career, when I started writing more or less full-time, I turned to her for help and advice.

In 2010, I told her that I had been mulling over her Hamilton speech ever since she gave it. I was fascinated by her belief that we need "to grow our capacity to deal with the 'Other'." But I thought that challenge encompassed even more than immigrants and global customers. The stranger at home and abroad was even more complex than she had suggested back in 2006, I said. And the threat of thoughtless and wholesale "otherizing" had grown. Globalization, media fragmentation, demographic change, political polarization, the rise of nongovernmental organizations, and the growth of online communities have created publics so unique that they constitute potential new "Others." They are first- and second-generation immigrants, acculturating to their new home and developing traditions from both cultures. They are nontraditional families born of continuing sexual and cultural revolutions. They are single-issue activists, passionate about rights they believe are being trampled or groups they consider ill served. They are customers, suppliers, and employees in far-off countries with their own histories, values, and customs. They are people of strong principle who disagree with the business community's values and question its true motives.

Paradoxically, their influence has grown in step with their sense that they stand outside the mainstream. They are foes of the status quo, and they are not passive observers of business. They are passionate advocates for their point of view. And they demand accountability. Companies have never been under greater third-party scrutiny. Businesses have no choice but to deal with these new publics, not only because they threaten a company's operating flexibility, but also because they represent a new opportunity. The companies that learn how to engage them productively will gain a competitive edge in developing new markets and creating products tailored to the needs of these new publics. Conversely, those companies that act on the comfortable assumption that everyone sees the world as they do are headed for disaster.

"There's a book in all this," I told Marilyn. "And I'd like you to help me write it."

At about this point, I paused for breath, and a long silence followed. Then Marilyn said, "I seem to have had a greater influence on you than I thought."

Talk about understatement.

We agreed to talk further about the project, and I made a mental note to spend more time on receive than transmit in our next meeting. Sadly, there would be no next meeting. Marilyn passed away less than three weeks later, succumbing to a brain tumor that had been diagnosed just months before.

So this book has a single author, who is solely responsible for its flaws. But its inspiration was a self-described "little Jewish girl from the Bronx" who climbed to the highest levels of American business, but never lost her sense of what it is like to be "Other." She admitted to that in one of our last conversations.

This supremely self-confident, almost cocky, trailblazer wasn't sure she could explain the secret to her success. Like many who "make it," her success was partly the chance meeting of talent and circumstance. Focus and hard work certainly contributed, even though the cost was less time and energy for the family she loved. And despite whatever personal doubts she might have harbored, she appeared resolutely fearless. A former CEO of AT&T once recommended her for a job no one else would touch, saying, "Give it to Marilyn. She's not afraid of anything."

More fundamentally, I think the secret to Marilyn's success was her ability to see things from the other guy's perspective. I used to call it "orthogonal thinking." She came at problems from unexpected angles. But then I realized that the angles were unexpected only to those of us who were trapped in conventional corporate thinking. Marilyn looked at every issue from a stranger's perspective. The ultimate insider still knew what it felt like to be an outsider. Ironically, that feeling didn't come from frequently being the only woman in the room as she progressed in her career. I always found it curious that, on balance, Marilyn considered her gender an advantage rather than an obstacle in her advancement. "I think maybe I was always able to speak my mind without fear, and with less repercussion, because I was less threatening as a woman, and it was clear that I was not competing for the topline-job," she told me once.

That doesn't mean she ever felt like "one of the boys."

"Looking back, there were negative effects. I see them now," she told me long after she had left the company. "I had a very collegial, and friendly, and warm relationship with many, many of the guys. But I was never invited into their social circles or homes. Guys never invited me out to lunch, you know, one on one.

"And it was many, many years before I realized that it was sort of unnatural that I didn't have the same kind of social relationships," she said. "I came to attribute that to the fact that men didn't want to be seen eating at a restaurant alone with a woman from work. I think they were nervous about it when they were married. I think they were nervous about it if they *weren't* married."

But Marilyn's gender isn't what made her feel like an outsider. What *did* was more a matter of geography and values. Although when we worked for the company, AT&T's headquarters had been in New York for more than a century, it was as Midwestern as a cornfield. Most of the company's senior executives—and all of its recent CEOs—went to school, married, raised their kids, and spent much of their careers in the big square states in the middle of the country.

Marilyn was born, bred, and educated in New York City. She spoke with its flat accents and directness. "It always seemed to me that the values that I was constantly engaged with were the values of the heartland of our country, with me representing the bicoastal values," she said. "I was Jewish and liberal in a company that was essentially Republican and conservative."

I can attest, from personal observation, that that mix made for stimulating discussions in business meetings, as well as in the executive dining room. It also gave Marilyn carte blanche to bring outside perspectives into the company's deliberations. In many ways, she was our peripheral vision. In fact, she saw it as her role to give the company's employees, customers, and the communities where it operated a voice in the boardroom.

In a world that rightly values experience and education, Marilyn Laurie had a unique kind of wisdom—she was OtherWise.

1

Who Is "Other"?

When our primordial ancestors dropped from the trees and started walking across the African savanna on two legs, survival favored those with an innate ability to work in small groups, as well as a deep hostility toward anyone not of the group. That had the double-barreled benefit of making it easier both to acquire resources and to keep them. Those characteristics were so critical that, over a number of generations, they became the norm. And they survive to this day.

We may be born into a world of blooming, buzzing confusion, as William James thought, but we start sorting it out almost as soon as we let loose our first cry. Our brains are not blank slates, but learning engines that follow patterns set into our Stone Age ancestors' brains even before they acquired the faculty of language. These same attitudes and behaviors have been bred into us by natural selection.

Mounting evidence suggests that we are born with a rudimentary sense of fairness and injustice, right and wrong. By one year of age, babies show signs of prejudice, preferring people who speak a familiar language and accent. Eventually, they slowly develop what is called a "theory of mind," the realization that other people have beliefs, desires, intentions, and feelings separate from their own. In most circumstances, this capacity blossoms into empathy. Sometimes, it stagnates in suspicion. This book explores both ends of that spectrum and suggests that the ebbs and flows between them may be the defining characteristic of our age. Relating to people unlike ourselves has always been important; today it may be the most critical life and business skill we can develop.

At the most fundamental level, our sense of self emerges in relation to others. The first "others" in our lives, of course, are the most significant—our mothers, our fathers, our siblings. But our personal identity is also intertwined with close relationships beyond our immediate family. Our clan and our tribe have defined who we are since the day of our hunter-gatherer ancestors. Everyone outside that circle is a stranger, neither one of us, nor one with us.

We are by nature labeling machines, which is one of the secrets to our survival as a species. We categorize and label everything—animals, people, situations. And then we act as if those categories define reality. Of course, they don't; almost everything we label could fit into more than one category. But in daily life, unless motivated to behave differently, we narrowly pigeonhole things willy-nilly because it's easier than analyzing and weighing their actual characteristics, similarities, and differences. That's especially true in our dealings with other people, who are orders of magnitude more complex than inanimate objects.

Purpose

Categorical thinking may have helped our prehistoric ancestors traverse the African savanna safely when anyone outside their tribe was a potential enemy, but in the second decade of the twenty-first century, it is a shortsighted and dangerous practice. Thanks to the digital revolution and everything caught in its slipstream, the world is smaller, communications more insistent, privacy less certain, and community less personal. There are more people on the fringes of our standard categories than ever before. Our sense of personal identity and security, which we have always interpreted in reference to others, feels threatened. The real threat, though, may lie in our inability—or unwillingness—to control what social scientists call "irrelevant category activations." In other words, we have to close down some of those pigeonholes.

At first, these issues may be seem to reside, at best, on the margins of a businessperson's ambit—something worthy of an hour on the agenda of an executive retreat, or perhaps a paragraph or two in a speech to the local Rotary. But acquiring the wisdom of dealing with people unlike ourselves is not touchy-feely stuff; it's a hardcore operational capability, essential in relating to people, markets, and all the third-party activists who have an increasingly influential voice in how and where a company does business.

The world's demography is changing more rapidly than ever. The population of developed countries is aging; the developing world and emerging markets have given birth to a new middle class; wealth is moving from the Northern Hemisphere to the Southern, from the West to the East. The United States itself is fast becoming a minority-majority, multiracial, multicultural, multigenerational society. Non-Hispanic white people accounted for less than 10 percent of America's population growth over the last decade. In fact, four states and dozens of the country's largest metropolitan areas—including the twenty-three counties that constitute the New York metro area—already have minority-majority populations. Businesspeople need to get wise to these changes; they need to acquire the wisdom of relating to people so unlike themselves that they appear to be wholly Other.

Who Is "Other"?

Not every stranger is Other with a capital O. The truly Other are people we consider so different from ourselves that we have trouble seeing beyond those differences to what we have in common. Even then, many of us consider ourselves quite accepting. For example, I never thought of myself as anything but an average, live-and-let-live, open-minded kind of guy. But as I delved deeper into the issue of diversity, I discovered that the depths of my ignorance about other ways of life were darker than I suspected. I was a lot less tolerant than I thought, and my presumed ability to relate to the Other was shaky at best. The tolerance on which I prided myself seemed inadequate and problematic. I had a lot to learn. And as it turns out, it had less to do with the behavior of others than with my own inner workings—the unconscious patterns of thought and feeling that cause us to see the world in terms of "us" and "them."

I have not tried to cover all the instances of "otherness" in American society. As we will see, the possibilities are virtually limitless since one's status as Other is largely in the mind of the observer. The most obvious case is that of women. Western society is moving with gathering speed away from the dark days when women were relegated to a separate existence unless their services were required. While female carpenters and firefighters are still a relative novelty, gender is no longer an occupational straitjacket. Indeed, while the United States lags behind other countries in the number of women elected to public office, about half of professional and management positions in U.S. companies are held by women. In fact, there are so many women in some lines of work—public relations, accounting, and the law, for example—that their male colleagues are actually worried about the feminization of their professions. It's not that women can't do the work—it's that their participation tends to devalue it. Women still make only about 75 percent as much as men doing the same job.

And too many women still run into the quiet bigotry of daily life, whether at the bank applying for a credit card or at the local gas station trying to get their car repaired. So there is still much to be said— and done—about continuing gender bias in our society.

But in terms of gender bias, there seems to be a more significant Other. But if biology is no longer destiny for American women, the dominant culture still excludes people—male and female—who have adopted a gender identity seemingly inconsistent with their sexual organs.

Something similar might be said of anti-Semitism, which has had a long and miserable history going back millennia. Only a fool would pretend that it no longer exists, but by the same token, in many parts of the Western world these days, Muslims are even more feared, shunned, and excluded than Jews. Even in America, many Muslims experience a form of toxic religious and cultural prejudice that was once reserved for Jews and Catholics. And while Islamophobia will hopefully never rise to the level of the state-ordered genocide of the Holocaust, in terms of religious otherizing, Muslims seem to be the more critical contemporary case.

Many people live outside the mainstream of American society and are clearly the subject of otherizing—Native Americans, the elderly, the disabled, fat people, mentally challenged people, militant atheists, and little people, to name just a few. My use of "Other" in the singular is intended to encompass all these "others." And while I don't treat them separately, the same principles apply.

Most important, my use of "Other" is not a concession that some people are unknowable and flawed in some way. On the contrary, it is to signal that too many of us are so blinded by our differences that we can't see our commonalities. If anything, we all need to become much wiser in the ways and whys of others.

Furthermore, my use of "Other" with a capital O is intended to communicate an ethical difference between *excluders* and the *excluded*. Usually, when we speak of others having a disagreement, we withhold judgment about which party is right. At least initially, we keep an open mind and give both parties moral parity. Well, when I refer to people as "Other," I *am* making a judgment—I am saying that they are being excluded through no fault of their own, not because of anything they did, but simply because of who they are. The Other in this book is not some Rousseauian "noble savage" in an exotic foreign land or in a dim, idealized past, but people on the fringes of our daily existence. They occasionally pass through our field of vision and may even play a limited role of some sort in our lives. They are near, but we don't think of them as one of us.

Ironically, everyone has the potential to be someone else's Other. African Americans have a long history of being otherized in this country, yet in the 1990s some African Americans did the same thing to Korean grocers who opened shops in their neighborhoods. Some Hispanics of predominantly European ancestry look down on those of mixed African and indigenous descent. And the forebears of many white Americans of European ancestry were once Other to a people long gone. Only now, as they have been assimilated, those memories are faint. Part of this book's purpose is to rekindle those memories and to press them into the service of becoming OtherWise—not in response to a "Can't we all just get along?" question born of race riots, and not under some disaster-driven "We Are the World" anthem. But as a practical response to opportunities lost.

As the psychologist Stanley Krippner has said, "Humanity is entangled. As long as there are strangers or subjugated people, we are depriving all of humanity of a source of strength, wisdom, intelligence, and creativity." As businesspeople and as citizens, we cannot afford to squander those gifts.

Roadmap

This book is not a twelve-step guide on dealing with people who seem "different." There are such guides, of course, each tailored to the specific characteristics of the group in question, whether a stranger at home or abroad, or just strange. There is some practical advice here, but in terms of twelve-step programs, this book largely resides at step zero, the foundation on which all the others rest, namely understanding the issue, its importance, and its implications. We'll be tramping through a lot of cognitive and social science here, but it really all boils down to one idea: Feeling is a way of knowing that has a profound effect on our perceptions and behavior. The Latin words *homo sapiens* literally mean "wise man," but our species' wisdom isn't most manifest in the taming of fire or the use of tools. It is most obvious in our dealings with each other. Ironically, that's when our simian roots are also most apparent, especially in the way we relate to strangers.

Each of us lives in a unique world shaped by the stories we have heard and, even more powerfully, by the stories we tell ourselves. Yet, like all stories, ours suffer from distortions and misinterpretations. One of this book's goals is to lay out the grounds for reexamining some of the narratives we spin about ourselves and especially about people at the edges of our lives.

Part One deals with the strangers among us, whether their strangeness is based on their recent arrival and its circumstances, their ethnicity, or their religion. The color of their skin may set them apart, or the language they speak, or their customs. Or maybe it is something rooted in our most elemental beliefs concerning sexuality and creed. In any case, they make us profoundly uneasy. We see only their differences. They cease to be individuals, but a caste to be shunned or worse.

Part Two expands the discussion to include strangers who live elsewhere. Once, we only had to deal with them when traveling abroad, but now we are dependent on their resources; their goods crowd our store shelves; their voices respond to our customer service calls; their parochial concerns reverberate through our economy; and our future prosperity and security seem to be entangled with theirs. Some of us struggle against such entanglements; others pretend they don't exist.

Part Three surveys the strange times in which we live—an increasingly fragmented, polarized world, in which technology has the power to bind us into self-righteous tribes, divided against other tribes and blind to any but our own truth. Paradoxically, digital technologies that promised to bring us together by making the world smaller have made *us* smaller by allowing us to create our own private worlds. Religion, sex, and politics—the trinity of topics unfit for polite discussion—cast new fissures across the social media landscape.

Finally, we end with a brief consideration of what our response to these developments should be, not in the fashion of a step-by-step recipe, but as a change in perspective and attitude. As Mother Teresa once said, "The problem with the world is that we draw the circle of our family too small." Too many of us live in a world of strangers. But we don't have to be saints to connect with people who are different. We don't even need to be psychologists or sociologists. We simply have to understand the hidden forces that shape their behavior as well as our own. To be willing to see ourselves as others see us and to see a bit of ourselves in others.

Part **One**

Strangers
at Home

2

Strangers Climbing in the Window

In poetry and legend, America is a nation of immigrants, with a welcome mat stretching from ocean to ocean and border to border. But in our most candid moments, we'll admit to being just a little wary of the Other—people who speak a different language, eat strange food, and follow odd customs, or have a different sexual orientation, worship an unfamiliar god, deny the deity's existence, or in other ways don't conform to what we consider "the norm."

No one should be surprised. In evolutionary terms, *Homo sapiens* is a relatively recent species. The psychological adaptations that caused us to allow some strangers into our kin-based tribes about 100,000 years ago may have sparked the development of everything from language and gossip to abstract thought. But we also retain an instinctual suspicion of people who don't look like they could be our kin. Or who act or think differently. That's especially true when we feel vulnerable, as in an economic downturn or in times of rapid social change. In fact, in the summer of 2009, at the height of the Great Recession, more than half the people surveyed by the Pew Research Center said they thought the principal source of conflict in American society is not between rich and poor, blacks and whites, or young and old, but between immigrants and native-born citizens.

Ground zero for that conflict has to be Arizona, which considers itself in the bore of an immigration tsunami rolling in from Mexico. And what has had Arizonans particularly upset is the impression that they are being swamped by "illegals," Mexicans who hiked in through miles of mesquite scrub or came on a visitor visa and never left.

Ironically, there are more illegal immigrants in New Jersey, of all places, and they account for a higher percentage of the state's workforce. But one-third of Arizona's total population is Hispanic and, although eight out of ten of them were born in the United States, many people mistakenly assume that most of them are here illegally. Arizonans are left with the impression that they are under siege. A trip to Home Depot or Wal-Mart as far north as Flagstaff seems like a quick run to the Mexican side of the border because of all the Hispanic day laborers milling in the parking lot. Parts of Phoenix have so much Spanish-language signage, many residents joke they need to carry a Berlitz phrase book in the glove compartment. The news reports that "Beirut may be safer than Phoenix" and that the city has become the "kidnapping capital of America" have others vowing to put a loaded gun there.

State politicians jumped on the bandwagon of anti-immigrant feeling and fought for the reins. The result was a series of state laws that put anyone with a Hispanic surname or complexion in the crosshairs of the state's full law enforcement apparatus, from the state police to the local constabulary. The laws inspired boycotts and lawsuits that will ultimately be decided by the U.S. Supreme Court. Of particular interest to anyone who would be OtherWise are the driving motives behind these laws.

Proponents of Arizona's restrictive immigration laws maintain that "illegals" represent a drain on state budgets, steal jobs from people who are here legally, and contribute to increased crime. But the Congressional Budget Office reviewed twenty-five studies and concluded that, after taking into account the taxes and fees undocumented immigrants pay, "the net impact on state and local budgets is most likely modest." Furthermore, most economists believe that immigrant participation in the workforce actually *expands* demand for goods and services, creating new jobs. Low-skilled immigrants compete largely with earlier immigrants. In the end, their participation in the workforce keeps jobs from being outsourced overseas and leads to the addition of higher-paying management positions in the United States.

Finally, it is very difficult to get reliable data on crimes committed by undocumented immigrants because few, if any, jurisdictions record immigration status in arrest reports. We do know, however, that the rate of incarceration for immigrants is about one-fifth that of people born here. Recently arrived immigrants have the lowest arrest rates of all. In fact, despite the hysteria about drug-addled illegals climbing in every bedroom window, Arizona has enjoyed record low crime rates in recent years. According to the U.S. Department of Justice, at the peak of illegal immigration in 2007, violent crimes in Arizona had dropped to their lowest level since 1983. And in any case, illegal immigration itself has declined by more than 60 percent from that peak, partly because of the recession, and partly because of expanding educational and employment opportunities in Mexico.

Nevertheless, two-thirds of Americans approve of Arizona's tough immigration laws. Twenty-two states, including some as far from a U.S. border as Nebraska and Kansas, considered legislation that mirrored it. Alabama passed a state law in 2011 that, among other things, requires elementary schools to screen children for their immigration status. The state's governor proudly proclaimed it "the strongest immigration law in the country," In fact, seven out of ten Americans would like to limit the number of immigrants entering the country by *any* means, whether in the back of a beat-up van crossing the desert or in a jumbo jet at LAX. Talk about "illegals" may actually be politically correct cover for a feeling that *overall* immigration should be reduced or curtailed altogether. There's more than a little irony here: The strangers at our borders want to get in, and the descendants of former strangers want to keep them out. Understanding the first group is relatively easy. They aren't coming here for the climate; they want jobs and an opportunity to build a better life for their families. Figuring out what really motivates the second group is more difficult, but no less important.

3

Strangers Making Themselves at Home

Most people take it for granted that the suit or dress they buy at the local mall was probably designed in one country and sewn in a second, using fabric woven in a third from thread spun in a fourth. And if they happen to be shopping in a foreign country, they think nothing of paying for their purchases with a credit card issued by their hometown bank. They might even use an automatic teller machine to dip into their home checking account for walking-around cash in the local currency.

The movement of money across borders represents the first wave of globalization; the global movement of goods, the second. And, notwithstanding misgivings about job losses at home and the exploitation of workers in developing countries, most of the world's people have accepted both as the new normal. The third wave of globalization is having an even more significant impact on our lives. But unlike the global movement of money and goods, there are no international organizations like the World Bank or the World Trade Organization to guide its course. Every country is on its own in dealing with the tides and currents of this new wave. And many people are still adjusting to its implications.

The third wave of globalization is the movement of people across borders.

The United Nations estimates there were about 200 million international migrants in the world in 2010 (not counting about 15 million refugees). That number has been relatively stable as a percentage of the world's population over the last five years. If all those immigrants lived in the same place, it would be the world's fifth-largest country. About 70 million of these immigrants live in the countries of the European Union. The United States is the adopted home of the second largest number—39.9 million in 2010, according to a Pew Research Center analysis of U.S. Census Bureau data. That's about 12.5 percent of the U.S. population, up from about 5 percent in 1960, when immigration was at historic lows.

The foreign-born populations of other countries reflect the same shift. According to the *OECD Factbook 2010*, Belgium, Spain, and Sweden all have essentially the same proportion of foreign-born populations as the United States. Germany, the Netherlands, and the United Kingdom are not far behind. Australia, Canada, Austria, Ireland, New Zealand, and Switzerland are home to even higher shares of foreign-born people. From Auckland to Antwerp and Atlanta, the public reaction to the rising tide of immigrants ranges from concern to alarm. According to Pew Research, large majorities in nearly every country—including the United States—want greater restriction of immigration and tighter control of their country's borders.

The global recession undoubtedly magnified people's personal financial concerns, but that doesn't seem to be the primary reason people want to pull up the gangplank before more immigrants get on it. Professor Joel Fetzer of Pepperdine University has analyzed survey data going back to the end of the nineteenth century in the United States, France, and Germany. Despite significant differences in the three countries' respective cultures, histories, and immigration patterns, Fetzer discovered that hostility toward immigrants is based not so much on economic factors, such as competition for jobs, but on fear that admitting large numbers of foreigners threatens a country's traditional customs and values.

More than twenty years ago, U.K. Prime Minister Margaret
Thatcher proposed ending immigration entirely to avoid "being swamped
by people of a different culture." In the years since, the countries of
Western Europe seem to have discovered unity in a common hostility
to immigrants. Political candidates campaign on anti-immigration plat-
forms—and get elected in growing numbers. Legislatures ban symbols
of "foreign" cultures, such as headscarves, burqas, and even minarets.
But for real irony one need look no further than the country that had
invited the world's hungry, homeless, and poor to its door.

Americans have been wary of newcomers since Revolutionary
days. Theoretically, America's ever-expanding borders were initially
wide open; in practice, most of the people coming here in the earliest
days were from the same European stock as the Founding Fathers.
America's history from the eighteenth century through the first half
of the twentieth is full of state action that, in the kindest interpretation, displayed overt wariness of immigrants. For example, Congress
passed laws to exclude certain people (such as Asians), to limit others (such as Jews, Italians, and Slavs), and to send some (such as
Mexicans) back where they came from. Black people were subject to
dehumanizing segregation in much of the country for a hundred years
after gaining their freedom, and even in the supposedly integrated
north, they were only slowly and partially assimilated into mainstream society. Through most of the twentieth century, immigration
from Western, Southern, and Eastern Europe was subject to quotas
that ensured the country would keep the same ethnic profile it had
in the nineteenth.

American culture evolved in its first three centuries. We added
pizza to our diets, French cuffs to our shirts, and polkas to our dance
music. And a people who didn't even come here under their own
steam made some of the most significant, enduring contributions to
American culture. Nearly every branch of American music owes a
deep debt to the rhythmic and harmonic contributions of African-
American jazz, blues, gospel, and most recently, rap.

But none of this fundamentally changed the character of the
American population, which remained in numerical terms largely
white, Anglo-Saxon, and Protestant. That didn't begin to happen until

Congress passed a new immigration law in 1965. President Lyndon Johnson traveled from the White House to Liberty Island in New York Harbor so that he could sign the Immigration and Nationality Act of 1965 at the foot of the Statue of Liberty.

That single law probably did more to transform American life than any other legislation in an era known for social change—even more than the Voting Rights Act and the bill establishing Medicare. Within a decade, the number of immigrants entering the United States every year reached levels not seen since the beginning of the twentieth century and, by the 1990s, it even surpassed the peak of immigration in the mid-nineteenth century. The benefits of this immigration boom were equally stunning. Immigrants have founded more than half of the Silicon Valley start-ups since 1995, including such successful high-tech companies as Google, Intel, Yahoo, and eBay. In fact, more than 40 percent of Fortune 500 companies were founded by immigrants or their children. More than two-thirds of U.S. scientists and engineers with a doctorate are immigrants. In fact, immigrant inventors accounted for more than a quarter of all U.S. patent applications in recent years, filing at a rate twice that of native-born Americans. The products and services they invented changed our lives, created new jobs, and turbo-charged our economy.

But eliminating immigration quotas had another effect. It literally changed the complexion of the country, altering the demographic course America had been on for nearly 300 years. In 1960, 85 percent of the U.S. foreign-born population came from Europe or Canada; by 2007, 80 percent were from Latin America or Asia. When the 1965 Act was passed, only about 15 percent of the U.S. population was Asian, Hispanic, or black; today, more than one-third are. And Americans of those backgrounds will almost certainly be in the majority by 2042.

That's precisely what bothers a lot of people. Some groups are openly racist, warning that what is at stake is "the ethnic cleansing of the founding European people" through "competitive breeding." They blame immigrants for everything from poverty and urban blight to crime and environmental ruin—not to mention an alleged Mexican plot to annex the American Southwest. Immigrants have been blamed for all sorts of social ills since the founding of the republic, but when a cable news anchor implores his viewers to "make more babies" because "half of the kids in this country under five years old are minorities," one has to wonder if the country's complexion isn't what's really bothering him. Of course, most people opposed to unbridled immigration are not racists. They are not concerned about the dilution of the country's racial pool or the loss of territory to our southern neighbor. They honestly worry that American "culture" and "values" will be watered down—or maybe even replaced.

For much of its history, the dominant American culture almost always seemed to win out in the pull and tug with immigrants over manners, customs, and even language. America was described as the great "melting pot," where immigrants happily shed their cultural differences and blended into the majority's lifestyle. It might take two or three generations, but assimilation was believed to be certain and irreversible. We now know that was a gross oversimplification and a misreading of history. Ironically, it was the son of immigrants, a proudly Irish pol—Senator Daniel Patrick Moynihan—who helped blow up the venerable myth of America as the great melting pot.

4

Bouillabaisse or Consommé?

The most celebrated tourist to ever visit America was probably a young French aristocrat, Alexis de Tocqueville, who came here in 1831 ostensibly to study America's prisons.

What resulted was not only a report on penology but *Democracy in America,* a well-received book that explored what Tocqueville called "American exceptionalism."

Tocqueville was struck that the American idea of "nationality" was different from Europe's. It was based less on common history or ethnicity than on common ideals. And those ideals were fairly unique for the time: Americans were distrustful of public authority, self-reliant, inclusive, egalitarian, and democratic. The other belief that Americans shared was the lively expectation that they could somehow make their lives better if they only worked hard enough.

Sociologist Peter Salins suggests that this "American Idea" constituted the core terms of a relatively straightforward social contract with new arrivals. As long as immigrants learned English, identified with their new homeland, and accepted what Salins calls the "American Idea" of equality, opportunity, individualism, and hard work, they were welcome to bring as much cultural baggage with them as they liked. "Time and again," he writes, "Americans learned to accept, socialize with, and eventually marry their immigrant neighbors because the American Idea made it the natural thing to do." Immigrants who bought into the contract were eventually assimilated into mainstream American culture. It might take a couple of generations, but all those foreigners would eventually learn English, largely abandon the ways of the old country, and become just like the Northern European offspring around them. That was the "melting pot" theory—America was a blended consommé of every nationality.

It might be a vivid metaphor, but Daniel Patrick Moynihan, observing the street life outside his New York City apartment, became convinced that the melting pot didn't hold water. Passing from one Manhattan neighborhood to another in the 1960s was like international travel. A single subway line could take you from Yorkville's mini-Germany on the Upper East Side to downtown's Little Italy, Chinatown, and something closely approximating Tel Aviv. Transfer to another line and the sights and sounds of Puerto Rico would surround you. Walk a few blocks, and you could wander into an Irish pub, as authentic as anything in Dublin. Blacks had their own neighborhood, too—a sprawl of tenements in the northern reaches of Manhattan above Central Park and between the Hudson and East Rivers.

Moynihan was a Harvard-pedigreed sociologist who spent much of his time in the Kennedy and Johnson administrations trying to figure out why African Americans were still struggling to integrate into mainstream society 100 years after the end of slavery. When his friend Nathan Glazer suggested they compile and expand a series of articles he had written about New York City's ethnic groups into a book, Moynihan saw an opportunity to turn over a few academic apple carts. Glazer did most of the heavy lifting; Moynihan wrote one chapter (on the Irish, naturally) and much of the conclusion. But they shared authorship for what became one of the most influential books of the 1960s, *Beyond the Melting Pot*.

A decades-old metaphor doesn't unravel easily, but twenty years after publication of *Beyond the Melting Pot*, Moynihan could tell the *New York Times*, "Empirical evidence has come along that proves us right. In the 1980 national census, for the first time they asked people what ancestral group they came from. Eighty-three percent of persons interviewed identified with at least one ancestor group. Only 6 percent claimed their ancestry was American. People in Tennessee still think of themselves as English, Irish, or Scottish, and they've been in those hills for centuries." What replaced the melting pot model of assimilation, he thought, was "multiculturalism," the idea that, in America, multiple ethnic communities live side-by-side, celebrating their heritage and choosing how deeply they would assimilate into mainstream culture, if at all.

Moynihan and Glazer saw this happening not only in New York City, but also in every other major city. The 1965 Immigration Act helped it along by bringing even more non-Europeans into the country. And each successive group established its own beachhead in one or another corner of the nation. Furthermore, the publication of *Beyond the Melting Pot* coincided with the heightened racial awareness of the civil rights movement. Black Americans were reconnecting with their African heritage, where they found a new level of validation and, in the process, appeared to confirm Moynihan and Glazer's thesis.

But then in 1993, Glazer began to have second thoughts about their book's premise. He wrote an essay for a scholarly publication in which he asked, "Is assimilation dead?" The answer, he concluded, was no, not by a long shot, despite what he and Moynihan had predicted nearly three decades earlier. Assimilation was real, but a number of social roadblocks—such as racial discrimination—made its progress uneven. It wasn't so much that immigrants didn't *want* to assimilate; the big problem was that some in the majority population threw obstacles in their path. The situation of blacks in America was an especially difficult case, owing to "the fundamental refusal of other Americans to accept blacks, despite their eagerness, as suitable candidates for assimilation." No wonder blacks were the most insistent of all ethnic groups on multicultural school programs. They separated themselves from mainstream society out of sheer frustration.

Glazer, who was age 73 at the time, may have been working from limited field data in suggesting that African Americans were ardent multicultural separatists. The sociologist Alan Wolfe interviewed dozens of black middle-class parents for his book *One Nation, After All* and found that few of them wanted their kids to be exposed to the kind of ethnocentrism that would put them in a parallel society; most thought that spending "five minutes on everyone," and encouraging a form of multicultural education that gave everyone a turn, was sufficient.

At about the same time, two other sociologists came out with a new, more nuanced theory that reflected the complexity of American society and the diversity of its immigrant populations. Alejandro Portes and Min Zhou suggested that assimilation is not an inexorable force that moves uniformly in only one direction. Nor does it occur in a vacuum. Portes and Zhou suggested that immigrants integrate at different rates, depending on such factors as their ability to speak English, educational levels, economic resources, support from family and friends, and how different the host society's culture is from what they are used to. For example, a German would probably find American culture more familiar than someone from Bangladesh would. And immigrants whose poverty forces them to live in substandard housing and to send their children to underperforming schools are obviously not going to assimilate into middle-class American society as easily as well-educated, English-speaking professionals from Asia. In fact, children of heavily disadvantaged immigrants sometimes reject their new homeland altogether.

The election of a black president did not eliminate race as an impediment to assimilation in America. The physical differences of Asian, black, mulatto, and mestizo immigrants still represent a barrier to upward mobility and social acceptance. They can't simply blend into the majority population. And many of them don't feel it is necessary. For example, unlike earlier generations, few of today's immigrants change their name to facilitate assimilation. Bernard Schwartz changed his name to Tony Curtis, and few people knew he was Jewish. But Yo-Yo Ma, by any other name, would still be Asian. Furthermore, inexpensive air travel and easy international communications allow immigrants to have much closer ties to their home countries than they might have had in the past. Finally, recent immigrants have come in such large numbers that they can get along just fine in relatively self-sufficient communities. For example, both the Hispanic and Asian communities have easy access to an even broader choice of

American and foreign-based in-language media than previous immigrant groups.

Nevertheless, many sociologists believe that eventually all these new immigrant groups will fully assimilate just as previous groups have. "We're basically a Northern European, Protestant culture," sociologist Claude Fischer told me, "and I haven't seen anything that will change that in the long run." He has a point. Adding pizza to our diets isn't quite as consequential as adopting the Italian form of government or social mores. And many fourth- or fifth-generation Italian-American families are just as likely to count Irish, German, or even Asian hyphenates within them. So maybe this new, "segmented" model of assimilation, in which immigrants retain some elements of their home culture, really is a "light form of multiculturalism," as Fischer terms it.

Indeed, although America's racial and ethnic mix is radically changing, the increasing rate of interracial and interethnic marriage suggests an eventual homogenization of our genetic pool. Eight out of ten Americans have no problem with whites and blacks dating each other, which is nearly twice the rate of approval in 1987. In fact, more than a third of adults (35 percent) say that they already have a family member who is married to someone of a different race. About 15 percent of new marriages in 2010 were between Hispanics and non-Hispanics or between people of different races—more than double the rate in 1980. As a result, people of multiracial or multiethnic backgrounds are one of the fastest-growing demographic groups in the United States. Some 9 million people, about 3 percent of the population, said they were multiracial on the 2010 census, an increase of about a third since 2000.

America's mainstream culture is not static, either. It is constantly incorporating elements from the cultures of its newest arrivals, as well as from those who have not yet fully assimilated themselves. So rap music influences mainstream media, and Asian foods show up in *nouveau* American cuisine. We may not be changing our fundamental political values and social mores, but the majority culture into which second- or third-generation immigrants assimilate is very different from the one in which their parents or grandparents lived.

And when the third of the U.S. population that is black, Asian, or Hispanic accounts for almost all of the country's growth, it is not all that clear how much longer America will remain basically "Northern European, Protestant." America is no longer a consommé of cultures, but kind of a stew—lumpy at times, but always flavorful.

Such cultural exchanges have enriched the American experience, but they also irritate or even scare many people. In fact, according to the Pew Research Center, about two-thirds of Americans believe that their "way of life needs to be protected against foreign influence." Having to punch a button to continue listening to a telephone recording in English suggests to many that the country's very language is under attack. In reality, though, immigrants are learning English at an even faster rate today than 100 years ago. According to census data, there were four and a half times more non-English speakers in the country in 1890 than in 1990. Nine out of ten Asian and Hispanic Americans have at least "some facility" in English; seven out of ten speak it "well" or "very well." There's a difference between not speaking English and being bilingual, which accurately describes many recent immigrants. The increasing number of non-English-speaking immigrants may require short-term accommodations, such as language training and bilingual signage, but it does not portend the demise of English as the nation's unofficial language. On the contrary, it could make the typical American something we've never been before: bilingual.

The historic reality is that American culture has always been relatively porous. In the beginning, American culture reflected the values and the beliefs of the Anglo Americans who founded and ran the place. That made it essentially English and Protestant, with several ideals—like equality, free speech, individualism, and the separation of church and state—that sharply distinguished it from the "old country." American culture evolved with every new wave of immigrants, while staying true to those founding values. And that stands in sharp contrast to the European models, which, at best, gave immigrants a binary choice of total assimilation or wary coexistence.

The countries of Europe tapped their former colonies and trading partners for cheap labor to aid in postwar reconstruction. They didn't try to integrate those workers because they expected them to eventually go home. Instead, those workers stayed, and now their children and grandchildren have the same low-paying, often dirty, and difficult jobs they had with little prospect of improving their lot. They live in crowded enclaves, and while free to follow the cultural standards of their country of origin, they are less than full members of the mainstream society around them. So, if a Pakistani family in Brighton agreed to marry off an underage daughter to a wealthy widower, the state would look the other way. But her brother, who is put down as a "Paki" and unable to get a decent job, might feel more allegiance to the local imam than to the country in which he lives.

Part of the problem, of course, is the difficulty of defining what it *means* to be French, German, or Italian when ethnicity is removed from the equation. British Prime Minister David Cameron suggests such a clear definition requires what he calls "muscular liberalism." "I believe a genuinely liberal country . . . believes in certain values and actively promotes them," Cameron told the Munich Security Conference in 2011. "It says to its citizens, this is what defines us as a society: To belong here is to believe in these things." True enough, but one of those "things" has to be a willingness to incorporate into the mainstream culture the best of immigrants' compatible values and traditions.

On that score, at least, the United States has a head start on the rest of the West. If anything, we should be celebrating that openness, not bemoaning it. The bottom line is that America can't *afford* to eliminate, or even dramatically limit, immigration. It is the primary driver of our population growth and the only source of the so-called prime age workforce of people ages 25 to 55.

The genius of America is that it has never really been a country in which different ethnic groups live side by side in varying degrees of harmony—although a snapshot at any one time may make it appear so. American culture is rooted in its own 'hoods and hamlets, as well as in the ethnic and religious customs immigrants brought with them. It is multicultural by history and design, Multicultural America is the product of give and take on both sides—one culture, one people from many. Just like it says on a dollar bill—*e pluribus unum.*

5

A New America

Back in the 1980s, Peter Francese used to find himself sighing a lot whenever he went on the road to promote *American Demographics,* the magazine he founded. Inevitably, he would find himself in the conference room of some big-shot chief marketing officer (CMO), trying to get him interested in the demographic changes that were going to radically change the world as he knew it. And Francese could hear his audience's brain slip into a daydreaming gear.

"He always seemed to be a guy in his early fifties, and the longer I talked to him, the more I realized that his only real skill was signing invoices," Francese remembers. "He was probably good at negotiating contracts, but he knew nothing about the marketplace." Undaunted, Francese would press on, throwing chart after chart on the screen showing how a tectonic shift in the market was about to upend the CMO's carefully laid plans. "Eventually," Francese says, "the guy would wave his hands and say, 'I get all I need to know from watching my friends and neighbors.' And that would be it."

Francese may have been slightly ahead of his time, but his magazine attracted the readership of 22,000 more enlightened marketing executives, before he sold it in 2004 to Crain Communications, which folded it into its flagship trade publication *Advertising Age.* Francese currently writes an occasional white paper for *Ad Age* and is the chief demographic analyst for the Ogilvy & Mather ad agency. It seems that the new crop of CMOs has a livelier interest in demographic change, which Francese can satisfy nicely from his node on the information superhighway in New Hampshire. Still, when Francese speaks to a large group of marketing and advertising people, he often conducts the same brief survey.

"How many of you think the majority of adults in the United States graduated from college?" he asks. Most of the hands in the audience go up.

"How many of you have parents who graduated from college?" Again, most of the hands go up, perhaps explaining the answer to the first question.

But the correct answer is that barely a third of the adult population in the United States graduated from college. "You're two generations away from working-class America," he tells the audience. "You don't have a clue how they live."

Francese told me, with a hint of frustration, that "most CMOs carry around this mythology of mainstream America as married couples with kids. They just don't get it. Married couples with kids are a niche market at best. They don't even represent one out of five households," he said. "Married couples *without* kids are another 28 percent. This is the first time in history that married couples account for less than half of American households." In fact, according to the National Survey of Family Growth, nearly half (42 percent) of children under thirteen years of age live with unmarried parents, more than the 24 percent who live with a divorced parent.

To Francese, all the averages are meaningless. "There is no more average," he says. "There's hardly a majority anymore." Indeed, the 2010 census showed that no racial or ethnic group—including non-Hispanic whites—represented a majority of the population in the country's ten largest cities. The United States is becoming a truly multiracial, multicultural society. Not just a society in which different races and ethnicities live side by side, but where the world's cultural heritages are blended with uniquely American traditions: literally a new people drawn from many.

America has also become a more multigenerational country, with the character of each generation molded by very different events. Consider the following:

■ The 80 million baby boomers, born between 1946 and 1964, came of age during the social change and controversy of the 1960s. Many of them protested the Vietnam War, marched for women's liberation, helped African Americans win greater civil rights, and were enthusiastic participants in the sexual revolution. Boomers are optimistic and ambitious. They invented the concepts of the "workaholic" and the "superwoman who can have it all."

■ The 70 million members of Generation X, born between 1965 and 1984, were raised in an era of two-income families, rising divorce rates, and a faltering economy. They saw the end of the Cold War and the fall of the Berlin Wall, but they also experienced runaway inflation, wage and price controls, gas lines, and the energy crisis of the 1970s. They are twice as well educated as the boomers, resourceful, and self-sufficient. Unlike their parents, they work to live rather than live to work.

■ The 100 million members of Generation Y, born between 1985 and 2010, constitute the first high-tech generation. They take personal computers, the Internet, and cell phones for granted. They are natural multitaskers and expect everything to happen quickly. The meritocracy and openness of the Internet has made them very impatient with hierarchy and information hoarding. Most of them lived through the dot.com, stock market, and housing booms, as well as the busts. They grew up adapting to innovation and change. They don't draw a sharp line between work and the rest of their life. They want to enjoy both.

In terms of buying power, for the first time in recent history, the oldest segment of the population is the fastest-growing, adding 3 million to 4 million people to its ranks every year. Baby boomers already account for half of U.S. consumer spending, and with longer life expectancies, that share is almost sure to increase. Many researchers also say that instead of passing their wealth on to future generations after they die, boomers are more likely to spend it now, on their children and grandchildren, as well as on themselves, as they pursue more active lifestyles than prior generations of "senior citizens." Even the younger baby boomers aged 47 to 64 are more attractive to marketers than their kids are. They are much less likely to be unemployed than adults in their twenties and thirties. And they have the highest median weekly earnings of any other age segment in the United States.

The marketing implications of the developing boom in older consumers are just dawning of many marketers. Sales and service representatives are taking courses on how to avoid language and behavior that reminds baby boomers they are getting older. Medical alert systems of the "I've fallen and can't get up" variety, marketed by companies like ADT Security Services, have been rechristened "companion services." The typefaces in ads and brochures are getting quietly larger; store shelves are being lowered; and the lighting is being turned up. Some companies are even putting their product designers in spacesuit-looking outfits that simulate the mobility, balance, and dexterity challenges of advancing age. As a result, companies are redesigning everything from the grab bars in bathtubs to the caps on pill bottles to make them more usable by aging consumers. Kimberly-Clark redesigned its Depend adult diapers to look more like regular underwear. One consultant has even tried to rebrand the whole experience of getting old, calling it "middlescence." It's like adolescence without the acne, and with about $2.5 trillion to spend.

Employers also have to be prepared for the fact that it is not only households that are multigenerational. Baby boomers are healthier than people over age 65 used to be, and they are staying at work longer, partly because their retirement nest eggs took a beating during the 2007–2009 recession and partly because they like what they're doing. But for the first time in history, three distinct generations share the same workplace: the baby boomers, Generation Xers, and "millennials" (as members of Generation Y are known). They are not only working side by side, but many members of the oldest generation are finding themselves in the uncomfortable position of reporting to people young enough to be their children or grandchildren.

Also for the first time in history, the majority of American house-holders (what used to be called "heads of household") are women. Part of the reason is that a record number of unmarried women are having children. In 2008 alone, about 40 percent of all births were to unmarried women. A little more than 10 percent of households are single-parent families, most led by women. Many of those unmarried women depend on their own parents to help them financially and directly.

In fact, for that and other reasons, many of the nation's 70 million grandparents are more actively involved in their kids' and grandkids' lives than ever before. About 10 percent of them actually live with their grandchildren. Combined with adult children who live with their parents because they can't find a job, or are stuck in one that doesn't pay enough for them to move out on their own, the 2010 census found a record number of three or more generation households—some 10 million. For the first time in a long time, major purchases like an automobile, a home, or a college education involve two generations of people.

Complicating matters further, the generations coming in behind the baby boomers are far more diverse racially. Less than one in five seniors belongs to a racial or ethnic minority, while nearly half of children under five do. And even within the same ethnic or racial groups, values differ markedly by generation. In the black community, for example, there is a sharp divide between the civil rights and hip-hop generations. Marketers who try to appeal to the entire African-American community through hip-hop culture are going to be speaking to a lot of deaf ears. Hispanic and Asian audiences are also divided by generation. Immigrant adults differ significantly from the younger U.S.–born generation in attitudes, values, and behavior. OtherWise marketers must either speak to each generation in its own voice or find messages that bridge the gap between generations.

Finally, marketers can no longer count on sheer population growth to fuel consumption. The baby boomers consumed more than preceding generations simply because there were so many more of them. But on a proportionate basis subsequent generations have been of smaller (Generation X) or similar (Generation Y) size. "What growth they see will have to come from product innovation and differentiated value," Peter Francese warns.

But that value will come only from a better understanding of an increasingly complex market that is multicultural and multigenerational, with no "standard" household type. "More than anything," Francese warns, "CMOs need to understand that their customers will never be like their friends and neighbors. They will not be like the people they see every day. Nothing like it." To many marketers, they will be the Other. Times like this call for more than an adjustment in advertising techniques; they require a whole new definition of marketing—a radical reorientation from upstream activities like promotions to downstream functions like product conceptualization and development. Marketing must be more than selling. It must become the engine of discovery and focused on fulfilling customers' deepest needs, values, and aspirations. And that, of course, must start by understanding who the customer is.

While a "market of one" is theoretically possible, the sweet spot is the break point between individual and culture, where needs, values, and aspirations coalesce. Ted Levitt, a professor at Harvard Business School, used to tell his students that no one needs a quarter-inch drill; they need a quarter-inch hole. People buy products to accomplish a job. That job may be functional (drilling a quarter-inch hole), social (fitting in on the job site), emotional (impressing your spouse), or aspirational (wanting to be a master carpenter like Norm Abram of *This Old House*). In most cases, it will be a combination. And in almost all cases, a person's cultural heritage will contribute to shaping that need. For example, ethnographic research done by General Mills has revealed that many first- and second-generation Hispanic-American women consider the preparation of family meals a particularly big part of being a "good mom." They invest a lot of time and energy in it because they believe that every mother should have her own individual recipes. This attitude is markedly different from the general American market, coming as it does from their country of origin where food was a magnet for gathering, managing, and nurturing multigenerational families.

As Mark Addicks, chief marketing officer for General Mills,

told me, "To the general American market, a brand like Hamburger Helper is about convenience and great taste in minutes [and] on a budget. In marketing Hamburger Helper to newly arrived Hispanic-American mothers, we still emphasize the convenience, taste, and value, but position the brand as the first step to dinner where you add your own special ingredients and ideas." To Hispanic-American mothers, Hamburger Helper is a recipe *element*, a base on which they can build a meal.

Expanding on insights like this, General Mills created a lifestyle brand for Hispanic Americans called *Qué Rica Vida* ("What a Rich Life"). "We realized that Hispanic-American women were very similar to the paradigm we saw in the 1940s and 1950s," Addicks explained. "At that time, millions of women were moving from rural areas to the suburbs and into a world of different types of people, foods, and behaviors." General Mills' iconic "spokeswoman" Betty Crocker helped women of an earlier generation adjust to their new lives. Through her cookbooks and recipe-driven television and radio shows, Betty Crocker gave women menu ideas and cooking tips, and she explained social traditions that might be unfamiliar to them.

Similarly, Qué Rica Vida showcases food ideas and lifestyle information designed exclusively for Hispanic Americans through a magazine with a circulation of more than 500,000, as well as through Spanish-language television, digital media, and store displays. It's as if a bilingual Betty Crocker decided to share recipes, time savers, and health tips with her Hispanic friends. More important, General Mills is celebrating the choice Hispanics made in coming to America, and it is showing them how they are going to have a better and richer life because of that very personal decision to live differently from their parents.

"What it takes to be a successful marketer today goes way beyond empathy," Addicks says. "You have to understand who your customers are, what they want in life, what makes them happy, what bothers them, what moves them."

In a sense, marketers may be the canary in the mine shaft for all businesspeople. Whatever our business card reads, we all need to take account of the breathtaking complexity of American society—

multicultural and multigenerational, traditional and nontraditional, simultaneously in a state of being and of becoming. Whether recruiting or managing our own employees, or interacting with customers, suppliers, and communities, we need to be sensitive to the needs of sharply different segments within the overall population, addressing them separately when it is appropriate and productive to do so. Even more fundamentally, we need to understand how our individual cultures shape the needs, values, and aspirations that we all share—and how that may be giving birth to an entirely new culture.

6

It's the Culture, Stupid!

When Bill Clinton was running for president in 1992, one of his advisers famously put a sign in the Little Rock campaign headquarters to keep the candidate on message. "It's the economy, stupid" became something of a slogan for the campaign. Marketers would be wise to do business under a similar banner: It's the culture, stupid.

All marketing is about culture. And as we have seen, one of the defining characteristics of American culture in the twenty-first century is that it is becoming increasingly diverse. In 2010, for the first time, more than half of all births in the United States were to Hispanic, black, or Asian moms. In fact, ethnic minority groups accounted for more than 90 percent of the country's population growth between 2000 and 2010.

According to the Selig Center for Economic Growth at the University of Georgia, the purchasing power of so-called multicultural communities now exceeds $2.5 trillion, accounting for nearly one of every four dollars that American consumers spend. The Hispanic-American market alone represents a larger opportunity than the countries of Canada, Spain, or South Korea. Indeed, America is the second-largest Hispanic country in the world, after Mexico.

Mark Addicks was a young brand manager for General Mills'

Cheerios in the 1990s when he first realized that multicultural marketing was a business imperative. "Basic math would demand that you market to Hispanic and African Americans," he says. "It was a simple matter of numbers. Moms buy cereal, and almost a third of new moms back then were multicultural. So you had to understand their palate, their cultural experience, their predispositions, how they approach motherhood." One thing Addicks discovered is that Hispanic mothers had a different point of view about breakfast. For one thing, they were heavy corn eaters, but Cheerios are made from oats. "They didn't understand why oats are good for their kids," Addicks remembers. "So we changed the way we marketed yellow-box Cheerios to them, giving them a lot more nutritional information. And we introduced them to MultiGrain Cheerios."

It no longer makes sense to pitch campaigns to European Americans, using money that spills off the table to fill "ethnic" gaps. Multicultural consumers are the new mainstream. They are young and culturally influential, setting trends in food, fashion, and entertainment. They live in larger households. They are very brand conscious. And most of them speak a language other than English, at least part of the time. But effective multicultural marketing requires more than a good bilingual dictionary.

Multicultural audiences have different cultural values and consumption patterns from those in the mainstream culture, and there are even differences within multicultural audiences. For example, Procter & Gamble research showed that African-American women spend at least three times as much on beauty products as the overall female population. P&G also found that 71 percent of black women feel they are portrayed worse in the media than any other racial group. That finding led P&G to launch a nationwide "My Black Is Beautiful" campaign to share beauty and lifestyle tips within the context of a discussion of issues of concern to African-American women.

Most Hispanic families have at least two wage earners, and they tend to be a whole person larger than average—3.4 people versus 2.4 for the average non-Hispanic white family. So they spend more of their income on food and clothing. In some ways, Hispanic families represent a throwback to America of the 1950s. Demographer Peter

Francese is particularly taken with the similarities. "Hispanics are about as young as the whole nation was in 1955," he points out. "They often live in large, traditional, married-with-children families, with lots of participation from grandparents. More often than not, they eat family meals at home and spend less than average on alcohol. They're moving to the suburbs, tend to be community-oriented, and have high aspirations for their children." That does sound a lot like America when the baby boomers were young. Francese says he wouldn't be surprised if one day we say something like, "It's as American as *dulce de leche.*"

In fact, flavors, textures, and traditional ingredients matter a lot. American marketers have been adapting their products to local tastes and preferences in foreign markets for some time. What's new is that the best of them are now adapting product formulations to distinct cultures in their home market. General Mills introduced a line of ready-to-eat cereals catering to the tastes of Hispanic families under the *Para Su Familia* brand and added three new Mexican-inspired soups to its line of Progresso soups. Frito-Lay did the same with Doritos, adding zesty flavors such as Salsa Verde and Flamin' Hot Sabrositos. In cosmetics, Revlon and P&G's CoverGirl introduced a wider array of product colors tailored to the complexions of African Americans, Hispanics, and Asians.

Finally, multicultural markets are anything but static. Customers' needs, desires, and values are in constant flux. As Esther Novak, founder and CEO of multicultural marketing agency VanguardComm, told me, members of this new minority-majority "select which elements of American culture they absorb and which elements of their native culture they intuitively retain." They may adopt the dominant culture's language and etiquette, while maintaining their own music, food, and social attitudes. In many cases, they may even switch back and forth to suit their own needs. And one generation may follow a totally different path from the last, or the next.

For example, Marian Prio-Odio, a psychotherapist in Miami, is a first-generation Cuban immigrant who arrived with her mother and father in the 1950s, when Fulgencio Batista took over the country through a military coup. Although educated largely in the United

States, she can go days without speaking English. Yet her children, now adults, speak nothing but English. "We sent both of our kids to study in Spain and speak mostly Spanish to them," she told me. "Yet they will only speak English to us, because they know we understand." Since it was Prio-Odio's father—Cuba's last democratically elected president—that Batista overthrew, you would expect her children to have a better reason than most to want to reconnect with their heritage.

"One thing social analysts don't see as clearly as we see 'from the inside' is the degree to which the second generation of Hispanics has been absorbed by the mainstream culture," Prio-Odio says with a hint of exasperation. "First of all, our kids speak English all the time to their peers and siblings and only occasionally throw in stock terms, such as *chico* and *oye*. Other than through their surnames, I can't tell which of my kids' friends are Hispanic."

VanguardComm's Novak, who is from Peru and had two children of her own with an American husband, takes a slightly longer view. "Being a foreigner is to love and hate simultaneously," she says. "You love that you have ties elsewhere that are very emotionally meaningful, but you hate being different." She remembers observing this sentiment in her own children as well as feeling it herself as a child. "They were completely bilingual until they went to elementary school and saw that no one else spoke Spanish," she recalls. "In that context, they didn't want to be different." Years later they reconnected with their Hispanic culture, and one of her sons even asked her to take a proactive role in encouraging his own children to speak Spanish. Novak says language and culture are complex issues that people adapt to in different ways at different times, depending on the context.

Still, Novak cautions that "most Hispanics are firmly bicultural. More than two-thirds of Hispanics were born in the U.S., yet even those who speak English most of the time are likely to describe themselves as Hispanic or Latino." Relevant cultural cues matter. Bill Cosby played the most acculturated of African-American pediatricians on television, but he wore sweatshirts from historically black colleges and hung art by black artists on the walls of his TV-set living room. "I myself respond to Hispanic cues," Novak confesses, "even though I conduct much of life in English. If I hear something that has a Latin beat to it or if someone throws a Spanish quip, like *oye*, into conversation, I'll resonate to it. Those small, subtle cues say that you're part of the circle, that you know and understand us."

Of course, those cues work in the other direction as well. If not chosen carefully, they can reinforce negative stereotypes. Unilever dropped one agency because every ad it produced for the Hispanic market featured a picnic with a revolving cast of Latin musicians. There is a very thin line between a positive cultural cue and a demeaning stereotype. "Cultural sensitivity often translates into seeing people through a lens of generalizations, and often poorly understood ones at that," warns Prio-Odio, "Connecting with people who are in some way different doesn't always mean addressing what is different about them. A more fruitful approach, I believe, is to recognize the presence of differences we cannot fully understand and focus on what we have in common." Indeed, to borrow a phrase from the poet Walt Whitman, each of us "contains multitudes." In some ways, we are just like every other person alive; in others, we are like all the people whose culture we share; and in still other ways, we are unique, unlike anyone else ever born.

The standard cultural briefing on Hispanics maintains that they typically have large extended families, are bound by traditional values (e.g., respect for elders, good manners, and a sense of personal honor), and faithfully celebrate religious rituals (e.g., saints' days, baptisms, marriages). Their politeness and warmth is reflected in the language, it is said, which is sprinkled with endearments such as *mi vida, mi rey,* and *mi corazón* that have no real equivalent in English. A literal translation would be "my life," "my king," or "my heart," but when applied to a person, a more accurate rendition would be "dear," "darling," or "honey." Such generalizations are relatively harmless, especially when compared with equally popular stereotypes of a Hispanic male's machismo or a Latina's "fiery sexuality."

Cultural generalizations may be useful in "one to many" communications, but generalizations can quickly deteriorate into stereotypes that skew our interactions with each other because they highlight differences. For example, on the most widely used measure of cultural dimensions, the United States is a highly "individualistic" country, rating 91 on a 100-point scale. By contrast, Latin American countries rate much lower—23 to 46 on the same scale. This can lead to misunderstandings if a Hispanic businessperson's indirectness and diplomatic language strikes an American counterpart as a sign of insincerity, while the American's directness and self-confidence appear egotistical and arrogant to the Hispanic. Of course, not every American is direct and not every Hispanic uses flowery language. Assuming differently can lead to just as many misunderstandings. Knowing where individual countries fall on cultural dimension scales is useful background information, but it's no substitute for taking an individual's measure.

Culture is more than skin tone or language. It's a common bond of shared values and beliefs; it is thinking and feeling the same way about the important things in life. At one level, all people want the same thing—our Founding Fathers defined it as "life, liberty, and the pursuit of happiness." But those aspirations are interpreted through a person's culture and experience. And America's cultural center of gravity is shifting, flattening old assumptions and raising new possibilities. When immigrant groups were small pockets of consumers in our largest cities, marketers could afford to sit back and wait for them to catch up with the majority general market, occasionally scheduling a few in-language ads in ethnic media. But multicultural consumers are the new mainstream. And while assimilation was once thought to move in only one direction—immigrants adopted the majority culture, end of story—we now know that it is actually a two-way street, changing *both* cultures over time. Multiculturalism doesn't describe only ethnic communities anymore. To some degree, it now applies to the whole of America.

Some marketers have their finger on the pulse of this new culture. For example, McDonald's discovered that its ethnic customers are trendsetters. A menu item developed specifically for Hispanics did well not only in the Latino neighborhoods of Los Angeles, but also in the chain's restaurants in Laguna Beach, a predominantly white area. When the same thing happened with Asian menu items and African-American promotions, McDonald's looked up from its cash register receipts and realized it was on to something. As a result, the company's mainstream menu and advertising has become more black, Hispanic, and Asian. McDonald's calls it "leading with ethnic insights." McDonald's is motivated by more than the opportunity of the ethnic market; sales are big enough that the company could run ad campaigns tailored to every ethnic group if it wanted to. But for a company that is dedicated to staying "forever young," keeping in touch with trendsetting multicultural customers is a no-brainer.

Smaller brands, which have to stretch budgets of $15 million or $20 million across all market segments, can't even afford the market research for multiple campaigns, let alone the executions and media buys. So many marketers are looking for the one Big Idea that will resonate across different cultures and market segments. Some have forced their various agencies into a sometimes-uneasy partnership to integrate their strategies and messaging. A few have gone so far as to reassign their "ethnic" business to their mainline ad agencies. And some have declared the end of multicultural marketing altogether; long live "cross-cultural" marketing dedicated to messages that "celebrate shared values and insights." The "multicultural" versus "cross-cultural" debate playing out in the advertising trade media probably has more to do with agency income statements than with the marketplace. Marketing is all about creating meaning, and it's hard to see how that can be done without reference to people's culture.

However the battle plays out, Francese doesn't believe it signals the end of ethnic specialization. "As the United States becomes more multicultural, everyone in an ad agency or a company's marketing department will have to understand what multicultural marketing is all about," he says. "But that doesn't mean ethnic agencies will disappear. They may become more integrated into larger agencies, but specialized programs need to be handled by specialists. In-language advertising is the most obvious example. With a million immigrants, mostly Hispanic, entering the U.S. every year for as far into the future as I can see, Spanish language media isn't going to go away," Francese adds, "but understanding the nuances of a culture is even more important. That can be the difference between saying something really stupid and connecting with customers emotionally."

Language can be a leading indicator that you are dealing with another culture. But it is no substitute for cultural literacy. Puerto Ricans and Columbians may both speak Spanish, but their cultural experiences and heritages are very different. And even companies that never run an ad in anything but English need to realize that, these days, they are multicultural marketers. As the man said, "It's the culture, stupid!"

7

Race Matters

Despite the rainbow of skin colors you see on the commuter train or in the office cafeteria every day, race is not real. It has no meaningful biological or genetic significance.

Genetically, two random Koreans are as different from each other as from any random Italian. There is very little genetic difference between any two human beings, and 85 percent of the variation that does exist occurs within any local population, whether the people live in sub-Saharan Africa or on an isolated island in the Pacific. While race may be a scientific fantasy, it is unfortunately a socially constructed fact. Race matters, if only because so many people *think* it does—and more significantly, because it plays such an important role in shaping the lives that people of color experience.

Color, in fact, is what most racial differences boil down to. Of all the physical traits that might characterize people of different races, skin color is by far the most obvious. It is also among the most arbitrary. In fact, anthropologists have devised a number of biologically based ways to categorize races, each equally valid and none making explicit reference to color. One method would assign Nelson Mandela to the same race as most Swedes. Another would put Italians, New Guineans, and Native Americans in the same race. Faced with so many differing systems of racial categorization, most anthropologists have abandoned the concept entirely.

But most people are not anthropologists, and all of us—including people of color—tend to categorize humans on the basis of their skin color. It shapes what we think of people, subconsciously puts them in an out-group, and justifies all sorts of discrimination. Though circumstances differ, so-called colorism is a universal issue, in countries from Saudi Arabia, China, India, and Japan to Brazil, Mexico, and Venezuela. Explanations for this widespread prejudice range far and wide, but a consensus of sorts maintains that it is the product of sexual selection. Since testosterone darkens skin, men tend to have darker complexions than women. That may be why men across virtually all cultures seem to prefer women with fair skin, and most women prefer men with ruddier complexions. According to anthropologist Peter Frost, in primitive societies, men of higher social status and wealth had their pick of marriage partners and tended to select partners with lighter skin. As a result, many of their offspring had fairer complexions, and eventually the upper classes as a whole were lighter skinned. Similarly, during the period of slavery in the United States and elsewhere, slave owners selected lighter-skinned women as sexual partners. Any children that resulted were given relatively lighter work than the physically demanding tasks in the fields the darker slaves were expected to do. This created some friction among the slaves, but it also supported the idea that lighter was better. Over time, lighter complexions became associated with higher status, which became part of the culture in most societies.

Whatever its history, there is little question that a preference for lighter-toned skin is widespread in nearly all cultures. *Washington Post* reporter DeNeen Brown calls colorism "the crazy aunt in the attic of racism." Whether you are white or a person of color, that old crank is likely whispering in the ear of your subconscious. And the consequences are serious. For example, a Harvard University study of state and national elections since 1865 showed that light-skinned blacks were four times as likely to be elected as dark-skinned candidates. The earnings of light-skinned African Americans and Hispanics are about $2,600 to $3,000 higher than those who are dark-complexioned.

From 1980 to 2007, African Americans were arrested on drug charges three to six times more frequently than white people, even though they engage in drug offenses at comparable rates. And darker-skinned African Americans convicted of a capital offense involving a white person are twice as likely to receive the death penalty as lighter-skinned black people convicted of similar offenses.

Studies of colorism *within* a community of color are more difficult to nail down, though anecdotes abound. For example, most Hispanic women remember hearing their mother's admonishment: *"Ya salte del sol, te vas a poner muy negra"* ("Get out of the sun, you will get too dark"). They seemed to intuitively know what studies have conclusively shown: Light-skinned Latinas are twice as likely to marry as their darker-complexioned sisters. And Harvard's research into implicit bias indicates that Asians and Asian Americans are even more prejudiced than whites on issues of skin tone—all of which helps explain why 60 percent of skin care sales in India are for skin-whitening products, and why, worldwide, skin lightening is a multibillon-dollar industry, worth even more than tanning.

So race and color are inextricably entwined in our minds, whether we are white or people of color. But that does not mean that blacks, Hispanics, and Asians are all in the same racial boat. Most Hispanic immigrants came to the United States from countries of unrelenting poverty, where the seam between master and laborer was permanently sewn into the fabric of society. They came here to better their lot, taking low-paying jobs nobody else wanted and settling in communities that were less than welcoming. Even then, as we have seen, they are often suspected of being in the country illegally.

Asians were excluded from immigration to the United States for decades, unless it was to undertake the back-breaking work of building the nation's infrastructure. U.S. citizens of Japanese descent were interned during the Second World War. And though the majority of recent Asian immigrants settle in suburbia, rather than in the ethnic enclaves of major cities, they still have to cope with their own social isolation and rootlessness, reinforced by their neighbors' casual stereotyping. Asian women are often fetishized as being docile and subservient. Asian men, often of unassuming physical stature and stereotyped as passive, are targets of opportunity for muggers. Marginalized as a "model minority," Asian Americans' loyalty to their adopted country is nevertheless questioned. According to a 2009 Harris poll, nearly half of Americans (45 percent) think Asian Americans are "more loyal to their countries of ancestry than to the United States." Incredibly, nearly half (46 percent) think that Asian Americans are "passing secret information to the Chinese government," reflecting a widespread inability to distinguish between Asian ethnicities.

Hispanic and Asian Americans deal with colorism, ignorant stereotypes, and institutionalized racism every day, as do people of other minority communities. But the history and experience of African Americans is unique, and the legacy of past racism has fundamentally poisoned the environment in which many of them live, making full assimilation difficult. Black Americans suffered two centuries of slavery and one century of Jim Crow institutionalized racism. That legacy can be seen in everything from black unemployment, which is nearly twice that of whites with the same education, to segregated neighborhoods, substandard inner-city schools, and urban crime. Those injustices distort the way black people are viewed by others—and even by each other. The African-American taxi driver who pretends not to see the black man trying to hail him from the curb is not necessarily a racist; he's reacting, at least in part, to the product of past racism, namely that he might be asked to take his fare to a dangerous neighborhood, where he'll either have trouble finding a return fare, be robbed, or both.

Richard Thompson Ford doesn't believe in looking for racists under every rock. But writing in the *Boston Globe,* he observed, "The biggest racial problem facing the country isn't discrimination, but rather the deep inequality that has created almost two different Americas." As a Stanford University law professor and an African American, Ford has a uniquely personal and professional perspective on the state of race relations in the United States. He is as likely to shoot down leftist agitators as right-wing bloviators when they try to play the race card. He is less a champion of diversity and multiculturalism than of integration and inclusion. And he worries that tagging every racial injustice as the product of intentional bigotry can actually get in the way of addressing the wrongs' real causes. For example, he is not among those who believe that blacks were the victims of racially biased disaster-relief following Hurricane Katrina. The real problem, he says, was neighborhood segregation, which itself is the legacy of *past* racism.

"Most of the racists responsible for the distinctly racial cast of the Katrina disaster are dead and gone," he wrote. "We can't undo the wrongs of the past; trying to imagine what any given neighborhood, profession, or individual would have been like 'but for' racism is idle speculation. But we can work to achieve the type of world we'd like to inhabit or leave to our children."

In Ford's view, racial injustices should be addressed as social problems to be solved collectively rather than as a series of wrongs perpetrated by bad people. For example, Ford believes past segregation has isolated poor black people from mainstream American society and the normal job market. As a result, in many inner cities, black youth develop dysfunctional social norms that erode their work ethic and feed immediate gratification. "Men, unable to support their families, abandon them; women become resigned to single motherhood; children suffer from broken homes and from the bad examples set by both peers and adults," Ford writes. "And this dysfunctional behavior reinforces negative racial stereotypes, making it all the harder for poor blacks to find decent jobs." So-called urban black culture is not the cause of black poverty; it is its natural consequence. Ford is not "blaming the victim." On the contrary, he is calling for aggressive public policy to break the cycle of poverty by reintegrating the victims of past discrimination into mainstream society.

The challenge of addressing past wrongs should be more personal as well. Perhaps ashamed of the racial attitudes of prior generations, most white adults have set a personal goal to be "colorblind." But paradoxically, bridging the gap between white Americans and Americans of color can only be accomplished by explicitly confronting the meaning and power of race in our shared experience. Race is a more potent and potentially explosive factor in relationships with African Americans than with any other group, not only because of slavery but also because of the long period of discrimination that followed. And it also bleeds into relations with other people of color.

Esther Silver-Parker is a friend and successful African-American businesswoman who has counseled corporations as large as AT&T and Walmart. She rose to the executive ranks of both companies and had the means to send her son to whatever prep school would offer him the best education. Yet even she found it necessary, when he was preparing to leave for college, to warn him, "Now don't you forget where you come from or you'll be hurt." She told me that she felt it necessary to remind him that he was black, and that some people would be suspicious of him—or even rude toward him—because of it. In fact, 60 percent of black people report being followed when they are out shopping. The racial profiling practice is so common in some high-end malls that it even has a name: "shopping while black." And there's a mobile version of it too, called "driving while black," in historically white neighborhoods.

Ironically, white parents don't talk to their kids about race. Because they want them to be as colorblind as they hope to be, they avoid discussing skin color or anything associated with the sad history of blacks in America. By contrast, most parents have no trouble discussing gender stereotypes from the earliest age. They tell their kids that women can be doctors and lawyers or bricklayers and plumbers. But they don't feel the need to do the same on behalf of blacks or other people of color, perhaps because most white Americans still have only "brief, superficial encounters" with African Americans. As a result, most senior executives are adults who never became comfortable with people of color. Pretending to be colorblind is ignoring the moose on the meeting room table. They should find ways to broaden their own circle of friends and colleagues to include people of color. And as they would for any issue of critical importance to their company and community, they should assume a leadership role in supporting public policies that promote equal opportunity and lessen inequality.

Most important, no one should underestimate the difficulty of reaching full racial equality. It is a multigenerational undertaking. White Americans typically think we have made more progress in racial matters than black people do. Whites typically compare the present to the past, while blacks compare the present to the racial ideals they envision for the future. Many blacks have had personal experiences with prejudice, from the mildly annoying to the truly horrific, which naturally makes them more skeptical. Some white people view gains in racial equality through affirmative action as good for blacks but negative for other whites, perhaps including themselves or their own children. Research shows that many white people see racism as a zero-sum game that they are losing. As overall perceptions of bias against black people have declined over the past forty years, whites' perceptions of bias against *white* people have increased. In fact, these changes have been so dramatic that many white people now consider anti-white bias to be a bigger societal problem than anti-black bias.

Furthermore, there is something perverse about racial problems in America today. We know that simply spending more time with people of color lessens unconscious feelings of racial bias. But the very prospect of inadvertently expressing—or being thought to have expressed—prejudice creates powerful feelings of anxiety. So people avoid those situations, and the cycle continues. Those who would be OtherWise must be prepared to break that cycle.

In matters of race and color, the first essential step in becoming OtherWise is to face up to a shameful fact: White people have privileges simply because of the color of their skin. Peggy McIntosh, associate director of the Wellesley Centers for Women, has termed them "unearned assets that I can count on cashing in each day, but about which I was 'meant' to remain oblivious."

Like most white people, I could understand why people of color are obsessed with racial issues, but I bristled at the suggestion that I was a member of a privileged class. After all, I was the first member of my immediate family to graduate from elementary school, not to mention college and graduate school. My parents were children of the Depression, the working poor who lived paycheck to paycheck when they had jobs and on unemployment checks when, as was too often the case, they didn't. I worked my way through college and up the ladder at work. Privileged? Nobody gave me anything on a silver platter. I earned everything I have.

Only when Peggy McIntosh unpacked her "invisible knapsack of white privilege" did I realize that I, too, had been carrying the same weightless assortment of special maps, codebooks, passports, free passes, and blank checks through the course of my personal and professional life. Like Peggy, I can wander through the local mall without buying anything, and no security guard will tail me. I can walk into any real estate office in town secure in the knowledge that I'll be shown every home in my price range. I can pick my nose in public, and no one who notices will put it down to my skin color. And I don't have to worry about how my grandchildren will be treated at school or on the playground; I don't have to worry about protecting them from people who will treat them with suspicion or worse. I had always associated racism with malicious acts, overt or insidious, that put some people at a disadvantage, not with systematic preferences that favor me and people like me. I'm not racist, but there is no question that I enjoy racial privileges.

If that wasn't discouraging enough, I also discovered that my deepest attitudes aren't as pure as I thought. Since 1998, scientists have been studying the phenomenon of "implicit social cognition"—the deep-rooted, unconscious assumptions that shape the way people process information about other people. Most of these assumptions are based on associations and memories that we accumulate indiscriminately as we go about our daily life. Unlike explicitly held knowledge, they don't go through fact checking and review as they are formed. They simply pop up, unbidden, as positive or negative attitudes that reflect what we like or dislike, favor or disfavor, approach or avoid.

Most people would repudiate many of those attitudes if they were consciously aware of them. Nevertheless, they do affect our behavior. For example, few people would agree with the proposition that height is an important leadership quality. Yet, while only 15 percent of the male population is six feet tall or more, 58 percent of corporate CEOs are that tall. In fact, multiple studies have concluded that an extra inch of height is worth an additional $1,000 a year in salary, all else being equal. Other studies show that people who are considered "beautiful" or "handsome" earn about 5 percent more per hour than the more ordinary looking. And the subtle, unconscious biases don't stop there.

Psychologists have long known that prejudice operates at an unconscious level, but many assumed it was a learned behavior. Now there is evidence that prejudicial thinking is so deeply rooted in our evolutionary past that it shows up in other primates as well, suggesting that it has been shaped by more than 25 million years of evolution. Some degree of prejudice is hardwired in everyone. Whether it goes by the name of kinship or in-group loyalty, it is a vestige of our primordial ancestors' adaptation to group living. Living in groups dramatically increased our ancestors' odds of survival by making it easier to acquire resources like water, food, and shelter. It also made it easier to find mates, to care for children, and to ward off predators. But the group itself needed to be protected. Outsiders could harm the group by spreading disease, fighting with group members, or stealing resources. Those who developed ways to identify outsiders had a better chance of survival. Over generations, this process of quickly evaluating others was so streamlined that it became the unconscious, automatic behavior we call prejudice.

We are born with an inclination to be suspicious of people who don't look or sound like us. In one experiment, behavioral economists at MIT and the University of Chicago sent out résumés to prospective employers in Boston and Chicago. In all cases, the candidates had similar backgrounds, experience, and qualifications, but half of them had names like "Emily" or "Greg," while the other individuals had names such as "Lakisha" or "Jamal." The "white-sounding names" received 50 percent more callbacks. Other researchers replicated the study with similar results: People with Asian, Hispanic, and African-American names all did more poorly in landing a job interview than those with white-sounding names.

Other research has demonstrated that the effects of unconscious negative racial attitudes extend into every aspect of life. Public officials are more responsive to white constituents than to black voters; doctors are more likely to prescribe life-saving care to white patients; people express less empathy toward someone in pain if the person is of a different race; and basketball referees subtly favor players with whom they share a racial identity. As Jon Hanson, a Harvard Law professor, once said, "Our brains, it seems, have a mind of their own." Our brain's "mind" operates at levels far below our awareness, and at frightening velocity. "What we think we know about what is moving us is only a tiny, and often a misleading, part of what is actually going on in those parts of our brains that elude introspection but that can nonetheless manifest in our perceptions, emotions, and actions," Hanson wrote. We don't choose our unconscious attitudes, but we are bombarded every day by cultural messages associating white with good and black with bad.

Maybe people of color aren't "obsessed" with racial issues; maybe they are just being realistic.

8

The Cost of Diversity

In the relatively tight-knit world of political scientists, Robert Putnam probably plays with the biggest ball of yarn. He's a professor at both Harvard University and Manchester University in the United Kingdom and the former dean of the Kennedy School of Government. He developed a widely used model that applies game theory to resolving international conflicts. And a paper he wrote for a scholarly journal with a circulation of just 1,631 in 1995 caused such a stir that it earned him a spot in the pages of *People* magazine and an invitation to meet with President Bill Clinton at Camp David. He expanded the original article into a full book—*Bowling Alone*—that still sells well more than a decade later.

Bowling Alone suggested that social capital—the lubricant that reduces the natural friction between people living in close proximity—was declining in America. The title came from Putnam's observation that, while bowling was growing in popularity, fewer people were bowling in organized leagues. It was a metaphor for his observation that fewer people were participating in social and civic organizations. Putnam considered that worrisome, because he believed that associating with people like ourselves for some important purpose made it easier to associate with others who were not like us. He believed that the "bonding" and "bridging" benefits of social capital reinforced each other in ways critical for a diverse society.

Ironically, Putnam's follow-up research on diversity touched off an even bigger furor. Putnam studied the social lives and attitudes of 30,000 people in forty-one U.S. communities around the time *Bowling Alone* was hitting the bookstores. But he was so perplexed and alarmed by the raw data he had accumulated, it took him seven years to publish his analysis in a Scandinavian academic journal. In the end, Putnam reluctantly concluded that living in highly diverse settings caused people to "distrust their neighbors, regardless of the color of their skin, to withdraw even from close friends, to expect the worst from their community and its leaders . . . and to huddle unhappily in front of the television." People in that situation "hunker down"—that is, they "pull in like a turtle," Putnam wrote, whether young or old, educated or not, rich or poor, and this behavior can be observed across all racial groups.

Remarkably, Putnam noted that trust was lower not just *between* the diverse communities—as in black people not trusting white people—but *within* the communities themselves. This finding ran counter to the standard theories of the time, which held that distrust between diverse groups was natural but declined as people from both groups got to know each other. But Putnam discovered that high levels of diversity made *everyone* more suspicious, tentative, and withdrawn—what Putnam called "anomie or social isolation."

Dr. Beverly Daniel Tatum, president of Spelman College and a clinical psychologist, was not surprised by Putnam's findings, but she doesn't believe that we are doomed to a long period of hunkering down, either. "What we know about human nature," Tatum told me, "is that we are pack animals. We identify who is in our pack and who is not. But a pack is also inclined to follow a leader, and a leader can shape how the pack is defined. If you have a leader who helps people see that they're part of this larger group and there's value in coming together, people will embrace that. If all you've got is rhetoric about being under siege and needing to circle the wagons, that's what people will do."

Fear of the Other is high. At the same time that America's economic might has proved more vulnerable than anyone suspected, and its global leadership is being challenged, our demographics are changing—and along with it our social narrative. "Given that the political—if no longer numerical—majority is white, it should not be surprising that racially fueled anxiety is high," Tatum says. The right kind of leadership can ease that anxiety. Sadly, though, some people used Putnam's findings to throw fuel on a bonfire they had been tending for decades, high-fiving each other that a noted academic had finally come clean about the perversity of diversity. Pundit and sometime political candidate Pat Buchanan opined that Putnam's research "makes hash out of the politically correct cliché [that] 'our diversity is our strength.'"

The controversy upset Putnam, who considers himself a political liberal. He believed his findings were often distorted to fit a nativist, anti-immigrant agenda, and almost always overly simplified, as if America could *choose* whether or not to become a multicultural society. Plus, while he conceded that his study accurately depicted the short-term costs of diversity, he felt many people ignore the long-term benefits. "It's not merely a fact that America's becoming more diverse," Putnam told one radio interviewer. "It's a benefit. America will—all of us will—over the long run, benefit from being a more diverse, more heterogeneous place. Places that are more diverse have higher rates of growth on average, and they have better cuisine. And it's just a more interesting place to live." Indeed, psychologists have discovered that being exposed to different cultures makes people more creative. Encountering different modes of behavior makes people more open to considering alternative possibilities in problem solving, rather than settling for the first thing that comes to mind. America's broad diversity could give it an edge in the global markets of the twenty-first century.

The big question, of course, is what we can do to speed the transition, minimize the pain, and gain the full benefits of diversity. Putnam suggests that it helps to start with a double dose of history and optimism. "I grew up in a small town in the Midwest in the 1950s," he recalled in the article that kicked off the controversy. "Of the 150 students in my senior class, I knew the religion of virtually every one." The reason had nothing to do with any early interest in social science, much less religion. It was actually quite practical. Religious intermarriage was uncommon in those days. So, for the most important aspect of any adolescent's life—mating—it was essential to keep track of the religious affiliations of one's peers. More than fifty years later, when it comes to romance, Putnam says most Americans consider someone's religious affiliation "hardly more important than left- or right-handedness." Putnam's surveys show that Americans have essentially eliminated religion as a social border over the last half century, even though religion itself remains personally important to them. In fact, most Americans consider their religious identity more important to them than their ethnic identity. It's not at all unusual to see people of all ethnic backgrounds worshiping in the country's mega-churches, many of which are in the historically less tolerant South and Southwest.

A 2012 Pew Research Center report suggests that race may also be playing a lesser role in the realm of romance and marriage. Nearly two-thirds of Americans (63 percent) say it "would be fine" with them if a member of their own family were to marry someone outside their own racial or ethnic group. In fact, nearly half (43 percent) say that interracial marriages have "been good for society." And the share of interracial marriages reached an all-time high of 8.4 percent in 2010, compared to just 3.2 percent in 1980.

So there may be cause for optimism. What seems unfamiliar—what people see as Other—can and does change over time. "What counts as being like yourself is not given by God," Putnam notes. "These divisions that we draw—these lines that we draw among ourselves—are things that change over time."

Putnam believes that human beings have an extraordinary ability to redraw social lines in ways that transcend ancestry. There's little reason ethnic identity cannot be replaced or, at minimum, coexist with more overarching identities such as a person's occupation or religion in a way that makes ethnicity less salient. Such a level of identity reconstruction would require wise policies in both the public and private sectors, however. For example, Putnam suggests building more community resources like day-care facilities, recreation centers, and parks in areas with large numbers of immigrants and offering greater support for English-language instruction. Obviously, the government needs to do the heavy lifting here, but business has an important role to play, too. In fact, some—like Dr. Tatum of Spelman College—believe that American business leaders are a step or two ahead of our political leaders on this score. "From what I have seen, business leaders are drawing the circle wider," she says. "Part of that comes from their understanding that they have no choice if they want to remain competitive in a global marketplace. They realize that they have to be able to relate to people different from themselves in order to be effective, and increasingly, that's what they're doing, not only in the context of international trade, but right here in our local communities."

More and more, the racial and ethnic makeup of American businesses reflects that of the communities in which they operate, even if their senior leadership ranks haven't quite reached that point yet. Putnam didn't study the effects of diversity within a business setting, but he suspects diversity has the same effect in the workplace as in the larger community. He believes employers need to take the problem seriously, and do more than tell people to treat everyone the same and to try not to offend anyone. "It requires a lot of conscious attention, not easy, happy-talk," he told *Human Resource Executive Online*. In fact, the wrong kind of diversity training can actually backfire. Giving people the feeling that they have to walk on eggshells to avoid offending anyone ends up erecting new barriers.

Putnam believes the central challenge of managing diversity is to create a more expansive sense of "we." Companies should focus employees on a common corporate identity that cuts across lines. The companies that can pull that off are almost always those that have a clearly articulated higher purpose than making money. McDonald's employees represent practically every race and ethnicity, but what unites them—beyond the Golden Arches logo on their shirt—is the knowledge that they are all about "food, family, and fun," whether they're taking orders, flipping burgers, or emptying the trash and cleaning the restrooms.

Tatum adds that it's also important to affirm people's strongest feelings of *personal* identity, which for many people of color may center on their race. "It is important to both affirm identity *and* build community," she notes. Tatum understands how this concept can seem foreign to many people of the mainstream culture, who believe that an ideal society would be colorblind. The logic of colorblindness is simple: if we don't notice race, we can't be biased by it. But that's easier said than done. Research shows that, beginning at the age of about six months, it takes less than one seventh of a second for us to notice someone's race. Furthermore, however pure our intentions, many African-Americans perceive efforts to appear "colorblind" as a sign of *greater* bias. And research suggests they may be right—people who sidestep mentions of race, even when relevant and appropriate, display *more* racial bias than those who openly talk about it.

"Being 'colorblind' is not a good thing," according to Tatum. "Race matters in our society, and it's important to acknowledge that fact, not to wallow in it or to point fingers, but to recognize that some problems are influenced by negative racial attitudes." Many white people—who would probably never think of describing themselves by their *color*— find this notion divisive. But Tatum suggests that, in fact, affirming someone's identity has just the opposite effect. It makes a person feel that the larger community cares about who she is. White people take their color for granted because it feels like the "normal" condition to them. That's not the case for those whose race, sexual orientation, or other characteristic places them outside the "norm." Indeed, the immigrant ancestors of many white Americans felt the pain of exclusion. Many found comfort in associating with each other in their own social clubs and take pride in celebrating their heritage in parades. For the most part, their children and grandchildren are now firmly in the mainstream, but many continue to celebrate their ethnicity in those same clubs and parades. Is it any wonder that people of color— who in some cases have been waiting more than a century to join the mainstream—continue to need the support of like-minded people?

That's why people in the same racial group often sit together in company cafeterias. It is a way of recognizing that they are not alone, that others share similar life experiences, if only for a half hour or so every workday. Many companies have established formal "employee affinity groups," not only along racial lines, but also for employees whose sexual orientation or physical disabilities make them feel different, as well as for those who are underrepresented in management ranks, such as women. Affinity groups are powerful mechanisms for demonstrating that the company recognizes and values its employees' heritage and traditions. "When people feel marginalized in an organization, they're less productive," says Tatum. "But when you create a space where people can get support from others who are having similar experiences, that support gives them energy and allows them to be more engaged." In fact, research suggests that most minorities who broke through to the top had mentors of their own ethnicity as well as role models of other ethnicities. Diversity in their personal networks proved to be more important in their development and success than in that of their white colleagues.

When people are secure in their own identity, they are more capable of bridging to another, broader identity, as Putnam suggests. Ensuring that business teams and task forces include members from varied backgrounds creates just that opportunity. And once employees realize that workers from other groups can help spark their own creativity, the mistrust starts to go away. In fact, research shows that the benefits of diversity don't accrue solely to the "diverse." Members of the "social majority" are actually more likely to voice unique and creative perspectives when they are working with a more socially diverse group. And that's true even when the people who are "different" don't express any unique perspectives themselves. The mere presence of social diversity makes people with independent points of view more willing to speak up, and others more willing to listen.

Employee affinity groups—or networks, as they are sometimes called—are also talent incubators, especially if a company looks to them for input on important projects or initiatives. For example, General Electric approaches the issue with the same Six Sigma rigor that it uses to manage the company itself. "Our affinity networks are really not about celebrating holidays with ethnic food in the cafeteria," Deb Elam, GE's chief diversity officer, told me. "We use them to attract, retain, and develop talent. They're about giving people of diverse backgrounds the opportunity to practice leadership in a safe environment."

In fact, GE is so serious about this undertaking that the employees who lead each of its five affinity networks are appointed by the company's senior management, based on an assessment of their job performance and leadership potential. The affinity networks themselves are quite large; as many as 1,700 members of the African-American affinity network convene for a three-day annual conference. In addition to participating in those annual conferences, GE's senior leadership—including CEO Jeff Immelt—reviews the affinity networks' plans quarterly. And those plans include much more than cultural celebrations and sensitivity workshops. GE leverages its affinity networks to deepen its relationships with its customers.

In fact, it was a question that African-American employees kept asking senior managers at GE—*When are we going to do something in Africa?*—that persuaded Immelt to finally get serious about expanding the company's business on the continent. Initially, GE's focus was philanthropic; it launched a multiyear, $20 million health-care initiative to reduce infant mortality rates. African-American employees volunteered to go to Africa on short-term "bubble assignments" to consult with local teaching hospitals within their area of expertise. The relationships they built with community and local business leaders, as well as with government officials, paved the way for business opportunities. As a result, the company's revenue in Africa expanded sevenfold in seven years, and Immelt added a senior executive for all of sub-Saharan Africa, rather than lumping it in with Europe and the Middle East, as most other companies do. So, in addition to helping senior executives learn more about people who may be different from them, affinity networks can act as a bridge to them. In fact, employee affinity networks are so ingrained in the GE culture that Elam says "it's almost socially unacceptable" for senior managers not to engage with them.

Affinity networks can also serve as bridges to the broader employee population. Raising the visibility of groups that have only minority representation within the overall workforce (or within management ranks) promotes a sense of inclusiveness and gives employees who might have felt marginalized greater confidence. More important, it lays the groundwork for the kind of personal interactions that can lead to a fundamental shift in attitudes toward people who are "different"—from tolerance to appreciation, and from political correctness to collaboration.

Affinity networks are not a panacea. Some white people think they smack of "special treatment" that can be divisive. Some people of color think they're a cynical way of sidestepping an open discussion of racial inequality. The key is to ensure that affinity groups are truly safe places to discuss each member's personal experiences without papering over difficulties and challenges. And to structure the network of groups in such a way that they encompass everyone—including white people. Celebrating each person's individuality is the point. What makes each of us unique includes not only our race, but also our family background and ethnic heritage. Why shouldn't we celebrate it? Tatum believes affinity groups can even help white people develop what she calls "a positive white identity."

"Few white people have given a lot of thought to the meaning of their racial identity," she says, "which is not surprising if they grew up in a mostly white community, went to a mostly white school, and work for a mostly white company." In fact, we don't give much thought to many aspects of our identity, especially if we think of it as the "norm." But as Putnam says, "race matters" in our society and, as someone who compiled his personal list of "white privileges," I asked Tatum what I could do about it, other than feel guilty.

"Affinity groups are also for people who made that list," she advised me. "Talk to other white people who made their own 'privileges' list and ask yourselves what you can do to give back to the community. For example, you can volunteer time to mentor young African-American youth, or support organizations that work for social justice." Being OtherWise isn't simply an intellectual exercise; it's the kind of wisdom that drives action.

9

Queerness

Few things are as changeable as politically correct language. Originally, *queer* had no sexual connotation at all; it merely described something "out of alignment" or "unusual." Then sometime in the early twentieth century, the word became an offensive slur referring to homosexuals, especially men who were the receptive partners in anal or oral sex. (Curiously, in those days, the "penetrators" were considered "straight.") Over the last twenty years or so, *queer* became the homosexual community's term of choice for people who are not heterosexual. There's probably a strain of righteous indignation in all this. "You want to call us 'queer' because of our sexual orientation and your own ignorant fantasies of what that means," they seem to be saying. "Fine, we'll embrace it. We're Queer and proud of it. Get over it."

The term now covers people who are lesbian, gay, bisexual, and transgender (LGBT, for short). In fact, a whole ideology—dubbed "Queer theory"—has arisen to describe gender or sexual identity outside the "norm" or the middle of the bell curve. Queer theory posits that people's sexuality and gender are not so much permanent physical characteristics as fluid social conventions. It is happy to let people be whatever they are and do whatever they do without imposing a label on them.

For an ideology founded on a deep skepticism of fixed identities, it is perhaps not surprising that there are probably as many versions of Queer theory as there are Queers. Even so, all of the proponents are very sensitive to what they see as heterosexist and homophobic language in modern society. They even promote the adoption of "preferred gender pronouns" (PGPs) to express whatever gender seems relevant at the moment. And if none of the dictionary pronouns quite fit the bill, people with nonconforming gender identities are welcome to make up their own, such as *ze* and *hirs,* words that connote both genders. At root, Queer theory is about protecting people's right to be different without being marginalized.

Sadly, that attitude is not broadly shared. And homosexuality is particularly offensive to the very people who claim to be followers of a man who made a show of associating with the Other of his day, whether the leper, the sinner, or the outcast. Christianity has been trapped in a lover's quarrel with homosexuals—Queers—for centuries. At best, Christians claim to "love the sinner, hate the sin." In reality, many are repulsed by the whole package.

Pastor Fred Phelps, for example, makes no bones about it. He believes that homosexuals who engage in sodomy should be executed. In fact, he believes that every tragedy in the world is God's retribution for society's tolerance and acceptance of what he calls the "homosexual agenda." In a sermon delivered just after the 9/11 attacks, Phelps thundered, "God hates America, and those calamities last Tuesday [September 11, 2001] are none other than the wrath of God, smiting fag America." As if that weren't incendiary enough, Phelps, his children, and his grandchildren—who constitute most of his congregation in a church run out of his home in Topeka, Kansas—regularly picket the funerals of soldiers killed in Iraq or Afghanistan with signs that read "Thank God for Dead Soldiers."

Phelps, an imposing man in his seventies, with a shock of white hair and piercing eyes, can be a spellbinding speaker. In his youth, he was an acclaimed civil rights attorney, feted by the National Association for the Advancement of Colored People (NAACP) for defending the rights of blacks. But his courtroom style bordered on the theatrical and reached an absurd climax in the late 1970s, when he cross-examined a witness about her sex life, accusing her of a variety of perversities totally unrelated to the case at hand. He lost the case and, when he was found guilty of perjury during his appeal, he was disbarred. Since he had been ordained a Baptist minister at age 17, he fell back on the ministry. In 1991, he began leading antigay protests, attracting national attention when he picketed the funeral of Matthew Shepard, the victim of a particularly vicious, antigay hate crime, with signs saying that Shepard was already burning in hell.

Phelps calls himself a "primitive" or "old school" Baptist. He believes that only a select few will be saved and that everyone else, no matter what they do in this life, will be cursed to hell in the next. Naturally, he considers himself one of the select few that God has chosen. And he finds plenty of textual evidence in the Bible that homosexuality is sinful and worthy of condemnation, even unto death.

In our day, Fred Phelps represents one, admittedly extreme, pole of religious thought regarding homosexuality. But more people than would like to admit it are closer to Phelps's end of the spectrum than to the other. About half of Americans believe that "sexual relations between two adults of the same sex is always wrong." Furthermore, hate crimes against homosexuals outnumber those against any other group except African Americans, who represent a much larger—and easier to identify—proportion of the population.

Standing at the other end of the spectrum is Mark Beckwith, a tall, thin man with a receding hairline and a graying beard. Beckwith has an easy smile and sparkling eyes. Were it not for his clerical collar and the pectoral cross hanging around his neck, he might be mistaken for a professor at the law school one block over from his office in Newark, New Jersey, or perhaps for a psychiatrist at the nearby University of Medicine and Dentistry.

Beckwith, who is married and has two children, is the Episcopal bishop of the diocese of Newark. He is the shepherd for nearly 30,000 souls spread across 113 congregations in the northern third of New Jersey. The Episcopal Church in the United States is part of the worldwide "Anglican Communion." While the archbishop of Canterbury, England, is considered the spiritual leader of all the Episcopal dioceses around the world, each diocese is run pretty independently. Beckwith, for example, was elected in 2006 by clergy and lay representatives from all the churches in the Newark diocese.

The election of bishops in the Episcopal Church has stirred controversy since 2003, when the New Hampshire diocese elected an openly gay priest as bishop. His selection offended many of the more traditional congregations in the United States, and at least six dioceses and some individual parishes announced plans to break from the Episcopal Church of the United States over the issue. That prompted the Anglican Church in England to ask for a moratorium on the consecration of gay bishops while it worked to prevent a permanent breakup in the church.

In the run-up to the selection of a bishop for Newark, the media were aflutter about the possibility that the notoriously liberal diocese might select a gay priest as its leader. Although many clergy in the Anglican Communion consider homosexuality a sin, by some estimates about a third of the Newark clergy are gay—the legacy of a former bishop who ordained thirty-five gay and lesbian clergy and took in dozens more who could not find jobs elsewhere. Indeed, among the six candidates for bishop of Newark in 2006 was a respected gay clergyman in San Francisco who had once lived and worked in the diocese of Newark and had maintained a loving relationship with another priest for twenty-four years.

Beckwith, who had also worked in the Newark diocese, won election on the third ballot. Even before he was consecrated, Beckwith joined seventeen other clergy in urging the legislature to vote on a bill giving gay and lesbian people the right to marry. Since Beckwith had less than a month under his miter when the law eventually passed, he politely declined opportunities to grandstand. And he professes to be untroubled by the controversy. "Religion has a fault line," he told me. "On one side is religion that reinforces difference, and on the other is religion that tries to build bridges. I subscribe to the religion that tries to build bridges between differences." Of course, he knows that many of his coreligionists base their objections to homosexuality on scripture. To them, it is a sin, an offense to God, not just a difference of opinion.

But Beckwith likes to point out that the Episcopal Church has lived in a tension between scripture, tradition, and reason for the 500 years of its existance. "The physicist Niels Bohr used to say the opposite of a fact is a lie, but the opposite of a truth is a competing truth," he says. "When you hold up that competing truth and sit with it for a while, it takes you to a new place." Beckwith believes that, in time, old disagreements can look a lot different. "Just as the Protestant/Catholic tension has eased off considerably, we're getting through the issue of gay priests and gay bishops," he says. "Not easily and not happily—but we're getting through it because more and more people have relationships with people who identify themselves as gay or lesbian. Young people see this as less and less of an issue."

Beckwith's comfort with ambiguity may have its roots in the two years he spent in Japan following graduation from Amherst College. He knew he wanted to go to divinity school, but he wasn't sure he wanted to be an ordained minister. He dabbled in Buddhism and was strongly attracted to Zen meditation. "That's where I was first introduced to organized silence," he remembers. In the end, he realized that there would always be dissonance between the Asian traditions in which Zen began and his own Western traditions, and especially with the centrality of Jesus in his own life. So when he came back to the states, he entered the Berkeley Divinity School at Yale. Nevertheless, he is probably among the least doctrinaire of religious leaders.

"To many people, faith is a matter of certainty," Beckwith says. "I believe certainty is the opposite of faith. The most vocal people express faith as certainty. I don't think that's faith; that's ideology." Like many of the rabbis and imams he knows, Beckwith is wary of certainty. "It's unyielding and static," he says. "But faith is always moving and changing." For Beckwith, "God is easy to experience, but hard to understand." He believes the Church has had that backward for at least 1,200 years, maybe longer. "[The Church] said you have to understand God this way, and when people had an experience outside of that understanding, the Church said it wasn't a valid experience. The gift of the tradition that I live in is that you can have four different people and have five different experiences of God."

So Beckwith's motto seems to be "honor differences." Consider them an opportunity to discover something new about the world and about yourself. That's what he meant when he wrote—less than a month into his new job—that sexual orientation, along with other differences like race, ethnicity, and class, was a "gift" to the Church. "We have the capacity to build relationships between people," he says. "But first we have to recognize them as people. My pet peeve is when we categorize people, as in 'the gays' or 'the poor.' Politicians love to do that because it gives them permission to paint with any brush they want. Bill Russell wouldn't let anyone call him a basketball player. 'I'm a man who plays basketball,' he'd say. He refused to be put in the box of overly tall black men."

Whether someone is born gay or becomes gay has yet to be definitively proven. But that's immaterial to people like Frank Bruni, the *New York Times* columnist who is quite open about his own homosexuality. "Among adults, the right to love—and to express it through sex and maybe, yes, marriage—is surely as vital to life, liberty, and the pursuit of happiness as a Glock," he writes. "And it's a lot less likely to cause injury." Whatever the gender of the person to whom one is attracted, certainly the expression of that love deserves respect, not condemnation.

Being homosexual can be both a sexual orientation and a lifestyle. Some gay and lesbian people celebrate their sexual orientation as the central characteristic that defines them. For others, it is only one important element in the assortment of characteristics that constitute who they are. In either case, it deserves validation and respect. Yet, members of the LGBT community in the United States are probably the ultimate Other to many people.

Homosexuality touches on such deeply personal behavior— bounded by so many taboos—that it borders on the mysterious. Homosexuality makes many people uncomfortable for reasons they often don't even understand themselves. It may be, as some psychologists suggest, a remnant of our primordial revulsion toward matters associated with bodily fluids. It may be the product of one's religious upbringing. It may be the result of social conditioning. It is almost certainly a mix of all three.

I know of a men's book club that somewhat reluctantly agreed to read and discuss the original short story and screenplay for *Brokeback Mountain*. When the men arrived for the meeting at the home of one of the club's members, they were ushered into a room with a large-screen projection television set to a baseball game. It was the first and, as it turns out, last time a TV was playing during one of their meetings, but that night it stayed on, as a wide-screen symbol of the group's enduring and decidedly masculine heterosexuality. During the discussion, some of the men confessed that they felt uncomfortable reading the story in a public place. One guy sheepishly admitted that he slipped it into a copy of *Esquire* when he was on a business flight. Yet no one could put his finger on precisely what bothered him. The good-natured "breaking of chops" that typically punctuated the discussion at these meetings suddenly assumed a mincing and effeminate tone as if to say, "If you can make fun of it, you don't have it." This was a group of sophisticated men—doctors, lawyers, investment bankers, business executives—but they were like little boys at their first coed dance. Bewildered, embarrassed, and awkward.

Studies suggest that the issue of sexual orientation is another area of life where familiarity breeds respect. People who know someone who is gay or lesbian are almost evenly divided on the issue of same-sex marriage, with 49 percent in favor and 47 percent opposed. There is also a growing generational shift: In 1988, young people were no more likely to favor same-sex marriage than their parents, by margins of 14 percent and 13 percent, respectively. By 2010, the generation gap was much wider, with about two-thirds of young Americans favoring it, compared to about half of their parents.

The natural process of generational replacement will likely lead to general acceptance over time, as it has on issues such as women with children working outside the home. Meanwhile, if the jury is still out on same-sex marriage, Americans are much clearer about the place of gay men and lesbian women in society. While nearly half of all Americans would have removed books about homosexuality from public libraries in 1973, fewer than a quarter would today. And while about half would have forbidden homosexuals from teaching back in the early 1970s, fewer than one-fifth of all Americans would today.

That's better than atheists are doing—half of Americans would deny them a teaching position in public schools.

But tolerance, which is all that may be attainable in the short run, is the cheapest virtue. In fact, it may be a false virtue. I hate mosquitoes, but I'll tolerate them at a picnic by the lake if I have to. Sadly, that's the approach many of us take toward people with a different sexual orientation. Doing better will require those who would be OtherWise to understand the source of their own feelings about homosexuality. And it requires us to see lesbian, gay, bisexual, and transgender people as complete human beings, not damaged by nature, but endowed with particular gifts they bring to our larger community, and as people struggling, as we all are, to live a fulfilling life.

10

Strangers with a Strange God

On September 11, 2001—the very day irony was said to have died —Miroslav Volf was addressing a United Nations prayer breakfast on the subject of reconciliation in a world of conflict.

He began his talk by quoting a poem about the Holocaust: Paul Celan's "Death Fugue." As he read the line "we shovel a grave in the air," neither he nor his listeners knew that two planes had just crashed into the towers of the World Trade Center, less than five miles away. And as Volf reminded his listeners of distant places where "rivers of blood have flowed and mountains of corpses have grown," word of the terror unleashed in Lower Manhattan was just beginning to filter through the room. Almost as soon as he finished his remarks, the South Tower fell, killing thousands of innocent men, women, and children. And as the full scale of the horror became clear, the prayer breakfast was brought to a swift conclusion. Volf and other visitors were quietly ushered out of the room and into the eerily quiet streets of Midtown Manhattan. The United Nations complex, which was later identified as a terrorist target, was locked down.

Compounding the irony, Volf had been invited to address the prayer breakfast on the strength of a book he had written following a six-week stay in his native, war-torn Croatia in the fall of 1992. There, broken windows, scarred facades, and burned and desolated houses bore stark witness to the power of tribal hatred. As a trained theologian, Volf turned to his faith to make sense of it all. He came to the conclusion that justice, repentance, and forgiveness were not enough. One actually had to "embrace" the oppressor to achieve peace. That was the message he had brought to the United Nations prayer breakfast that day.

Years earlier, Volf's theological mentor, Jürgen Moltmann, had listened to him expound his theory at a conference. "Well and good," Moltmann thought, but afterward, he asked Volf a simple question: "But can you embrace a *cetnik*?"

Volf remembers thinking, "The notorious Serbian fighters called *cetnik* had been sowing desolation in my native country, herding people into concentration camps, raping women, burning down churches, and destroying cities. I had just argued that we should embrace our enemies as God has embraced us in Christ. Can I embrace a *cetnik*—the ultimate Other, so to speak, the evil Other?" Volf pondered the question for years.

Now he had been presented with another "evil Other." Would he have the same answer? More to the point, would he have delivered the same message had the U.N. prayer breakfast been held one day later, on September 12, 2001?

Miroslav Volf is a man of contradictions. He is a Croat who was raised in Serbia, a Christian who lived among communists. At one point, he was even conscripted into the Yugoslav army, though he later discovered that many of the men in his unit were assigned to spy on him because he was the son of a minister, had studied abroad, and at the time was married to an American, which made him suspected of being a CIA spy. "For four or five months, all my conversations were recorded," he remembers. "Then for another three or four months, I was interrogated. They showed me transcripts of my conversations and photos of me going into this or that building, taken from crazy angles. They threatened that I would be sent to prison for years because I had said this or that against our great communist country." When Yugoslavia began disintegrating into ethnic and religious conflict, Volf was teaching at a seminary in his Croatian hometown, Osijek. The entire seminary went into exile and people watched their homes being destroyed on TV.

Theologically, Volf is hard to categorize. He was raised in the Pentecostal tradition, but now considers himself an Episcopalian and teaches at Yale's Berkeley Divinity School. He doesn't subscribe to the idea that religion should be taught as a social science, though he values the insights psychology, sociology, and anthropology can bring to theological thought. He can plumb the intricacies of religious dogma like the Trinity with the best in the Vatican Curia, but he also writes compellingly on practical topics like finding meaning in work and developing a generous soul. He is also former British Prime Minister Tony Blair's partner in studying the intersection of globalization and religion, with particular attention to points of conflict and reconciliation.

In another bit of irony, Volf concedes that many conflicts stem from religious differences. While globalization pushes us together, religion often seems to pull us apart. Indeed, the tensions have rarely been as strong as they are today. At the same time that Christian, Muslim, Hindu, and Jewish groups are fighting poverty and disease around the world, most of the world's conflicts have a religious dimension. Many of the world's major religions think they are the ultimate arbiter of a moral life and the only path to God. Sometimes it seems that the great "Clash of Civilizations" appears to be developing along the lines Samuel Huntington predicted—the primary source of conflict in the world is not so much economic or political as cultural and religious. Differing views on women's role in society and on the limits of religious freedom are just two of the most obvious flashpoints.

Volf told me he's not sure that Huntington's analysis is entirely accurate, but one statistic strikes him as particularly alarming. "There are 1.6 billion Muslims in the world and 2.2 billion Christians," he points out. "And some say that 60 percent of each group intensely dislikes the other. That's close to 2.3 billion people! One of the issues that moves me as a theologian is figuring out how these two great world religions can live in peace." That particular statistic may be the fuzziest of guesstimates, but there is no question that Volf's larger point is correct. Relations between the largely Christian West and the increasingly global ranks of Islam haven't been this bad since the Crusades. Many Muslims believe that their religion is under attack— eight out of ten say that America's top foreign policy goal is to "weaken and divide Islam." In fact, to many Muslims, this is simply the continuation of a story that dates back to the Middle Ages. At the same time, many Westerners believe that Islam is not so much a religion as a political movement determined to impose its seventh-century values on the rest of the world.

The most obvious cause for Western wariness is that Muslim terrorists were behind the 9/11 attacks. Of course, people don't really think that *all* Muslims are terrorists. But radio and Internet pundit Glenn Beck believes that "ten percent [of Muslims] want to see us dead." Evangelist Franklin Graham says, "The teaching of Islam is to hate the Jew, to hate the Christian, to kill them. Their goal is world domination." And former Speaker of the House of Representatives Newt Gingrich is so convinced that Islamists want to impose traditional Muslim law, known as sharia, in the United States that he has proposed a federal law to prevent it.

In fact, however, most American Muslims are about as radical as Justin Timberlake or Taylor Swift. A 2009 Pew survey described American Muslims in decidedly 1950s, Ozzie and Harriet terms as "middle class and mostly mainstream." They are generally as well educated and as financially well off as the general population. Three-quarters enthusiastically subscribe to the American Dream, saying that in the United States, most people who want to get ahead can make it if they are willing to work hard. Two-thirds say Muslim women have a better quality of life in the States than they would have in most Islamic countries. About three-quarters are concerned about the rise of Islamic extremism around the world, just a bit less than among the general public. And about eight in ten say that suicide bombings or other forms of violence against civilian targets can never be justified, even to defend Islam from its enemies. A 2008 study showed that American Muslims' civic engagement and agreement with democratic values even *increased* with their religiosity.

Of course, as within any large group, there are outliers. A few younger Muslims try to justify suicide bombings. African-American Muslims are less likely to condemn Al Qaeda entirely and are more disillusioned about life in America. And about a quarter of American Muslims still refuse to believe that Arabs were behind the 9/11 attacks. In general, though, American Muslims are well integrated into American society—in fact, far more deeply than their coreligionists in Europe, which is home to proportionately twice as many Muslims as the United States. In some European cities, such as Marseille and Rotterdam, Muslims account for as much as 25 percent of the population. Many people in Western Europe—the most secular society since the fall of the atheistic Soviet Union—are particularly wound up that this foreign cultural virus is disguised as a religion, and one that recognizes no boundaries between private and public life, at that.

The reality on the ground, in the United States as well as Europe, is much more nuanced and complicated. Muslims vary as much in their interpretations of Islam as followers of other faiths do with theirs. In fact, Muslims do not greatly differ in religious behavior from other Europeans. A study by the demographer Michèle Tribalat found that 60 percent of French Muslim men and 70 percent of women were "not observant," though the great majority respected "cultural attachments" by abstaining from eating pork or drinking alcohol and by fasting during Ramadan. And while it is true that Islamic nations are highly conservative on issues of sexuality and gender equality, Western Muslims don't necessarily share those values to the same degree.

Surveys show that the basic values of Muslims living in Western societies fall roughly halfway between the values of the country they left and those of their new home. This is probably due in some degree to self-selection: People who migrate from an Islamic country to the West are likely more open to Western values. It probably also reflects a general adaptation to Western culture. Notes one researcher, "Muslim migrants do not come to Western countries with rigidly fixed attitudes. Instead, they gradually absorb the values prevalent in their host society. Living in a given country has a stronger impact on people's belief systems than their specific type of faith." So an American Muslim has more in common with an American Catholic than with a British Muslim.

Americans themselves are more like Europeans when it comes to Muslims. About half of Americans told the Gallup organization they are at least "a little" prejudiced against Muslims. According to the Pew Research Center, nearly half of Americans—including about two-thirds of conservative Republicans and white, evangelical Protestants—believe that Islam is more violent than other religions. But scholars at the University of Maryland say anti-Muslim feelings are based on something more fundamental than a fear of terrorists. "We are less likely to trust or tolerate people who seem different from ourselves," they wrote, "and Muslims' religious beliefs and practices, cultural orientations, and ethnicities have long made them different in key ways from the Judeo-Christian mainstream." Muslims belong to the age-old "band of Others," they say—a group that includes people of different races or religions, such as African Americans and Jews, as well as people with distinctly different values and behaviors, such as gays and lesbians. In that sense, Muslims are a "twofer"—different in *both* religious beliefs as well as cultural behaviors.

To Western eyes, many aspects of Muslim culture seem to be stuck in the seventh century, especially in its treatment of women. Of course, it is just as easy to find misogynistic texts in the Old and New Testaments as in the Quran. And Islamic culture is not immutable. It is subject to as much change and flux as any other culture. In fact, as Muslim scholar Mohammed Ayoob points out, Islam is practiced in very different contexts in theocratic Islamic states like Iran as compared to Muslim democracies like Turkey and Indonesia. The so-called Arab awakening in the spring of 2011 demonstrated a strong desire for greater freedom and economic opportunity among Arab youth in countries from Syria and Tunisia to Egypt and Libya.

For their part, only about one-fifth of Americans count an actual Muslim among their friends. And most Westerners don't know enough about Islam to cull the sensationalistic misinterpretations from the actual doctrine. Indeed, Fareed Zakaria reminds us that "the Quran is a vast, vague book, filled with poetry and contradictions (much like the Bible)." Like many holy books, it speaks through allegory and indirection. Look hard enough and you can find great sweeping exhortations for tolerance and equally fierce condemnations of unbelievers. According to Zakaria, "Quotations from it usually tell us more about the person who selected the passages than about Islam."

For his part, Miroslav Volf sees many points of intersection and overlap between Islam and Christianity. What binds Muslims to Christians and religious Jews is "a common belief in one God and a shared commitment to love God and neighbor," he has written. True, they understand God somewhat differently, but the similarities in their convictions about God are much greater than the differences. Muslims, Christians, and Jews share fundamental values, including some version of the Golden Rule that we treat others as we want to be treated. And then there's the actual role that religion plays in people's lives. "If faith were simply a matter of how one feels—awe in the face of the unknown, for example—or even if faith were simply a set of beliefs that can be neither proved nor disproved, if that's all faith were, it couldn't have the kind of power it has," Volf cautions. "But faith is a major way people think about themselves and how they fit in the world. Religion is both a set of spiritual values that deal with things like how to live a good life, and a badge of identity that provides continuity in one's life." It is as a badge of identity that religion separates us, which sometimes has nothing to do with matters of faith. Volf jokes that "90 percent of Serbs are Orthodox Christian; 60 percent even believe in God."

Ironically, that badge of identity becomes even more important when people feel that they are under attack. For example, the oldest mosque in America is in Cedar Rapids, Iowa, the town where Grant Wood painted "American Gothic." Every year, the city's Islamic Center attracts young Muslims from around the world who study in local colleges. But the staff has noticed a troubling trend. "Many foreign students, including a substantial number that had never been to a mosque or practiced Islam before they came to America, report that their American experience has led them to a search for identity and religious roots," a staff spokesperson says. It's not that they are inspired by the way Muslims have been accepted in America. (And if anyplace in America should inspire such feelings, it is Cedar Rapids, where Muslims began settling in 1895.) No, it's just the opposite—they leave the United States convinced that Americans are "hostile to Islam." And what speaks most eloquently to them are the Christian broadcasters who call Islam "wicked" and "evil." "These Muslim students are absorbing the notion that Christianity is hostile to Islam, and translating it into hostility toward America and toward Christianity in general," the Islamic Center's staff believes. "Many of them are being turned by their American experience into anti-Western, anti-Christian Islamic revivalists." Talk about ironic.

Miroslav Volf, who knows a thing or two about irony, understands. As a twenty-year-old, he left Yugoslavia to study at Fuller Theological Seminary in the United States, and he remembers that "some among the student body were suspicious of me, coming as I did from a communist country. They were scandalized that I didn't speak with animosity about the godless communists and celebrate the American system without qualification. They thought the communists of Yugoslavia were totalitarians who would not let people out of the country, and if they let you out, they kept you in their service. Maybe I was a communist spy." To say Volf was disappointed is to gloss over his personal history. "By that time, I had been beaten up by a mob because I was a Christian, I had been jailed and interrogated because I was a Christian," he says. "Then I come to this country, and I'm suspect because I'm not quite the kind of Christian that they think I ought to be. I realized that notwithstanding what people say, nation is a much more palpable and important goddess than the invisible Creator, especially if people feel threatened."

Volf had something of the same feeling when Pope Benedict XVI gave an address in 2006 in which he quoted a medieval emperor accusing Islam of being "evil and inhuman." It was a public relations disaster for the Vatican and infuriated the Muslim world. To Volf, it was just one more example of stressing differences rather than commonalities. "In encounters with others, if we see only differences, the result is exclusion; if we see only commonalities, the result is distortion," he has written. "Only when we see both—undeniable differences that give others a peculiar character, and commonalities that bind us together—are we able to honor both others and ourselves." The West's differences with Islam—real and imagined—are well known. It is time to examine what we have in common.

It will be impossible to protect ourselves from the terrorism of radical Islamists without the active support of all law-abiding Muslims. Prejudice against Muslims feeds the victim narrative extremists use so effectively. And it risks alienating the moderate Muslims who are potential partners in a generational battle for mutual understanding. "We need to strengthen the voice of moderate Islam," Volf says. "Demonization is good for fighting and for politicians, but it is bad for statesmanship. It's certainly not good for peacemaking."

Many so-called moderate Muslims are ready to condemn those who would use their religion to incite hate. They want to reconcile Islam with the values of liberal democracy, while preserving the Islamic foundations of their society, just as Judeo-Christian principles animate most Western societies. But they need to see some evidence that those of different faiths truly respect theirs. Moderate Christians can begin by denying their coreligionists tacit permission to use God as a prop in their private crusades and fund-raising. Mutual respect requires religious literacy on both sides. It demands what Volf calls "a more empathic understanding of the Other."

And what of the "evil Other"? Could Volf bring himself to embrace even them? He knew what he wanted to answer: "No, I cannot—but as a follower of Christ, I think I should be able to." Still, that question—or maybe that answer—haunted him for years. In the end, he decided that rejecting the possibility entirely would lessen himself. For Volf, embracing an enemy is a matter of both Christian charity and of self-respect. "If you think of yourself as apart," Volf says, "you do violence to yourself and others."

As the Good Book says, "We have made you nations and tribes that you may get to know one another." That particular Good Book, of course, is the Holy Quran.

11

World Values

With his balding head and carefully trimmed chin curtain, the University of Michigan's Ron Inglehart could easily pass for an Amish farmer, but what he tends is a massive body of empirical data from multiple waves of standardized surveys, fielded over three decades, in countries with nearly 90 percent of the world's population.

Inglehart directs the World Values Survey, which tracks the beliefs, values, and motivations of people around the world. It covers societies with per-capita incomes of as little as $300 a year to as much as 150 times more—everything from free-market economies to socialized welfare states, from long-established democracies to authoritarian monarchies. It's a veritable cornucopia of data for social scientists.

In analyzing the data, Inglehart and colleague Christian Welzel discovered that just two dimensions account for 70 percent of the variation between countries: the role religion plays in people's lives and whether they are focused more on sheer physical and economic survival or on their quality of life. In broad brush strokes, the data seem to indicate that human development follows separate arcs in each dimension, moving from a search for physical security to opportunities for self-expression, on the one hand, and from adherence to traditional religious values to more secular-rational standards, on the other. For example, most people in industrialized, economically advanced countries pretty much take physical survival for granted and pay much more attention to quality-of-life issues such as freedom of speech, social tolerance, and environmentalism. In contrast, across large swaths of the Middle East, Africa, Latin America, and South Asia, most people are primarily concerned with keeping a roof overhead and finding their next meal. This perhaps commonsense finding has been confirmed by other studies.

A related finding from the World Values Survey is even more intriguing. It seems that once people set off on the road to economic development, they not only become more concerned with so-called quality of life issues, they also seem to become less religious. This pattern appears to hold across a number of countries and a variety of faiths. For example, about half (48 percent) of lower-income people in predominantly Catholic Mexico say religion is very important to them, while only about a third of the more affluent do. Largely Hindu India has a similar religiosity gap between lower- and higher-income people (72 percent to 60 percent, respectively). And in Malaysia, which is majority Muslim but has significant Buddhist, Christian, and Hindu minorities, the gap is 86 percent to 60 percent.

Marx and Nietzsche to the contrary, this does not mean that better-educated, higher-income people are rejecting religion; rather, religion is simply playing a different role in their lives. While the World Values Survey shows church attendance declining in almost every developed country, it also indicates that people in those countries are still just as likely to say God plays an important role in their lives. In fact, they are *more* likely to spend time "thinking about the meaning and purpose of life."

Declining religiosity is only one symptom of a more systemic value change. As people's economic situation improves, their values overall seem to become less absolute and more relative. This applies not only to matters of religious precept (e.g., modest dress), but also to family and social issues, such as gender roles, deference to authority, sexual norms, and patriotism. The World Values Survey shows that people who are struggling to survive are more inclined to accept inflexible norms and rules of behavior. When survival is less of an issue, they are more prone to think things through for themselves, and standards become more relaxed.

Not every society moves along these arcs at the same speed, however. Values seem to shift back and forth generationally, depending on the pace and direction of a society's economic development. Because people's values are generally fixed in adolescence and early adulthood, a generation that enters adulthood during a war is likely to be more focused on the day-to-day struggle for survival than on the fulfillment of self-expression. The following generation, reaching adulthood in a booming postwar economy, is more likely to take good times for granted and have greater quality-of-life concerns. For the same reasons, the older generation is likely to have traditional attitudes toward authority and religion, while the subsequent one is likely to take a more rational approach. And that's precisely what a time series analysis of the World Values Survey shows. In developed countries that have experienced dramatic economic growth since 1950, younger people have much more secular-rational worldviews than older people. The difference is less pronounced in countries that had lower rates of growth. And in low-income countries, both groups tend to have traditional worldviews.

But there is one very significant exception to the rule that the arcs of religiosity and economic development tend to move together, if at different rates and in different directions. America is the most economically advanced country in the world. Its culture is all about self-expression and quality of life. But according to the World Values Survey and a separate study by the Pew Research Center, Americans adhere to what can only be called "traditional values." In fact, according to recent surveys by sociologists Robert Putnam and David Campbell, the United States is unique among developed countries as a highly religious society. They estimate that only about 6 percent of Americans are true atheists who believe there is little or no truth in any religion. Another 5 percent are "agnostics" who are not quite sure they believe in God. The rest of us have unusually high levels of what sociologists call "religious belonging, believing, and behaving." Some 83 percent of Americans belong to an organized religion,

80 percent are absolutely sure there is a God, and 59 percent pray at least weekly. By contrast, only 38 percent of the British say they believe in God.

The United States may have become an exception because of the particular way religion and politics influenced each other from the country's earliest days. Many of America's first settlers came here to escape religious persecution, and most of its Founding Fathers were suspicious of state religions. The result was a clear separation of church and state. But that didn't mean Americans gave up on religion. On the contrary, Alexis de Tocqueville speculated that religion played an important role in balancing the American ideal of individual freedom with concern for the good of the community. Religious and political beliefs moderated each other. No church institution was pulling political strings, yet the belief that we should treat others as we want them to treat us tempered the potential excesses of a free-market, survival of the fittest free-for-all.

Furthermore, joining a church has historically been the most common form of association in the United States, even surpassing sports and other leisure activities. But if most Americans are highly religious, we are also religiously tolerant, believing there are basic truths in all religions. Only 10 percent to 12 percent of us believe that salvation is available only to our coreligionists. And even these true believers don't think someone needs to believe in God to be a good American. As a result, Americans are a rarity in human society—religiously devout, diverse, and tolerant.

But the nature of American religiosity may be changing in subtle but important ways. Americans traditionally inherited their religion—it was part of their ethnicity. Many sociologists expected people's religiosity to wither, just as the salience of their ethnicity had. They would be Catholic at Easter and Christmas, just as they are Irish on St. Patrick's Day. That hasn't happened; Americans are still relatively religious. But they are much more likely to *choose* their religion rather than simply going with the generational flow. Putnam and Campbell estimate that more than a third of churchgoers have changed from the religion in which they were raised. Religious intermarriage accounts for much of this change. Most new marriages these days are between people of different faiths, but even people who retain their family's traditional religious affiliation shop for a particular congregation or parish that better suits their social and political beliefs. "Cafeteria Catholics" fit in this category. So do Protestants who move from a mainline congregation to one that is more "evangelical," and vice versa. And Jews who move between Orthodox, Conservative, and Reformed synagogues.

Putnam and Campbell also found that the fastest-growing segment of religious adherents—already about 18 percent of Americans—consists of people who believe in God and an afterlife, but have not adopted *any* particular label. Some may simply be between affiliations, but the religious beliefs of many of them are relatively generic. They don't feel the need to join one denomination or another.

Ironically, if religious belief makes less of a difference in the church Americans join, in recent years it has played an increasingly important role in our choice of political party. Since 1980, when the Republican Party included an anti-abortion plank in its campaign platform and the Democrats took the opposite position, a very strong correlation began to develop between high religiosity and the GOP. Ironically, of the two major presidential candidates that year—Ronald Reagan and Jimmy Carter—the Democrat was clearly the more evangelically religious. But whether intentionally or by happenstance, the Republican Party in 1980 exploited the tendency of highly religious people to consider sex and family issues important, while the Democrats focused on women's rights, including the right to choose. The Republicans' subsequent opposition to same-sex marriage solidified its God-fearing credentials. In fact, according to Putnam and Campbell, whether someone is "highly religious" or "not at all religious" accounts for a shift of 40 to 60 percentage points in opposition to abortion and same-sex marriage. As a result, even today, the highly religious are much more likely to be Republican, with the notable exception of African Americans, who are overwhelmingly Democrats. And even nonreligious voters have the impression that Republican candidates are "friendly" to religion while Democrats are at best "neutral."

Over time, sex and family issues may lose their stickiness as the glue that holds the religious right together. As we have seen, public attitudes toward homosexuality are clearly shifting in the direction of greater tolerance. And even highly religious young people are more likely to allow abortion in some cases—such as rape, or incest, or to protect the life of the mother—than to outlaw it completely. But the gap between the highly religious and the determinedly secular can only widen since each group already tends to see the other as intolerant and selfish. In addition to abortion and homosexuality, they have sharply different views on a range of issues, from gambling and R-rated movies to premarital sex and in vitro fertilization. And while relatively small in number, unlike the more easygoing majority in the middle, both groups have the passion of unshakeable convictions.

For their part, Europeans are somewhat baffled by American religiosity, finding it hard to fathom how more Americans can believe in the Virgin birth than in evolution. And the differences in values don't end there. For decades now, Pew has been asking Americans to assess their personal values on a scale ranging from "extremely conservative" to "extremely liberal." From the late 1980s to 2008, Americans' self-assigned score has never wavered much more than a tenth of a point above the middle of the graph, indicating a very slight conservative bent. Nine in ten Americans describe themselves as very patriotic. Nine in ten believe society should ensure equality of opportunity. Nine in ten regard voting as a civic obligation. Seven in ten claim to have "old-fashioned values" about family and marriage. About two-thirds believe that government should help those who can't take care of themselves. Western Europeans generally live at the other end of the spectrum; they are "secular-rationalists" who believe religion is a personal, optional matter; patriotism is not a big concern; and children have their own lives to lead. So, in terms of fundamental values, most Americans are in a class by themselves when compared to our European cousins.

But there are a lot of people in the shallow ends of every bell curve. And the best survey is only a blunt instrument in trying to figure out what's going on at a level *below* people's conscious beliefs. For that, we need someone like Jonathan Haidt, a social psychologist at the University of Virginia.

12

Gut Values

Jonathan Haidt's thick shock of black hair shows just enough salt and pepper to compensate for a boyish face and the brawny build of a jock. But no one who hears him speak—or reads one of the more than seventy-five articles he has written or cowritten since receiving his PhD from the University of Pennsylvania in 1992—would mistake him for an overeducated frat boy.

Haidt's PhD thesis—"Moral Judgment, Affect, and Culture, Or Is It Wrong to Eat Your Dog?"—was an early tip toward his eventual field of study, as well as the irreverent approach he would take. He studies people's moral values and the largely unconscious norms that cause us to think something is good or bad, right or wrong, worthwhile or worthless, disgusting or . . . not. Haidt (pronounced "height") likes to say that morality is "one of those basic aspects of humanity, like sexuality and eating, that can't fit into one or two academic fields." Nevertheless, the intersections of philosophy (his undergraduate major at Yale) and psychology (his graduate degrees) would be a good place to start.

Haidt believes that the so-called culture wars in the United States spring from the different weights people give the moral intuitions that evolution has hardwired into us. Those "gut feelings" developed tens of thousands of years ago, before the invention of language, when the only thing standing between our ancestors and a dinner of mastodon was an inclination to selfishness. The early hunters who were inclined to work in groups survived and had offspring who learned the same cooperative behavior. The loners and the free riders didn't do so well (the former weren't much of a match for mastodons, and the latter were tossed out of the cave for not pulling their weight). Of course, working in groups wasn't the only behavior that benefited from those gut feelings. Hunter-gatherers who bit into rotten meat didn't live as long as those who were disgusted by it. In fact, it was Haidt's initial interest in feelings of disgust (as in the reaction people have to the idea of eating the family dog) that prompted him to comb through the literature on anthropology, evolutionary psychology, and cultural variation looking for common ideas about morality across cultures, across disciplines, and even across species.

Haidt initially came up with five innate emotional mechanisms that are common to most cultures. Two of them are practically self-evident: It is wrong to harm someone else and it is good to be fair. The three others aren't as intuitively obvious, but clearly play a role in forming human cultures. They are loyalty to one's group, respect for authority, and a sense of purity or sanctity. Haidt's insight is that because morality predates the development of language it is based on emotion, not reason. Everyone has felt repulsion at seeing someone harmed or, conversely, felt a strong urge to care for someone in need. Those feelings are visceral. So, too, are the other four moral emotions, though everyone doesn't feel their effect to the same degree. "Moral judgments, like aesthetic judgments, are best understood as quick gut feelings, not as products of reasoning," he writes. "We engage in reasoning too, but reasoning is slow and it takes place within a mental workspace that has already been pre-structured by feelings."

Haidt believes our moral feelings and intuitions are as much a part of our DNA as our taste for sweets and fats. He concedes that culture plays a role in the refinement of our moral reasoning. We use reason to explain and systematize our moral feelings or to convince others of our beliefs. Societies develop their own languages to describe and teach virtuous behavior. That's why moral standards vary so widely from culture to culture. But at root, all people make their initial moral choices based on a mix of these five gut feelings.

Haidt has tested his theory through an ingenious mix of experiments and surveys in the United States, Europe, Brazil, and India. (He not only is a prolific author, but also oversees at least six websites, in addition to his personal web page.) He has found that people who describe themselves as "conservative" tend to give equal weight to all five moral feelings, while people who describe themselves as "liberal" give far more weight to the first two moral intuitions (harm and fairness) than to the other three (group loyalty, authority, and purity/ sanctity). In fact, U.S. liberals generally minimize the last three (see Figure 1). They celebrate diversity, not in-group identity; they question authority; and they think judgments of what is pure and sacred are entirely personal and subjective. So liberals don't think the government should concern itself with people's sexual and reproductive choices, while conservatives believe family issues have serious implications for the country's social structure. Liberals and conservatives even have different standards of fairness and care. Liberals believe it's only fair for the government to tap the rich to help the needy; conservatives think the government is unfair when it rewards failure and punishes success. In the long run, they say, the needy will be better off if they work to better themselves. In Haidt's view, the culture war is basically a disagreement about the proper balance of these moral intuitions. But there's no reason to question each other's motives. In fact, Haidt believes questioning someone's motives should be made "as inappropriate as smoking." When liberals fight for same-sex marriage, from the perspective of many conservatives, they are endorsing impure behavior. So no one should be shocked that there's a backlash.

Yale psychologist Paul Bloom, confirming some of Haidt's work, has discovered that conservatives are more easily moved to disgust than liberals. "Everybody is disgusted by things like dog poop, the smell of urine, or rotten meat," he says, "but conservatives are more easily disgusted than liberals . . . by certain sex acts or by male homosexuality. Disgust has had a very ugly history. People used to be disgusted by interracial marriage. They used to say 'I can't explain why it's wrong, but it's just gross. Ergo it's wrong.'"

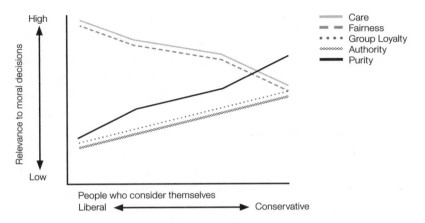

SOURCE: Reprinted courtesy of Jonathan Haidt, University of Virginia.

Figure 1. Factors liberals and conservatives consider in making moral decisions.

Seen in this way, the U.S. culture wars seem to make sense. For example, people who base their moral decisions on only two questions—who is hurt and what's fair?—are likely to defend same-sex marriage because doing so is compassionate and just. It's only fair. And they have great difficulty understanding why anyone would oppose it. But people who base their moral decisions on all five moral emotions are just as likely to see homosexuals as flamboyant outsiders who reject authority and base their very identity on offensive sexual acts.

Haidt, who confesses to being a "moderate liberal," doesn't believe that the conservative position on same-sex marriage is morally correct. But he rejects the notion that the conservative position is irrational or the product of people's twisted minds (though he concedes that might be true of some conservatives). He sees the position as the natural product of conservatives' moral emotions. Most of all, Haidt believes that it is a mistake to dismiss conservatives out of hand. He believes that the search for order and unity is a high value. There's a place for sanctity in modern life. Those who measure progress only in terms of achieving fairness and avoiding harm are missing something. "Self-righteousness is the normal human condition," Haidt says. "We all believe we're right." It takes moral humility to entertain the notion that the other side in any debate might have a point. Part of the problem is that many people live within morally isolated enclaves, associating only with people who agree with them, reading only opinions they share. "Because we cloister ourselves in these zones of zero moral diversity," Haidt warns, "we become morally colorblind; we lose the ability to see part of the moral spectrum."

Becoming OtherWise means learning to understand *why* others believe what they believe, and do what they do, and to appreciate its value. Perhaps even more important, becoming OtherWise means understanding the scaffolding of our own values and our own moral intuition, which can be even more difficult to acknowledge.

13

Second That Emotion

Businesspeople of both sexes are decidedly ambivalent about emotion in the workplace. At best, it is awkward and better be over quickly. At worse, it is a pollutant clouding the cold, data-driven reasoning that business supposedly runs on.

But for at least two decades, an alternative view has been struggling to take hold in corporate America. Its popularity has waxed and waned with the economic cycles, perhaps reaching a low point during the Great Recession. Still, a 1998 *Harvard Business Review* article on "emotional intelligence" ranks as the magazine's bestselling reprint of all time, even though the editors studiously avoided the term in the title. There are psychologists and sociologists who find the whole concept hopelessly "fuzzy." Nevertheless, the article spawned a library's worth of follow-up articles and books, not to mention an entire industry of online courses, conferences, seminars, and consultancies. What had once seemed like the softest of business concepts turned into hard currency for armies of consultants.

Charles Darwin would have approved. He pretty much established that animals need emotions to survive. Fear causes them to avoid predators. Anger triggers aggression that helps them protect their young, their mates, their food, and anything else necessary for the species' survival. Humans also need emotions. They help us make quick, often complex decisions when we have to, and they feed our more deliberative judgments, whether we realize it or not. They focus our attention, make things easier to remember, and even play a big role in our moral development. Emotions tell us what's important; they are the seat of our values. They help structure our social lives and are the scaffolding on which our self-concept rests.

Most people have experienced the six primary emotions before they learn to talk. They are happiness, surprise, fear, sadness, disgust, and anger. As we mature and our playpen expands, we acquire social emotions such as embarrassment, jealousy, guilt, shame, and pride. Emotions play such a big role in our lives that there are more than 600 words in English to describe them verbally, not to mention forty-three facial muscles to express them physically. And although human beings speak more than 6,000 languages, about 90 percent of people across different cultures have no trouble figuring out if someone is registering happiness, surprise, or disgust just by looking at the person's face. We are supersensitive to the slightest shift in people's facial expressions, especially if they are registering fear or anger.

We are not slaves to emotional cues and triggers. We can use reason to evaluate our emotions, interpret them, and even reassess our initial reaction to them. We can soften their impact or shift their meaning. In other words, we can control our own emotions as well as the effect that other people's emotions have on us. In fact, the ability to detect, assess, and control one's emotions is one of the predictors of success in relating to the Other. So, somewhat paradoxically, connecting with the Other depends on developing a deep understanding of ourselves—what triggers our strongest emotions, and how the emotions we show impact others. For example, an executive who understands that looming deadlines bring out the worse in her won't schedule an important meeting if she has work piling up. A manager who knows that talking about certain subjects tends to get him angry will think twice before reacting to an opinion that would normally set him off.

Self-awareness and self-regulation are only two aspects of emotional intelligence. But they are fundamental, and they can be learned. Unlike other management skills, however, they are not the product of higher reasoning and logic. Like emotions themselves, they originate largely in the brain's most ancient depths—in the limbic system, which governs feelings, impulses, and drives. Research has demonstrated that learning anything that involves the limbic system requires determination, lots of practice, and honest feedback from a spouse, trusted colleague, or coach.

Regulating one's emotions doesn't mean that we should all become placid automatons. On the contrary, showing the right kind of emotion at the right time can be a powerful means of communication in its own right. A manager who pretends to be unmoved by significant events, such as a major layoff or the death of a colleague, risks appearing clueless or insensitive. On the other hand, someone who flies off the handle at the slightest provocation is not only disruptive, but risks losing people's trust. The trick is modulating one's emotions and expressing them appropriately.

People who understand their own emotions are more capable of dealing with those of others. I once worked for a CEO who told me the worse part of his job was serving as the "corporate psychiatrist." He hated dealing with the steady stream of senior executives who came into his office looking for reassurance. The man was so supremely confident and optimistic that he probably never had a self-reflective thought in his life. So he didn't realize that his bluster and micromanagement style was actually the source of whatever doubts the other senior executives harbored about themselves. He interpreted their apparent lack of confidence as "wimpiness."

I once showed this CEO an employee survey indicating that people's confidence in the business was indirectly proportional to their management level. In other words, the further they were from him, the more likely they were to think the company was going the right direction. He focused on the great scores at the lower levels and completely ignored the dismal results among the people reporting to him directly. What the survey told me is that the CEO was a great communicator, but a lousy boss. Naturally, he was never able to build a strong senior team and eventually left with a division that he sold off to another company, which eased him out a year later.

Being starts with being OtherWise keenly self-aware.

14

Feeling What Others Feel

Kip Williams was a young psychology professor sitting on a picnic blanket with his dog when a wayward Frisbee flew into his back. He turned and saw two students not far away looking hopefully in his direction. He stood and tossed the Frisbee back to one of them and was surprised when it came scaling back to him.

Before he knew it, Williams was involved in their game, catching the Frisbee from one and then tossing it to the other in a wide triangle. Then, all of a sudden and without a word, the other two players went back to their original back and forth. Williams waited patiently for the Frisbee to come his way again, but it never did. At first, he watched their game with feigned interest, then pretended to be fascinated by something on the ground at his feet, and finally returned to his dog on the blanket. He was surprised how hurt he felt. He didn't know these guys, had not planned on playing Frisbee, and hadn't tossed it back and forth more than half a dozen times. Still, he felt excluded somehow.

Decades of research and a newfound expertise were born in that chance encounter. Williams devised a way to replicate his experience in the laboratory to plumb the emotional impact of exclusion. He ultimately found that social pain triggers much of the same neural machinery involved in the experience of physical pain, and that people's coping mechanisms can make them more inclined to antisocial behavior, as well as to positive efforts to regain their self-esteem. "There are two possible reactions to social ostracism," Williams has written. "Either a man emerges determined to be better, purer, and kindlier, or he goes bad, challenges the world, and does even worse things." Sadly, the research seems to indicate that the latter "is by far the commonest reaction to stigma." People who feel little hope of regaining that sense of inclusion, or have a high degree of anger over their ostracism, are especially likely to react aggressively. In fact, Williams's research draws an almost direct link between feelings of exclusion and horrific acts of violence, from the shootings at Columbine High School to similar incidents at a school in Germany and an amusement park in Tasmania.

Of course, not all who are Other are prone to violence. But by definition, the Other feel excluded, outside the mainstream of society. And the deeper their otherness, the greater their pain and despair. The obvious solution to exclusion is *inclusion,* but that isn't as easy as it sounds. When a group of people has been excluded for a long time—when they can look back at generations of outsiders like themselves—they are naturally suspicious and wary. Someone long held at arm's length doesn't expect the next move to be an embrace. In fact, although those who are Other usually develop a wide range of coping mechanisms, in the final analysis, since they are our creation, we are the only ones who can release them from exclusion. Being OtherWise is not a purely intellectual exercise; it requires more than memorizing the differences that divide us into in-groups and out-groups. It means seeing the world through the Other's eyes and feeling what they feel.

To be OtherWise, in Barack Obama's words, is to "make a habit of empathy—to recognize ourselves in each other." When inflammatory and divisive remarks by his Chicago pastor forced then-candidate Obama to confront the uncomfortable issue of race during the 2008 presidential campaign, he demonstrated a keen ability to see—and feel—the issue from multiple perspectives. He spoke of the anger and bitterness that many blacks still felt because of past segregation

and degradation. But he also acknowledged a similar and no less legitimate anger in the white community, as during this campaign speech:

> Most working- and middle-class white Americans don't feel
> that they have been particularly privileged by their race. Their
> experience is the immigrant experience—as far as they're con-
> cerned, no one's handed them anything, they've built it from
> scratch. They've worked hard all their lives, many times only to
> see their jobs shipped overseas or their pension dumped after a
> lifetime of labor. They are anxious about their futures, and feel
> their dreams slipping away; in an era of stagnant wages and global
> competition, opportunity comes to be seen as a zero-sum game, in
> which your dreams come at my expense. So when they are told to
> bus their children to a school across town; when they hear that an
> African American is getting an advantage in landing a good job or a
> spot in a good college because of an injustice that they themselves
> never committed; when they're told that their fears about crime in
> urban neighborhoods are somehow prejudiced, resentment builds
> over time.

By identifying with the fears and resentments of white people,
Obama made himself a little less "unconventional," to use his own
word, and perhaps even a little less Other. For someone often criti-
cized for being aloof and cool, Obama demonstrated emotional reso-
nance with white voters. He put himself in their shoes and had the
appropriate emotional reaction. They saw a little of him in themselves
because he showed a little of them in himself.

Now, empathy is no cure-all. It is easily manipulated, no more
motivating than a good three-hankie movie, easier to muster for those
who are near, and highly vulnerable to bias and selectivity. Ironically,
Obama demonstrated some of these shortcomings when he was later
caught complaining that "bitter" small-town Americans "cling to guns
or religion." The nuanced and deep understanding he demonstrated
on the issue of race became a hoary caricature when he spoke off-
the-cuff about small-town values. In speaking about race, he was on
familiar territory, not only in terms of his own experience, but also

because it was a subject that he had wrestled with intellectually over many years, alone and in discussions with close friends of different races. On race, he had the benefit of multiple perspectives.

What psychologists call "perspective taking" is the first step in developing a greater capacity for empathy. Generically, it is the ability to see things from a point of view other than our own, to develop a mental representation of the thoughts, feelings, and motivations of others. At this point, we don't actually feel what others feel; we are just able to describe it, more or less accurately. Perspective taking is an act of higher-level reasoning, but it is a necessary step to developing true empathy. As children develop, they begin to realize that other people have thoughts and feelings of their own. Over time, this realization usually blossoms into empathy—strong feelings stimulated by seeing others in emotionally charged situations. Such feelings are usually involuntary and highly dependent on our closeness to the other person. Empathetic feelings are stronger for a close relative or friend than for a stranger and may be practically nonexistent for an outcast under normal circumstances.

But a long series of experiments have demonstrated that the simple act of purposefully considering someone else's point of view can reduce prejudice and deflate stereotypes, even of outcasts, expanding the ambit within which empathy can take root. No one is sure exactly how this mechanism works, but it seems that simply learning more about other people makes them less threatening to us, while revealing how similar they are. There is even some suggestion that imagining what someone else's life is like increases our *own* self-esteem and reduces feelings of prejudice. Unfortunately, there is also evidence that most of us are emotionally lazy, adjusting our own perspective only enough to reach what feels like a satisfactory facsimile of what the other party might believe or feel. True perspective taking requires greater discipline and a willingness to let go of our preexisting beliefs and attitudes. Refining our natural empathetic feelings and expanding their reach to include the Other is not easy. But once we allow ourselves to truly understand how someone else feels—even an outcast—we can actually tune into the other person's emotions and feel their reverberations within ourselves. Of course, none of this can be done from the safety of our office or den. We have to get out in the field and meet on the other person's turf.

The prospect of meeting with someone we consider "Other" is about as inviting as a rendezvous with an extraterrestrial. Few of us are ready, or feel equipped, for a personal encounter with someone so unlike ourselves. Author Elizabeth Lesser (a regular on Oprah's Book Club) has a less-threatening suggestion: Take the Other to lunch. And she has a more approachable Other in mind for a lunch companion. "Anyone whose lifestyle offends you," she suggests, "or whose point of view makes smoke come out of your ears." Lesser would like to see diners everywhere filled with liberals hosting conservatives, straights breaking bread with gays, antigun feminists picking french fries off some rednecks' plates. She realizes that inevitably things would only degenerate into a food fight unless the participants agree to some basic ground rules. So she has some.

Remember that the goal is to get to know one person from a stereotyped group—like a neighbor who practices a different religion or a work colleague with extreme political views. In the interests of seeing beyond those differences, stifle any urges to correct, persuade, defend, or interrupt. On the contrary, be curious and conversational. Ask honest, agenda-free questions and listen to the answers instead of thinking of a snappy reply. And repeat what you heard in our own words before following up with more questions.

When Lesser made this proposal at a conference dominated by liberal intellectuals, it got some appreciative laughs. But she was dead serious. "The worst eras in human histories start with negative otherizing," she said, "and then they morph into violent extremism." She could have been describing remarks made at that very conference or at any of thousands of similar meetings hosted by partisans on both sides of the political spectrum. And her final admonition is good general meeting practice: "Speak up when you hear otherizing talk that feeds paranoia and inflames the other side," she said.

Some of Lesser's listeners probably considered her pitch too idealistic for the real world—maybe even unnecessary. But while social anthropologists have long believed empathy is hardwired into our brains, that wiring is coming loose. Scientists at the University of

Michigan have discovered that college students' self-reported empathy is in sharp decline. Almost 75 percent of students today rate themselves less empathetic than the average student did thirty years ago. No one knows precisely why, but psychologists have long known that even our most basic inherent emotional responses can be altered by our social context. Precisely what is sapping young people of their natural impulse to feel for others is unclear, but one candidate is Americans' increasing social isolation. Educators complain that today's kids appear to be detached from the world, because they don't follow the news, and even relatively detached from their friends, because they communicate largely in fast, frequent, and impersonal bursts of brief text over a cell phone.

Another candidate is the general decline in reading. That's not as random as it might seem. Reason and emotion are not at the opposite ends of a continuum. They are intertwined, reinforcing and regulating each other. People who have suffered damage to the part of their brain responsible for generating emotions are literally incapable of making decisions because they don't know what they want and value. Educating your emotions is just as important as sharpening your reasoning. In fact, the two are related. Immersing ourselves in art—highbrow or lowbrow—exercises our empathic muscles and hones our sensing skills. Indeed, great literature allows us to experience someone else's emotions and helps us articulate our own feelings by giving us the vocabulary to describe them.

Whatever the cause of our empathy deficit, there seems little doubt that the empathic skills of those just entering the workforce could use improvement. And that does not augur well for the future. Emory University biologist Frans de Waal has spent his career studying our closest primate relatives to better understand why we are who we are. In fact, he lays much of the blame for recent economic problems at the door of "bad biology, which resulted in a gross oversimplification of human nature." By "bad biology," he means the notion that we are the product of intense evolutionary competition that sorted the strong from the weak and produced progeny motivated only by their own self-interest. According to that theory, society as a whole is better off when every individual does only what benefits himself, without regard to the needs of others. Believing that, many Americans in the 1980s and 1990s turned John F. Kennedy's famous admonition on its head. "Ask not what your country can do for you," was their motto, "ask what you can do for yourself." The torch had been passed to yet another new generation, and this one believed in the power of greed. They foresaw all kinds of benefits trickling down from the haves to the have-nots, in the comfortable conviction that free-market competition is the self-regulating, economic equivalent of natural selection.

De Waal doesn't deny the process of natural selection, but he thinks the "trickle-down theorists" have drawn the wrong lesson from it. "The fundamental yet rarely asked question is why natural selection designed our brains so that we're in tune with our fellow human beings and feel distress at their distress, and pleasure at their pleasure," he writes. "If the exploitation of others were all that mattered, evolution should never have got into the empathy business. But it did, and the political and economic elites had better grasp that in a hurry."

De Waal has seen evidence of something like empathy in many species of animals, and he can trace it to some of the oldest structures in our brain. Empathy is so ingrained in us that it almost always finds expression, giving us subtle cues to the state of other people's minds through their expression or posture. It can be suppressed when necessary, as when doctors and nurses have to shove it aside to treat a grievously injured patient. Some call this process "psychic numbing." Habit and social conditioning can also stunt our natural empathy, as we have seen. Most important, empathy can and must be enhanced. "Empathy for 'other people'," he writes, "is the one commodity the world is lacking more than oil."

Part **Two**

Strangers Abroad

15

Strange Places

Prematurely bald with a brush mustache, bushy eyebrows, and piercing eyes, the late Ted Levitt looked like the demanding overseer of a busy loading dock. For more than forty years, he trafficked not in goods but in ideas, great pallets of ideas that are still taught at business schools around the world. Officially, he chaired the marketing area at the Harvard Business School, but through an unusually productive life that included a four-year stint as editor of the *Harvard Business Review* and a prodigious output of books and articles, Levitt influenced generations of the world's business leaders.

Levitt's remarkable writing career was bookended by a dry-as-dust doctoral thesis entitled "World War II Manpower Mobilization and Utilization in a Local Labor Market" and, nearly three decades later, an outrageous *New York Times* opinion piece that claimed "every sustained wave of technological progress and economic development everywhere has been fueled by greed, profiteering, special privileges, and megalomania." The two pieces neatly demonstrated his evolution from a scholar of economics to an agent provocateur.

One former student likened Levitt's genius to grabbing businesspeople by the lapels and shouting "Wake up!" One of Levitt's loudest wake-up calls appeared in the *Harvard Business Review* in

1983. That's when he coined the term *globalization* and convinced a generation of MBAs to focus outside U.S. borders for future growth. Levitt didn't get everything right in his article, "The Globalization of Markets." For one thing, he foresaw a homogenized worldwide market for standardized products that differed only in the language used in their packaging and instruction booklets. On that, he may have been ahead of his time by a century or two. The homogenized global market Levitt envisioned has yet to materialize. Local competitors have consistently outflanked companies that attempted to offer standardized products around the world. And companies that acquired local brands and tried to manage them from U.S. headquarters lost touch with their customers. But Levitt did call the shape of the coming world correctly. It would no longer have the United States as its dominant center, at least not in terms of marketplace growth.

From the vantage point of the early twenty-first century, it is hard to understand how radical Levitt's suggestion seemed just two decades ago. When Levitt wrote his piece in 1983, a long-distance phone call to London from New York cost about $1.44 a minute. The same call to Tokyo cost $2.31. Today, both calls cost pennies and can even be made free over the Internet. And thanks to the introduction of containerization in the 1960s, the cost of shipping goods internationally today accounts for so little of their value that some economists consider it essentially "costless."

In the early 1980s, foreign trade was only about 10 percent of U.S. gross domestic product (GDP). By 2010, it accounted for more than 25 percent. Today, about half of the S&P 500's revenue comes from products produced and sold outside the United States. And even though less than one percent of all U.S. companies qualify as "multinational," they account for about 20 percent of private sector jobs and for about three-quarters of private R&D spending. That mirrors what's going on in other countries. In 1969, the export of goods and services represented only 12 percent of World GDP. In 2004, the latest year for which data is available, it accounted for about 26 percent. In the 1980s, about $500 billion in foreign currency was traded daily on the world markets; in 2010, about $4 *trillion* changed hands every day.

U.S. companies initially focused their globalization efforts on the countries of Western Europe, which were the most familiar to American management. That's not particularly surprising. Companies usually start internationalizing by entering countries that are culturally close to them. Toyota, for example, began by exporting cars to Southeast Asian countries. Nevertheless, some companies made naive mistakes even in what they considered familiar territory. For example, mint-flavored Crest toothpaste was one of Procter & Gamble's bestselling products in the States when the company introduced it to the United Kingdom in the 1950s. P&G didn't even have to change the packaging much; it shipped pallets of the stuff to Southampton. But it gathered dust on store shelves. It wasn't until product developers at P&G, the company that invented consumer research, actually talked to potential customers that they discovered the problem. Brits at that time associated spearmint with a liniment to be spread on aching muscles, not with something you would brush on your teeth.

Globalization requires more than just shipping products across borders; it is fundamentally an interaction between companies and societies that creates something new for both of them. MTV, for example, is the exemplar of the very technological and social phenomena that inspired Levitt's globalization insight. And indeed MTV entered Europe in 1987 with pan-regional, advertiser-supported English programming. Within a few years, however, MTV discovered that the sum was smaller than its parts—local ad buys tallied to a much bigger figure than pan-European purchases. There simply weren't many advertisers who offered the same product across Europe because preferences varied so much by country. Furthermore, while young people shared many musical tastes, there were also sharp differences from country to country. When local competitors, such as VIVA in Germany and MCM in France, began to exploit these differences, MTV quickly changed business models. Instead of beaming the same programming across Europe, it created a number of local channels, tailored to local cultural tastes with a mixture of national, regional, and international artists, along with locally produced and globally shared programming. Today, MTV has about two dozen different program channels across Europe and another twenty or so in Canada, Asia, Australia, Latin America, the Caribbean, and Africa. MTV is neither a "multinational" company offering local products in multiple nations, nor an "international" company shipping a standardized product across borders. It is a "global" company intimately engaged with local societies to satisfy universal needs that Levitt described as "the alleviation of life's burdens, and the expansion of discretionary time and spending power."

At about the same time Levitt was writing "The Globalization of Markets" in the 1980s, the Japanese coined a term for the overall phenomenon of simultaneous globalization and localization. They call it *dochakuka*, a word that consists of three characters: *do, chaku,* and *ka,* meaning, "land," "arrive at," and "process of." A literal translation of *dochakuka* conceptualizes not *where* a company does business—globally or locally—but *how.* It means to be assimilated or "nativized." To the Japanese, a people very aware of their status as an island nation separated from the world by vast oceans, a company arriving in a new country must act in ways that not only show respect for local customs, but also adapt to them, just as a farmer would adapt his agricultural techniques to the land he is cultivating.

In the 1990s, sociologist Roland Robertson translated the term as "glocalization," a neologism of "global" and "local" that captured the paradoxical nature of globalization, which could be, as Robertson wrote, "in and of itself, simultaneously homogenizing—making things the same —and at the same time, making things different." In marketing terms, it means that multinational companies have to deal not only with worldwide considerations, but also with the particular conditions and preferences of every country in which they do business. McDonald's recipes are identical everywhere down to the millimeter width of the hamburger patties. But it also serves McLaks (grilled salmon sandwiches) in Norway and McHuevos (poached egg hamburgers) in Uruguay, and even beer where that product is expected, as in Germany. And courtesy is such a precious value in Asia that McDonald's restaurants in Beijing assign five to ten female receptionists to take care of children and talk with parents. Not only is that unnecessary—and unaffordable—in Western countries, but it would probably be looked on suspiciously.

Globalization requires more than a passport, a Berlitz guide, and a local "fixer" to make introductions and set up appointments. Successful global companies invest heavily in understanding the cultural values of the countries in which they do business. Perhaps remembering its U.K. experience, P&G spent three years studying the consumer market in China before introducing its first product there in 1988. The first expat the company sent to China was Berenike Ullmann, a Mandarin-speaking Swiss woman who had just graduated from Cambridge University. Her initial assignment was to test corporate ads in Beijing and Shanghai, but she was soon talking to consumers and observing their daily lives.

Ullmann found that the Chinese had very low expectations of laundry detergents. They really didn't care whether a detergent got their clothes whiter or brighter. Based on that insight, the company completely changed its initial plans to manufacture Tide detergent at a state-run factory it had purchased in Guangzhou. Instead, it shifted production to Head & Shoulders shampoo because Ullmann had also discovered that the Chinese were concerned about dandruff, which meant they had high expectations of shampoo.

Eventually, P&G sent people to live with typical Chinese families to observe how they went about such daily tasks as brushing their teeth, changing the baby's diapers, doing the wash, etc. When the company introduced a new toothpaste to the Chinese market, it had the flavor of jasmine tea because many local consumers consider tea a natural cure for bad breath and jasmine is the most popular flavor. Today, P&G not only has the bestselling toothpaste and shampoo in China, it is the country's leading consumer products company, with revenue of more than $1 billion. Its major foreign competitor, Unilever, on the other hand, has just $300 million in sales and lags behind P&G in every segment where they compete.

P&G's goal in new markets is to be as common as it can be and as different as it needs to be. That means spending a lot of time with consumers who are neither easy to reach nor to approach, in places like the jungles of Brazil, the slums of India, and the villages of rural China. That's essential to ensure that customers derive the right meaning about a brand or product—one that it is modeled on their unique needs, values, and aspirations.

But as writer and marketing consultant Jeff Yang points out, local knowledge ages very fast. "Who would have predicted just a decade ago that Korean pop culture would flow across the world and that Korea would take manufacturing leadership away from the Japanese?" he asks. "What's critically important is to develop the principles and processes to ensure that whatever comes next, you're ready." Since principles and processes are only as good as the people who use them, smart companies look for people who are inclusive and adaptive— people who are OtherWise.

16

Roots, Not Branches

Reynold Levy has the rounded shoulders and gray mien of someone who spends untold hours in a comfortable armchair, spectacles perched on the end of his nose, reading some thick tome. It's a mistaken impression. He does read a lot, usually following ten or twelve hours at his day job. But he's anything but a monkish recluse. He counts among his closest friends a long list of bold-faced names from the worlds of business, finance, the arts, and politics.

Standing in conversation, he is likely to wrap his arms around his torso, hugging himself, as if to better control the torrent of perfectly constructed sentences that flow from his mouth in a quiet, mellifluous tone. Many of those sentences are in the form of rhetorical questions, such as, "What would one think of a CEO whose secretary—upon being queried by a visitor—volunteers that she has not placed an international long-distance phone call for him in the past thirty days?" Few who know him would proffer a response, knowing that his question is simply the prelude to a lengthy, erudite, and perfectly constructed argument on the failures of some companies to fully appreciate the risks and opportunities of globalization.

All this was delivered impromptu, standing at the coat check of Lincoln Center's eponymously but incongruously named haute Italian restaurant, Lincoln. Just as oddly, it was Levy's first visit to the place for a meal, even though it is superb and had opened months before—not to mention that he is Lincoln Center's president, a fact not lost on the restaurant's attentive staff.

Before joining Lincoln Center for the Performing Arts, Levy was CEO of the International Rescue Committee, a humanitarian organization that shelters and repatriates refugees from places like Darfur, Kosovo, and Afghanistan. In five years, he eliminated the organization's financial deficit, tripled contributions, and doubled grants and service contracts, greatly expanding assistance to displaced people in the world's most dangerous trouble spots. Levy's impact at Lincoln Center has been similarly remarkable. In another productive five-year period—much of which coincided with the worst recession since the 1930s—he raised more than a billion dollars to fund a widely praised reconstruction of the center's aging sixteen-acre campus. And as that project neared completion, he began an ambitious initiative to market Lincoln Center's programming and management expertise to other cultural organizations, signing a consulting agreement with the developers of a new performing arts complex in Tianjin, China's fifth-largest city.

As you would expect of someone with both a PhD and a law degree, Levy has a nearly flawless memory. He is also a lifelong learner. And one of the things he's studied most closely is how institutions approach existential challenges. Globalization is one of the most daunting challenges facing most U.S. businesses. It is simultaneously the surest source of future growth and the biggest hole in their bench strength. Complicating matters further, population growth is shifting from the familiar developed countries of the North, like those of Western Europe, to the more exotic developing countries of the South, like China, India, and Brazil. In 1990, nearly a third of the world's population lived in the developed North; by 2000, less than one in five did; and by 2050, demographers project just 10 percent will. Levy puts the problem in easily grasped terms: "The State Department tells me that, as best they can estimate, about 33,000 Americans speak Mandarin Chinese. I was just in China. And they told me that their best estimate is that there are more Chinese who are fluent in English than there are Americans."

As AT&T's vice president for international government relations in the 1990s, Levy lived through the company's initial forays into foreign markets. AT&T had enviable strengths—talented managers, relationships with every telephone company in the world, access to the best consultants money could buy, and vaults of money. Sadly, consultants can size a market, but they can't penetrate it. The most talented managers are pretty impotent if they don't speak the language, don't know the territory, and seldom leave hotel conference rooms. The local telephone companies weren't thrilled about the idea of sharing their market, even with their rich American aunt, Ma Bell. And a fat wallet only makes it harder to see your own limitations. "AT&T, like many American companies, thought it could penetrate foreign markets with a well-armed band of expatriates, at least at higher levels of management. But those poor souls didn't have a clue," Levy remembers. "They literally lived in gilded ghettos, separated from the locals behind locked doors and high walls. Even in Japan, where the whole country is gilded almost, they'd still find a place to isolate themselves from the Japanese and talk among themselves. And all the conversation was about housing and restaurants. They saw the whole experience as punching a ticket, and they counted the days until they could get back to the states."

Ironically, on Levy's next career stop, at the International Rescue Committee, ticket-punching expats were a luxury he couldn't afford. A nonprofit organization like the IRC is forced to face its limitations every day. By necessity, it has to source talent where the market is. "When I was there, the IRC had 4,000 workers in Afghanistan," Levy remembers. "Only four of them were expats." Levy thought he understood the value of nongovernmental organizations (NGOs). After all, he had run one early in his career when he was executive director of the 92nd Street Y. And at AT&T he had helped fund the programs of organizations ranging from UNICEF to the IRC itself. But he didn't fully appreciate what a valuable resource they could be for global companies until a cocktail party conversation with one of his top lieutenants.

At the time, John Keys was the IRC's country manager for Rwanda, the African country that had been wracked by genocidal conflict in the early 1990s. As it happened, the country's new leader, Paul Kagame, fascinated Levy. "He seemed to me like Golda Meir," Levy recalls, "surrounded by threatening states, reasserting country pride, at least ostensibly trying to reconcile Tutsi and Hutu, and not taking any grief from the countries around him." Levy had read everything about Kagame he could get his hands on, but Keys was telling him things about Kagame and his points of view that he hadn't heard before. "John, how do you know this?" he asked. The answer was an epiphany of sorts for Levy. "Well, my wife has the same hairdresser as Mrs. Kagame," Keys said. "They see each other all the time, and that's what they talk about."

Levy remembers thinking that "the last thing in the world that a major corporation can do—[even] with its big, vaunted government relations apparatus and its market intelligence from expensive consultants—is get close enough to the ground to understand what the head of state is doing through the eyes and the mouth of his spouse. That's the kind of on-the-ground intelligence that NGOs can bring at their very best. They live in the country. Moreover, unlike many companies, the best NGOs put a big emphasis on hiring local nationals and have a very thin layer of expatriates." Companies can learn a lot about foreign markets from the nonprofit community and, in Levy's view, they are making a very big mistake in ignoring those intellectual resources, which he believes have become more and more potent. Instead of viewing NGOs as potential petitioners who would love to siphon corporate resources, CEOs should consider them on-the-ground sources of intelligence that can facilitate market entry.

NGO influence has exploded in the last sixty years. An estimated 60,000 international NGOs are active on the world stage; more than 2,000 have consultative status with the United Nations. Edelman's annual "Trust Barometer" consistently shows public confidence in NGOs outpacing that of governments, businesses, and the media. In fact, the 2011 Edelman survey shows that nongovernmental organizations are the most trusted organizations in the world "to do what is right." Some say that NGOs are to the twenty-first century what nation-states were to the nineteenth century. Their financial resources and expertise in community development, education, and health care often exceed those of the governments in the countries where they operate. Even larger countries, including the United States, depend on them to deliver much of their foreign aid, especially following natural disasters. The combined resources of international NGOs even exceed those of the entire United Nations system (excluding the World Bank and the International Monetary Fund).

"However a company is organized on the ground, its local managers should be plotting to find the levers to market entry, the intellectual capital about the country, its institutional memory," Levy says. "And more often than not, they'll find it in the NGO community, which will also have a longer length of stay than any for-profit they could possibly find." In addition to providing intelligence on the new market, NGOs also bring perspectives that can help avoid missteps in a local landscape littered with social and political issues as foreign to corporate managers as the indigenous language. Partnering with NGOs has another benefit—it demonstrates a company's interest in the country's future, not simply in its ability to sign contracts. "That was [former AIG CEO] Hank Greenberg's genius," Levy observes. "He was genuinely eager for China to thrive, not just for AIG to gain market share. That's quite unusual for most company executives." But it is an example that an increasing number of enlightened companies are emulating. For example, food giant Cargill has been partnering with the U.N. World Food Programme for nearly a decade on school lunch and deworming programs in Latin America, Africa, and Indonesia. Both Coca-Cola and Pepsi are working with NGOs on water development projects in countries throughout Africa and Asia.

But NGOs can be reluctant partners. Beyond politely answering a few questions, they have no real interest in helping corporations; they are totally dedicated to furthering their cause. Furthermore, they are very protective of the independence that is the wellspring of their credibility. They are paranoid about anything that would create the appearance of compromising their independence or their accountability to stakeholders. And the best NGOs will work only with companies that can demonstrate that they are not only serious about change, but also well positioned to influence activity across their industry. Similarly, companies should partner only with an NGO that has a track record of constructive relationships. As in any other partnership, both partners need to understand how the other benefits. At the very beginning of the partnership, the roles, rules, and even the risks of a partnership need to be crystal clear to all parties. Both partners need to agree to the scope of their work together, their mutual expectations, how they will make decisions, how they will evaluate progress, and how they will resolve conflicts. It can work. Leading companies like General Electric, Walmart, McDonald's, FedEx, and UPS have partnered with the Environmental Defense Fund to reduce their packaging, lower greenhouse emissions, and find sources for more sustainable food and forest products.

Some companies have tapped NGOs for their on-the-ground experience and capabilities. For example, in the mid-1970s, Merck scientists discovered an effective treatment for river blindness, a parasitic disease common in the developing world. The drug promised to be safe and effective—one annual dose could treat the disease and prevent blindness, and if an entire community was treated for the twelve- to fourteen-year lifecycle of the worms that caused it, the disease could be totally eliminated.

However, the company didn't have a presence in the countries where the disease was most common. So Merck made an open-ended commitment to give the drug away until river blindness was no longer a threat to public health. In 1988, the first year of the program, it lined up half a dozen NGOs to distribute about 100,000 doses. Today, more than two dozen NGOs facilitate the distribution of 90 million doses a year. The World Health Organization projects that Latin America could be free of the disease in a few years, and the goal even seems within reach in parts of Africa. Merck has gained valuable experience in dealing with NGOs and health ministries. More important, it has developed a reputation as a trusted partner in countries that may someday be important markets. Other pharmaceutical companies have even adopted the same model of working with NGOs to battle other tropical diseases as well as malaria, tuberculosis, and HIV/AIDS.

In the beginning, many NGOs were moral absolutists incapable of compromise. Obsessed with a single issue, their driving purpose was to block an action. Their default setting was for high-profile media campaigns, designed to embarrass their opponents into submission. They used companies or brands as springboards to publicize their cause. Nothing generates ink (not to mention contributions) like a good fight, especially with a well-known brand. It became such a staple in their kit bag that even the threat of bad publicity could move big companies. But over the years many NGOs realized that this inherently negative strategy was self-limiting. Randall Hayes, founder of the Rainforest Action Network, explained it well in a talk to other activists: "If you [as an NGO] are not talking to business, you are just preaching to the choir. Real change . . . is going to come from the business sector; we can't depend on government regulation to solve our problems."

That's not to say that NGOs don't have their share of critics. Sebastian Mallaby's book about former World Bank president James Wolfensohn argues that NGOs are often ill informed and incoherent, unaccountable and uncompromising, and even damaging to the development causes they proclaim to champion. Indeed, the NGO world is not monolithic. NGOs sometimes disagree among themselves, not only on tactics, but also on goals. The World Wildlife Fund, for example, does not oppose recreational hunting—as long as it doesn't endanger a species. The equally moderate International Fund for Animal Welfare, on the other hand, opposes all hunting on the grounds of cruelty. And in some countries, the term "NGO" may be too organized to describe the gangs and other loose-knit organizations that have a particular axe to grind.

With all those caveats and cautions, developing a good working relationship with selected NGOs is an effective way for global companies to enter global markets, where the key to being OtherWise is to share people's cares and dreams, sinking roots rather than just opening a few local branches.

17

Political Attunement

A self-described "realist," Richard Haass was a senior foreign policy official under both Presidents Bush. But Vice President Dick Cheney considered him so insufficiently hawkish that he had his phone tapped. Having his advice ignored is the least of the indignities Haass has suffered in public life.

As president of the prestigious Council on Foreign Relations (CFR), Haass is arguably in a more influential position now than when he was at the State Department. He's a regular fixture on TV news shows and the lecture circuit. Journalists solicit his opinions. Presidential candidates, as well as sitting heads of state, seek—and sometimes even follow—his advice, not to mention foreign secretaries, ambassadors, and business executives chasing a rapidly globalizing economy.

"Ideas matter" could be Haass's unofficial motto, and ideas—big, world-affecting ideas—are the CFR's stock in trade. But Haass has few detectable pretensions. His desk, and the floor around it, is piled with books and papers, and the gentle ping of incoming e-mail sounds frequently during an hour's conversation. He handles his own e-mail, firing off brief, to-the-point missives free of capital letters. A mobile of five globes hangs above the sitting area at one end of his office.

Looked at more closely, each of the globes is the earth at a different point in time, with political boundaries that shift from globe to globe and across the centuries, as if to remind him and visitors that the world is constantly changing. Asked about the mobile's significance, Haass says, "I like globes and maps, and this one made sense, I thought, given my background and job." Then, perhaps remembering the diplomat's rule of inscrutability, he quickly adds, "Not to mention that sometimes a mobile is just a mobile."

Haass looks more like a hard-charging executive in shirtsleeves than the Oxford-educated author of twelve books—eleven of them on American foreign policy and one on management. Even that one-off volume, *The Bureaucratic Entrepreneur: How to Be Effective in Any Unruly Organization* (Washington, DC: Brookings Institute, 1999), could have been inspired by his government service. I was a little surprised, then, by his answer when I asked what businesspeople needed to do to be OtherWise. "They need to learn from politicians," he said. "Their operating environment is fundamentally different than it was just a generation ago. Increasingly, business leaders have to contend with people who can't be told what to do and, at best, they can only try to persuade. Whether it's union officials, government officials, regulators, the media, special interest groups, suddenly they're dealing with people who have a degree of independence and an even greater say in what businesses can do. It increasingly reminds me of the world in which politicians and public officials operate."

Haass says this is particularly true in global markets, and expanding internationally is no longer merely an attractive option for American companies. "The United States accounts for 5 percent of the world demographically and about 25 percent economically, but that share is going to fall," he cautions. "I think it's going to become the exception for an American company not to do most of its business overseas. A lot of American companies are going to have to be global to make it, simply because that's where the growth is going to be. And doing business internationally involves nothing less than a fundamentally different way of doing business. It means dealing with a wider and more powerful group of constituencies and being proactive, not reactive, with them."

Haass thinks the best CEOs have a lot in common with the best public officials. "The savviest executives are those who understand the nuances of government and how to balance the concerns of broad, highly varied political and social constituencies," Haass says. That, as it happens, is what the Council on Foreign Relations is all about.

Businesspeople don't join the Council on Foreign Relations for the prestige and name-dropping potential, even though almost every foreign leader of any consequence has hobnobbed with its members in its wood-paneled drawing rooms. The CFR's home base is a handsome limestone mansion, just off Park Avenue on Manhattan's Upper East Side. Coming in through the lobby entrance, you can almost imagine young ladies in long silk gowns gliding down its winding staircase to the marble foyer. And, in fact, many probably have, since the building is rented out for wedding receptions. But most of the five-story structure is a workaday warren of offices and conference rooms. The building is the scene for about 250 events a year, including panel discussions, lectures, interviews, symposia, town hall meetings, film screenings, book clubs, and conference calls.

Those events represent an opportunity for business executives to engage in "unobserved learning," that is, gain new insights into the intersection of politics, economics, and business. As companies expand their global footprint, they soon discover that they are living in the swarm and gridlock of that intersection. Indeed, they may sometimes feel as if they are stuck on a traffic island in the middle of the intersection and can't get off. New social and political demands assail them from every side. Social activists and nongovernmental organizations (NGOs) assume a role, alongside governments, as their de facto regulators. The business risks they are paid to calculate multiply exponentially. "Risk control these days requires a richer analysis," Haass warns. "Not only do businesses have to gauge the political risk that a country's laws will change, the economic risk that its currency will falter, or the market risk that demand will decline, they now have to consider larger geopolitical forces at work in the world." Months before the popular uprisings in the Middle East, Haass told me that "in order to do intelligent analysis about Egypt, you need something complementary to traditional, 'inside-out' analysis. You also need 'outside-in' analysis, because Egypt isn't operating as an island. You should look at what is likely to happen in the Islamic world."

Global businesses operate in a complex, crowded, and uncertain environment. Even more critical than the complexities of language, cultural, and legal differences, they have to deal with more independent actors—ranging from sovereign nations to nonstate actors, special interests, NGOs, and the media—all of whom can affect their operating ability. Sovereign states increasingly find themselves in exactly the same position. "In every facet of international life," Haass says, "there's a gap between the dimensions of the challenges and the arrangements governments have put in place to deal with them."

The gap is so large, in fact, that Haass has suggested the development of new mechanisms to give nonstate actors a formal role in regional and global governance. He isn't proposing that Microsoft, Amnesty International, or Goldman Sachs be given seats in the United Nations General Assembly, but he does believe that representatives of such organizations should participate in regional and global deliberations to address cross-border issues, if they have the capacity and the willingness to do so. "Today's world is increasingly one of distributed, rather than concentrated, power," Haass observes. "It's folly to think anyone can really address climate change, for example, without involving the major energy companies, as well as key NGOs, local authorities, OPEC, and a host of other nonstate players who have a stake in the issue—and the capacity to address it." Haass sees a new world of "designer multilateralism," where the people addressing an issue will be whoever has "the greatest potential to get us to the goal." "In virtually every case," he adds, "you'll have players who are nonstate actors. You have to go way beyond people who have a seat at the U.N."

Haass seems unperturbed that suggestions like that play right into the hands of a small but vocal group of activists who accuse the Council on Foreign Relations of being a shadowy conspiracy of corporate and academic elites dedicated to the establishment of a global government. He says he's just being realistic. And in fact, state/nonstate hybrids have been around for decades. The International Telecommunications Union, for example, was founded in 1865. Nongovernmental organizations have been assisting refugees and doing development work on behalf of Western countries for decades. From Haass's perspective, the rapid globalization of the world economy has only accelerated the trend. Globalization challenges one of sovereignty's fundamental principles: the ability to control what crosses borders in either direction. "Sovereign states increasingly measure their vulnerability not to one another," he has pointed out, "but to forces beyond their control." Global corporations are—and are seen to be—among the most powerful of those actors. With the opportunities of globalization come obligations—in his view, obligations to make a difference.

"Take climate change," Haass says. "This is one of the few areas where many businesses are actually in the vanguard. They're discovering that sound environmental decisions are often financially beneficial. Rather than there being a price to pay, they often turn out to be good for the bottom line."

Another area Haass believes is at the intersection of business self-interest and societal need is female literacy. "There is the potential for great impact," he says. "If more girls learn how to read, it has tremendous consequences for everything from the rate of infant mortality to the economic success of the society." It can even help reduce the intolerance that plagues some Muslim communities and perhaps prevent the radicalization of some of their youth.

Haass doesn't particularly like the phrase *corporate social responsibility* because "that marginalizes the practice and reinforces the temptation to silo it, to keep it separate from what the company is really about." He sees social responsibility as a set of mainstream activities that contribute to the bottom line over time. Rather than something ancillary to the business, it is the way a company *does* business. "If you're doing things that develop human capital, broaden education, modernize infrastructure, improve land use, [and] contribute to people's health, it may not feed the bottom line today," he says, "but you're building better markets, you're investing in the future. And that's smart business." That's why Haass doesn't think those activities should be delegated to the PR or public affairs departments. "There is a danger in thinking you can channel those interactions or concerns to narrowly based functional offices rather than headquarters and the executive suite," he warns. "The new world calls for a different sense of how the CEO orders priorities."

PepsiCo CEO Indra Nooyi agrees with the contention that today's business leaders need a fundamentally different set of skills than those of the past, including the ability to work closely with public officials and to exhibit emotional intelligence toward employees. Skeptics might scoff that they wouldn't expect much else from a self-described working mom—and a sari-wearing native of India, at that. Nooyi's background may not be typical for a Fortune 500 CEO. But her performance hasn't been, either. In her first four years as CEO, despite a worldwide recession, PepsiCo's average annual revenue and profit grew at double-digit rates. The company also returned $29.3 billion to shareowners in the form of dividends and stock repurchases. "My honest belief is that corporations are little republics in their own way," she has said. "Look at PepsiCo. Our market capitalization is almost $100 billion. We're bigger than many countries. We have enormous influence in the world. But we cannot be guided purely by the earnings cycle, or we might end up adding costs to society. We have a profound role to play in society, and we have to make sure that we are constructive members of society."

CEOs and their companies needn't be apologetic about their global operations, secure in the knowledge that they increase the prosperity of underdeveloped nations and contribute to reducing child labor, increasing literacy, and improving the social and economic standing of women. But they also have to realize that the events surrounding the Great Recession of 2007–2009 undermined people's confidence in the business community. People are naturally going to question corporate leaders' competence and values when economically important companies go financially bankrupt, as in the cases of Lehman Brothers and General Motors, or suffer the reputational equivalent, as in the cases of BP, Goldman Sachs, Toyota, and too many others. The business community lost more than money in the recent recession. It lost legitimacy.

"In addition to economic performance as determined by economic outcomes, organizational decisions are also judged by the criteria of legitimacy," according to PepsiCo's Nooyi. "A legitimate organization is one that is perceived as pursuing socially acceptable goals in a socially acceptable manner." For PepsiCo, that has meant removing trans fats from its products, reducing sodium and saturated fat in its snack foods, and making products in calorie-specific serving sizes to help people manage their diets. In developing countries, like Mexico, it has meant working with local farmers and NGOs to ensure a reliable source of high-quality potatoes, corn, and sunflower oil near its factories. Those initiatives produced higher incomes for the farmers, more work for local communities, and lower transportation costs for PepsiCo.

But the key learning here comes not so much from the specifics of such initiatives as from the political attunement from which they spring. For a company like PepsiCo, social responsibility is not a "nice to do" sideline; it is the way it conducts its core business. That's not idealistic fantasy; it's hardcore realism. And part of being OtherWise.

18

Management Across Borders

Back in the first half of 2001, when the world was less on edge, a British psychologist named, appropriately enough, Richard Wiseman set out to find the world's funniest joke. He and his colleagues constructed a website that would collect jokes and ask people to rate them on a specially designed "giggleometer." (Patent pending, I suppose.)

In a year, they collected more than 40,000 usable jokes—after culling out all the dirty ones—which were rated by more than 1.5 million people around the world. Here's the joke that had the most universal appeal, since dubbed "the world's funniest joke":

> Two hunters are in the woods when one of them collapses to the ground and his eyes roll back in his head.
>
> His companion whips out his cell phone and calls emergency services. He gasps, "My friend is dead. What can I do?"
>
> The operator says, "Calm down. I'm sure we can help. First, make sure that he's dead." There's silence on the line, then a shot can be heard.
>
> Back on the line, the guy says, "Okay, now what?"

The winning joke was submitted by a thirty-one year-old psychiatrist in the United Kingdom who said he liked it because it reminds people that there's always someone out there more stupid than themselves.

Professor Wiseman and his team analyzed the data every which way, and some of the results are fascinating. For example, the Germans found almost all the jokes equally funny. On the other hand, the Canadians barely moved the giggleometer's needle. The Irish liked wordplay, such as:

Patient: I have a strawberry in my bum.
Doctor: I've got a cream for that.

Americans liked jokes that made them feel superior, such as:

Texan: Where are you from?
Harvard Grad: I'm from a place where we don't end our sentences with prepositions.
Texan: Okay. Where are you from, asshole?

Many Europeans liked jokes with a touch of surrealism, such as:

A dog goes to a telegraph office, takes out a blank form, and writes, "Woof, woof, woof, woof, woof, woof, woof, woof, woof."
The clerk looks at the form and says, "There are only nine words here. You could send another 'woof' for the same price."
The dog replies, "But that wouldn't make any sense at all."

By the way, jokes about ducks seem to be funnier than those about any other animal.

The good news here, I suppose, is that everyone in the world seems to have a funny bone, even if it is less highly tuned in some places than others. There's also a serious message in all these chuckles—people really are different. To some extent, we are each the product of the society in which we grew up, and that is reflected in what makes us laugh. And in what makes us tick.

Trading companies have recognized this fact for centuries. The Dutch East India Company, which was chartered in 1602, was a global powerhouse for more than 200 years. But because Holland was a relatively small country that didn't enjoy the military power of France, England, Spain, or even Portugal, it approached foreign trade in Asia with "more anthropological learning, greater cultural sensitivity, and better political skills" than its larger European neighbors. So it is fitting—and perhaps not too surprising—that a Dutchman, Geert Hofstede, has arguably done more than anyone to increase our understanding of other cultures, in particular, the different ways people brought up in diverse settings think, feel, and act. Anyone who has traveled more than 100 miles from home instinctively knows that people in far-off places sometimes seem to behave or perceive the world differently, but Hofstede's breakthrough was to explain the dimensions along which these differences typically manifest themselves. In his own parlance, he helped shed light on "the unwritten rules of the social game."

It is also fitting that Hofstede first developed his approach by studying one of the icons of modern global trade: IBM. Hofstede worked for the company back in the late 1960s and had access to a large database of more than 100,000 employee surveys covering more than seventy countries over six years. From his analysis of the responses, supplemented by surveys distributed to his own students at an international business school, he constructed a framework for differentiating cultures by their respective "values," which he defined as "broad tendencies to prefer certain states of affairs over others." Initially, Hofstede's framework had four primary dimensions (here, highly simplified):

1. *Whether the Culture Is Individualistic or Collective.* Are people and their families essentially on their own, or do they belong to strong groups from birth onward?
2. *How Power Is Distributed Within a Culture.* Is the culture hierarchical or nonhierarchical? Is unequal distribution of power expected and accepted?
3. *How a Culture Handles Uncertainty.* Are people comfortable in

unstructured or new situations, or do they like familiar situations and strict rules and standards?
4. *How "Masculine" or "Feminine" a Culture Is.* Are the men assertive and competitive or more modest and caring? Are women
modest and caring or competitive and assertive?

While these dimensions can help us understand a culture, it
would be a mistake to assume that they work mechanistically. For
example, it is generally accepted that the culture of the United States
leans toward the "individualistic" end of the scale, while Latin and
Asian cultures tend to be more "collectivist." But even within those
broad generalizations, further refinements are appropriate.

A group of Stanford University researchers studied the conditions
under which Citibank employees in different countries would agree
to help a colleague with a task. They could have had any of a range
of reasons for complying with the request: the rank of the employee
making it, the requestor's past cooperation, or maybe they just liked
their colleague. Their actual reason tended to follow a similar pattern, depending on the country. As expected, in the United States,
employees usually asked, "What's this guy or gal done for me before?"
In the individualistic culture of the United States, reciprocity was
the key motivator. In China and Spain, employees reflected the culture's collectivist leanings, but in different ways. The Chinese asked
themselves, "Is the person making the request connected to someone
of higher authority?" while the Spaniards asked themselves, "Is the
requestor connected to any of my friends?" The Germans, also in a
collectivist culture, asked, "What do the rules require?" Even though
people in each culture behaved in ways consistent with their country's position on the individualistic/collective dimension of Hofstede's
framework, they approached the request very differently.

So Hofstede's research, though groundbreaking, is only a starting point in understanding other cultures. Hofstede himself has been
careful not to oversell his work. He is very aware of the natural human
tendency to ascribe much more homogeneity to cultures other than
our own. The further removed we are from a culture—or really any

situation—the fewer nuances and differences we see within it. A conservative might be highly sensitive to the differences between Newt Gingrich's and Sarah Palin's brands of conservatism, but still consider all Obama Democrats the political equivalent of European socialists. Similarly, most liberals don't see much ideological difference between Palin and Gingrich.

The cultural dimensions Hofstede identified are not directly observable and can only be inferred from what people say or do. They are not absolutes—there is no "ideal" set of cultural dimensions. One nation's culture can be described only relative to another's. There is also nothing magical about the specific labels Hofstede used to describe these cultural dimensions, nor is their number absolute—he started with four and, as more data came in, he added two more: (1) whether a culture's orientation is toward the future or the past and (2) whether a culture fosters immediate gratification or restraint. Furthermore, the "unwritten rules about how to be a good member of the group" change only very slowly, if at all, but we can always improve our understanding of them. Finally, while these cultural dimensions help explain people's behavior and the way they see the world, they cannot predict what people will actually do. Hofstede is dealing with the central tendency within one culture as compared to others. But there is always variation around a central tendency—the "standard deviation," in math-speak. Sometimes, that variation can be even more useful, interesting, or dangerous than the central tendency.

When Procter & Gamble entered China, it hired twelve graduates from Sun Yat-sen University and the South China University of Technology. But first, it carefully screened them to ensure that they would be comfortable in a Western management culture that placed more emphasis on decisiveness than consensus building. Because P&G knew Chinese culture scored relatively low on Hofstede's dimensions of individualism and uncertainty, for example, it structured its interviews to tease out those particular values. Soon, the company was hiring as many as 200 graduates a year, even raising the hackles of provincial officials who couldn't believe the country's top graduates would rather sell soap than work in defense industries. Today, P&G is a net exporter of talent from China to other countries, meaning that there are more Chinese P&G people abroad than P&G people from other countries in China.

On the other hand, when I was working at AT&T, I was once sent into a negotiation with the telephone authority of Singapore. The lead negotiator on our side wanted me to make a proposal that he knew the Singaporeans would not accept. "They're going to nod affirmatively all the time you're talking," he warned me. "But they're not really going to like this idea. They're very hierarchical and nonconfrontational. They'll just say the idea is 'very interesting,' and it'll buy us a couple of days while they review it with the home office." I did exactly as instructed, and sure enough, all the heads on the other side of the table were bobbing up and down as I spoke. But then, when I was finished, their lead negotiator looked me right in the eye and said, "No way in hell we're going to do that." Either the idea was even worse than we thought or he was off the chart culturally.

The actual explanation is probably much more prosaic. The lead AT&T negotiator emphasized my rank in introducing me and made a point of mentioning that I reported directly to the company's CEO. If our Singaporean colleagues were awed by my august title, it apparently tripped no unconscious cultural scripts. While it is theoretically possible to manipulate people through their culture, they retain a good deal of control over their actual behavior. A person's culture is not a straitjacket. Michael Morris, who was the principal researcher on the Citibank study and now teaches at Columbia University, cautions that one's culture is seldom all-pervasive and inescapable. "Those who take this approach assume the 'lens of culture' is like a permanent contact lens, implanted in your eyes in childhood, which then continually and pervasively affects what you see," says Morris. In contrast, he says culture is "more like sunglasses—tools that you carry around with you but which shape your perceptions only when they are put into use." That doesn't mean controlling culture's influence is as easy as slipping on some shades. "Cultural knowledge structures automatically activate under certain conditions to filter the information from the world that the individual processes," Morris says. "They act more like those sunglasses that automatically darken when you walk into the sunlight."

On the other hand, in a series of experiments around the world, Morris found that cultural differences are magnified when people are under pressure, either by a looming deadline, a pile of work, or being asked to defend a decision. For example, in Morris's experiments, U.S. participants tended to give more weight to individuals' priorities in solving managerial problems, while participants in Hong Kong tended to emphasize the priorities of groups. Even more intriguing, it appears to be possible to activate such behavior simply by reminding people of their culture, even indirectly, by displaying their nation's flag or playing its music. That kind of "priming" happens, Morris says, "when an American manager living abroad sees a John Wayne movie, and then, without intending to, thinks about the next problem he encounters in more American terms." In fact, according to Morris, "People engage in active self-priming all the time. Expatriates surround themselves with reminders of their homeland—cuisine, music, photos, movies— so as not to forget their distinctive cultural feelings and habits."

Hofstede's cultural dimensions have obvious application in managing people. For example, people in cultures that rate high on avoiding uncertainty generally prefer well-defined situations and tasks. They do better with detailed instructions and written rules. On the other hand, people in cultures that rate low on avoiding uncertainty tend to be motivated and challenged by novel and ambiguous situations. Of course, companies and other institutions have cultures of their own. OtherWise leaders have a deep understanding of the interplay between national and organizational cultures.

19

Organizational Culture

The media love to trot out references to the "slow and lumbering culture" of big companies like AT&T, General Motors, and IBM, especially when they can be contrasted with the "quick, entrepreneurial cultures" of tech companies like Apple, Facebook, and Google. And there is some truth in their observation. Small companies generally do act more quickly and decisively than large ones; start-ups are, by their very nature, less risk-averse than long-established companies.

But Geert Hofstede's research (see Chapter Eighteen) shows that organizational cultures differ mainly at the level of symbols, heroes, and rituals, which are more superficial than the cultures of nations. The cultures of organizations are rooted in practices that can be learned and unlearned; the cultures of nations are rooted in values that are instilled deeply and early in each individual's life.

Having said that, Hofstede undertook a separate research project into the cultural differences among twenty organizations in Denmark and the Netherlands in the 1980s. He identified six sets of distinctive practices: the extent to which the organization was (1) process-oriented or results-oriented, (2) job-oriented or employee-oriented, (3) professional or parochial, (4) tightly or loosely controlled, (5) pragmatic or normative, and (6) reliant on open or closed systems.

Hofstede concluded that an organization's profile on these dimensions is partly determined by the business or industry the organization is in. Obviously, a pharmaceutical company would have a different culture from a movie studio. Key, however, is that managing a global business requires handling differences in both national and organizational culture at the same time. Organizational cultures can be managed to some extent, while national cultures are pretty much a given. According to Hofstede, "common organization cultures across borders are what holds multinationals together." Many researchers have built on Hofstede's work to answer some fairly practical questions. For example, what leadership styles work in different cultures? How should a company assess a manager's suitability for foreign assignment?

Robert House, a professor at the Wharton School of Management, for example, led a team of 170 researchers in a study of business leadership in sixty-two countries. They defined leadership as "the ability of an individual to influence, motivate, and enable others to contribute toward the effectiveness and success of the organizations of which they are members," and they collected data from 17,300 middle managers in 951 organizations. Realizing that leadership is exercised within a particular context, the researchers built on Hofstede's original research to identify nine cultural dimensions that differentiate societies and organizations. For example, Hofstede's original "masculine/feminine" dimension became a culture's "assertiveness" and "gender egalitarianism." They also asked the respondents about dozens of leadership attributes, ranging from orderliness to communications and team building. And in addition to measuring what a practice *is* within a culture, they also asked what it *should be*.

In the end, House and his colleagues discovered that what people expected of leaders—what they could and could not do, as well as the status they were given—varied widely from country to country. People in different parts of the world have very different conceptions of what constitutes effective and ineffective leadership. Consider this example:

> The best leaders: Are friends with their subordinates but make decisions on their own. Compete with their own direct reports and make sure they are better than others. Speak honestly, but take

into account others' status. Use indirect language and metaphors rather than get straight to the point. Avoid taking risks.

As it happens, that is the actual leadership profile of an ideal leader in China, as described by Chinese managers. American managers can be forgiven for believing the exact opposite is what it takes to get good results out of people. You have to be a total jerk to ignore your direct reports when making a decision. How can you expect people to know what you want if you beat around the bush? And what's this about taking someone's status into account? Of course, other parts of the Chinese leadership profile look more typically "American," but the devil is in the differences.

Despite such sharp differences, House and his team identified twenty-two leadership attributes that are universally positive, such as being "trustworthy," "motivating," and "oriented to excellence." Another eight attributes are universally negative, including being "irritable" and "dictatorial." But they really hit pay dirt when they uncovered thirty-five leadership attributes that are culturally contingent; that is, in some countries, they are viewed as promoting good leadership, and in others, they are seen as impeding it. Among these attributes are being "cunning," "evasive," "class conscious," and "sensitive." One of the most significant findings in the whole study has implications for the very exercise of leadership itself. "When individuals think about effective leadership behaviors, they are more influenced by the value they place on the desired future than their perception of current realities," House wrote. "Our results, therefore, suggest that leaders are seen as the society's instruments for change. They are seen as the embodiment of the ideal state of affairs."

Not every manager is equipped to be an "instrument for change" in a global setting, however. It takes more than a seminar on intercultural relations and foreign etiquette to prepare someone for an overseas assignment. And, in truth, some managers simply do not have the necessary capacity for a successful foreign posting. That realization is what prompted Mansour Javidan, a professor at Thunderbird School of Global Management, who collaborated on House's project, to design an assessment tool to identify those managers who have the greatest potential for success in global markets. Based on personal interviews with more than 200 global executives, and surveys of 1,000 managers, Javidan believes it requires a triple play of intellectual, psychological, and social capital.

1. *Intellectual capital* includes knowledge and understanding of global markets, competitors, and political systems, along with an ability to deal with high degrees of complexity.
2. *Psychological capital* includes traits such as openness, flexibility, respect for and understanding of other cultures, and a willingness to work with people of diverse backgrounds.
3. *Social capital* includes empathy for other cultures, diplomatic skills, and the ability to build trusting relationships with people who are different.

Javidan and his colleagues developed an online tool to measure what he calls a manager's Global Mindset. The basic format consists of 150 self-administered questions that take about ten minutes to answer, but it is also available in a version that invites a manager's colleagues, subordinates, and superiors to fill out the questionnaire, giving a full 360-degree view of the manager's suitability for a global leadership position. By early 2011, more than 10,000 managers from more than 200 companies around the world had used the Global Mindset instrument. And the results, by country, correlated very well with other assessments of national cultures, such as the World Values Survey.

Americans have not traditionally had a global outlook, but that may be changing. In fact, Javidan says that when he compared the Global Mindset scores of managers from ten different countries, American managers were firmly in the middle of the pack. Of course, the managers who used the Global Mindset instrument represent a self-selected group of people who are, almost by definition, interested in global markets. Javidan points out, however, that the attention any society pays to other countries is a function of its historical need to do so. "Canadians pay attention to what is going on in the United States every minute of the day," he says, "because what happens in the U.S.

has a huge impact on what happens in Canada. But most Americans don't know anything about what's going on in Canada, except the people are friendly and it's cold up there, because what happens in Canada doesn't have much of an impact on what happens in the U.S." Historically, Americans didn't *need* to pay much attention to other countries. But that has clearly changed. As we have seen, American business is becoming increasingly global, and the salience of what is happening in other countries has grown for many U.S. managers. Three-quarters of Fortune 100 CEOs have spent at least two years working in a senior position overseas. The percentage of other senior executives with overseas experience has jumped to 71 percent from 48 percent ten years ago.

These days, all businesspeople need to acquire a global perspective. "At the end of the day, it's all about diversity of thought," Javidan says. "Human beings grow up learning how to live and work with people who are like them. Managing diversity of thought is not something kids learn growing up in most societies." Even so, according to Javidan, it is possible to improve our Global Mindset. We can keep abreast of international news through media sources such as the *Economist* magazine, the *Financial Times,* the BBC, and the Al Jazeera English channel. We can improve our cultural literacy by reading novels, watching movies, and listening to music by artists in other countries. Before interacting with people from a different culture, we can read about the history, traditions, and etiquette of their country. When traveling internationally, we can eat in local restaurants and stay in local hotels, not in an anonymous international chain. And we can expand our knowledge of foreign affairs by joining a local chapter of the World Affairs Councils of America.

But OtherWise managers know that, no matter how much they learn about another culture, there will always be subtle differences in how people see the world—even when they seem to be speaking the same language.

20

We Are What We Speak

English is the undisputed *lingua franca* of international business. It is the official language of companies as diverse as Sony of Japan, Nestlé of Switzerland, Siemens of Germany, and Alcatel-Lucent of France. And even though most multinational companies make it a practice to hire local nationals, communications with headquarters—and often within the ranks of higher-level local managers—are often in English.

One would assume, then, that foreign language acquisition would rank pretty low on the requirements for being OtherWise. Indeed, a U.S. Department of State administrator once remarked: "Selecting, training, and promoting Foreign Service officers on the basis of foreign language skill is a little like picking chorus girls for moles and dimples. From the balcony it doesn't matter."

It may not matter in a chorus line, but it does make a difference in business. Executives don't need a second language in anticipation of conducting business in a foreign tongue. Unless they end up on the Spanish or Chinese version of TV's *Undercover Boss*, that's relatively unlikely. While it is always nice to impress foreign visitors by greeting them in their native language, it doesn't require all that much fluency. And although they might appreciate the gesture, most global executives would probably prefer to continue in English, which they likely speak as well as their host.

The real reason to learn a second language is because it is a window into other cultures. Language is more than a neutral vehicle of communication; it reflects and affects the way people perceive and value the world around them. People who know only one language live in one-dimensional space. Worse, they are unaware of it. And it's not even uncommon for them to devalue people who don't speak their language. Bob Selander, the former CEO of MasterCard International and now its chairman, began his career at Citibank. Early in his career, he spent some time traveling through Latin America. He brushed up on his high school Spanish by taking some Berlitz courses, but when he visited bank branches in Brazil, he was relegated to reading body language and smiling a lot. Many of the local managers spoke only Portuguese, and while there are similarities between the two languages, he didn't know what anyone was saying.

At first, Selander understandably focused on the English-speaking Brazilians, who he thought had more potential for higher management. But as the day wore on and he began to figure out what was going on, his view changed. "I realized that [the Portuguese speakers] were excellent managers even though they didn't speak English," Selander recalls. "They might have to learn English to move up in the company, but they were serving the company very well—maybe better than the English speakers—right where they were."

Selander's experience was not atypical. Two Canadian researchers captured the phenomenon very neatly in the title of their paper— "They think you're as stupid as your English is"—which examined attitudes toward foreign domestic workers in Toronto. Another study in the *Journal of Experimental Psychology* indicates that Americans are generally distrustful of people with accents, even if they find some—such as French and British—more sophisticated.

There is mounting evidence that the language we speak shapes— or at minimum reflects—how we think. A young immigrant from Belarus who learned English as a teenager is at the forefront of research into the intersection of language and our patterns of thought, what college course catalogs call "linguistics and cognition." Lera Boroditsky is attractive enough to have earned a rating of "hot" from her MIT psychology students back in 2004. One male student even confessed to an "intellectual crush" on her. Of course, that was at MIT. She now teaches at Stanford, where she had earned her PhD. She's still attractive, and she has a particularly seductive sense of whimsy—the photo on her personal web page sprouts Grouch Marx–style eyebrows, mustache, and spectacles when a cursor alighted on it—but her looks had nothing to do with her appointment. Early in her career, when she was still a young assistant professor at MIT, Boroditsky investigated how speakers of Mandarin perceive and speak of time. The paper that resulted showed dramatic differences with English speakers. And it rekindled a debate about language and cognition that was supposed to have been settled back in the 1970s, before Boroditsky was born. Colleagues who were decades more senior attacked her methodology, but later studies confirmed her results.

Boroditsky claims not to have anticipated how controversial her findings would be, but she is unapologetic about them. "What we have learned is that people who speak different languages do indeed think differently, and that even flukes of grammar can profoundly affect how we see the world," she says. Today, Boroditsky is the self-described "short dictator of Cognation—a sovereign state devoted to the study of Cognition." According to her lab's website, "in her spare time, she impersonates a professor of Cognitive Psychology at Stanford." Based on the number of articles she has written in just the past five years, spare time must be pretty scarce. Her lab has collected data from China, Greece, Chile, Indonesia, Russia, and Aboriginal Australia, demonstrating that language does indeed affect the way we think. Boroditsky is not, however, a complete throwback to earlier theories, popular in the 1940s and 1950s, suggesting language was a straitjacket, isolating people from concepts that were not part of their vocabulary. That theory held that because some languages don't have words for certain concepts, it is difficult—if not impossible—for people who speak that language to understand the concept. Practical experience debunked that idea.

The *New York Times,* for example, once erroneously claimed that Eskimos had 100 words for snow, depending on its various characteristics while English had only one. Whatever the actual number, English can express the same concepts, whether our Eskimo friends are talking about frosty sparkling snow or snow that's been peed on. It simply might take a few more words. There's no English word for *schadenfreude,* but we all understand the concept of taking pleasure in someone else's misery. The TV networks, after all, have built entire forms of entertainment on it. (Watch, for example, *Jersey Shore* or *The Housewives of Wherever.*)

To Boroditsky, it only makes sense that the language we speak—which, after all, predates our entry onto the scene—is shaped by the culture into which we are born. It reflects what was important to the people who came before us. For example, picking up on Geert Hofstede's theories (see Chapter Eighteen), one might expect a highly individualistic culture to place more emphasis on agency—who did what?—than a more collectivist society would. In fact, Boroditsky's research shows that English speakers are more likely to assign blame for accidents than people who speak, say, Spanish. For example, if an English speaker saw a flower vase shatter in pieces on the floor after someone brushed against it, he might say, "She broke the vase." Such a description would be relatively typical and appropriate in English even if the event were clearly an accident. By contrast, in Spanish, it would be equally typical to say *Se rompió el florero* (roughly, "The vase broke") to distinguish accidental from intentional actions.

Boroditsky has studied this phenomenon within the context of eyewitness testimony. English and Spanish speakers were shown videos of several events, featuring different people. In half of the videos, the event was intentional (e.g., a man breaks a pencil in two and smiles with satisfaction); in the other videos, the event was accidental (e.g., a man breaks a pencil in half while writing with it and reacts in surprise). After viewing the videos, each participant was asked, "What happened?" (*¿Qué pasó?*) In the case of intentional events, both the English and Spanish speakers described the event as the action of an agent; for example, "The man broke the pencil." But even in the case of the accidental events, the English speakers were much more likely than the Spanish speakers to describe the event as the action of an agent. Other experiments showed the same difference in the way English and Japanese speakers reported intentional and accidental events. It appears that the language we speak influences our view of agency and causality.

Languages differ not by what they can express, but by what they can express *easily*. And that often reflects a culture's world-view. A concept that can be expressed in a single word probably has greater significance to a society than one that requires circumlocu-tion. Translators, for example, have noted that French words *réalisa-tion* and *accomplissement* don't adequately express the full meaning of the English word *achievement*. Similarly, there is no equivalent Japanese word for *decision making*. That doesn't mean that the con-cepts can't be expressed in those languages. It simply means that it requires some verbal gymnastics. And it suggests that the concepts themselves, while not unknown within those cultures, have relatively less importance. Of course, as concepts and concrete objects grow in importance in different cultures, they often commandeer the words originally used to express them. So a small heated room in which people lock themselves for long sweaty periods is a *sauna* whether you are in Sweden or Glasgow. And a Chinese man-about-town can have as much *savoir-faire* as a boulevardier in Paris.

Linguists and cultural anthropologists are also beginning to believe that our native language influences our minds not because of what it allows us to think, but rather because of what it habitually *obliges* us to think about. For example, when the highest bridge in the world, the Viaduc de Millau, opened in 2004, it was widely acclaimed. French newspapers praised the "immense" "concrete giant." But Ger-man papers described it as "floating above the clouds" with "elegance and lightness." Were the French and Germans looking at the same bridge?

Boroditsky thinks she can explain the striking differences in their descriptions. French and German both assign a gender to inanimate objects, but there's no consistency between them. In German, the noun for bridge, *brücke,* is feminine, while the French *pont* is masculine. The gender of nouns or any "small fluke of grammar can have an effect on how people think about things in the world," Boroditsky says. Thus, German speakers saw prototypically female features in the Millau Bridge; French speakers, masculine ones. Boroditsky has confirmed the theory through a series of clever experiments. In one study, she asked German and Spanish speakers to describe objects that happened to have opposite gender assignment in their languages. They gave descriptions appropriate to the grammatical gender the word had in their native language. For example, the word for "key" is masculine in German and feminine in Spanish. When asked to describe a particular key, the German speakers used words like *hard, heavy, jagged, metal, serrated,* and *useful.* By contrast, the Spanish speakers described the same key as *golden, intricate, little, lovely, shiny,* and *tiny.* This was true even though all testing was done in English, a language without grammatical gender.

Of course, all this begs the question: Do people think differently because of the language they speak, or is their language constructed as it is because of the way their culture has taught them to think? To get at this issue, Boroditsky taught English speakers a new way of talking about time. People who speak English usually use spatial metaphors in speaking of time—e.g., a "movie is long" or "an event is far off." In her lab, she taught some volunteers to express time in size metaphors as Greek and Spanish speakers do (e.g., "a movie is big"). Once the volunteers learned the new "languages," their cognitive performance began to resemble that of people who speak Greek or Spanish. Large objects appeared to be on a slide screen longer than small objects, matching the reactions of Spanish and Greek speakers. On the other hand, English speakers who were not taught the new "language" saw no difference. "In practical terms, it means that when you're learning a new language, you're not simply learning a new way of talking, you are also inadvertently learning a new way of thinking," Boroditsky says.

The ways different cultures think about key concepts such as time involve more than the metaphors they use. They extend to the very concept itself. When Boroditsky established a lab in Indonesia, she began by studying Indonesian verbs. Unlike in English, the Indonesian language doesn't have verb tenses to indicate when an action is taking place. In Indonesia, it is perfectly acceptable to say a girl "eat a cookie." In one experiment, researchers in Boroditsky's lab showed photos of a man in various stages of kicking a ball to two groups of people and asked them to describe the photo. English speakers used verbs with time markers 100 percent of the time; that is, they said "the man is kicking the ball" or "had kicked the ball." Indonesian speakers, on the other hand, used time markers only 50 percent of the time. But subjects who spoke both Indonesian and English, when tested in Indonesian, used markers 85 percent of the time. Learning English seemed to make them pay more attention to when an action takes place. Boroditsky offers an explanation:

> Each language provides its own cognitive toolkit, and encap-
> sulates the knowledge and worldview developed over thousands of
> years within a culture. While language is a central part of cognition,
> there is nothing magical about how language shapes thought. Lan-
> guages shape our thinking in the same ways that going to medical
> school or learning to fly a plane also build expertise and transform
> what we can do. Different languages encourage different kinds of
> cognitive expertise in their speakers, and as a result, speakers of
> different languages end up thinking differently.

Boroditsky's experiments have demonstrated how language reflects and shapes the way people in different cultures think about space, time, colors, and objects, though the differences are admittedly subtle. Other studies have found similar effects on how people construe events, reason about causality, keep track of number, understand material substance, perceive and experience emotion, choose to take risks, and even choose professions and spouses. "Taken together, these results show that language is central to our experience of being human," Boroditsky says. "And the languages we speak profoundly shape the way we think, the way we see the world, the way we live our lives." Scientists are just beginning to explore these impacts. But anyone who speaks a language other than his own finds it easier to appreciate how it subtly shades meanings and shifts perceptions. The rest of us aren't doing much better than Steve Martin, who once expressed mild shock at discovering that "the French have a different word for everything."

A good manager must be aware of differences, not only to avoid offending people, but because our differences often color what really matters, which are our commonalities. In the end, the key to becoming OtherWise is not to focus on differences, but to use what we have in common to build bridges to a deeper understanding of each other.

21

Horizontal Empathy

Brigitta Tadmor's speech has the rolling *r*'s of someone who learned English as a second language, but she's been speaking it daily ever since college. "The first lab I worked in was in Zurich," she says, "and it was all English." It was the same in Israel, where she earned her PhD in molecular biology at the Weizmann Institute and, of course, at Harvard, where she did postdoctoral work, before moving on to MIT and eventually to the Novartis Institutes for BioMedical Research as global head of diversity, inclusion, and health policy.

"It's amazing how global the scientific community is," she says. "No matter where you go, it's just scientists speaking broken English everywhere." Not that she hasn't seen people cluster by language. "Even technical people tend to self-segregate by their first language in social situations," she says. It isn't unusual for many high-tech company cafeterias to have a Japanese table and a German table, just like there used to be a jock table and a nerd table in the high school cafeteria. On the other hand, Tadmor has seen scientists give more weight to colleagues' English-proficiency than scientific expertise, just because it's easier to get a quick answer to a question.

Language aside, Tadmor knows that culture matters. "Anyone who works in a company nowadays needs to deal with cultural diversity.

Even if they don't have operations outside their home country, they're probably dealing with suppliers and customers who do." Indeed, the Novartis organization she works for has 6,000 people in labs spanning from the United States and Europe to China and India. But in Tadmor's view, "The big difference for scientists is not when you talk to someone from another country, it's when you talk to someone from another discipline."

"As a biologist," she remembers, "the first time I talked to a physicist, I came away thinking *Wow, that was strange.* So much of our view of the world and our problem-solving skills are the product of the scientific training we undergo for ten years that the disciplinary boundaries become formidable. But that's where the real insights often lie. To me, the most obvious place we need diversity—and the most difficult place to get it—is in training people to work across disciplines." In fact, at MIT, Tadmor had helped launch an interdisciplinary PhD curriculum to train a new breed of scientists who could work at the interfaces of biology, computing, and engineering. "I was already at Novartis when the first PhDs in the program graduated [in 2009]," Tadmor says.

The Novartis Institutes for BioMedical Research had become a test bed for interdisciplinary research and development years before. In what some people considered a "pretty crazy experiment" in 2002, Novartis had redesigned its R&D organization around an interdisciplinary approach to developing medicines. It moved R&D headquarters from Basel, Switzerland, to an old NECCO Wafer factory in Cambridge, Massachusetts, and put a noted cardiologist with no pharmaceutical experience in charge. He quickly began supplementing the organization's specialty chemists with people from other disciplines, including biologists, geneticists, pharmacologists, and clinicians. And instead of basing development decisions on a medicine's commercial potential, Novartis focused on better understanding patients' medical needs and developing a deeper insight into basic science, such as the genetic and molecular pathways that control multiple diseases. Initially, the result was an intellectual collision between very smart people who were brought up in relatively narrow disciplines. The company quickly discovered that the chasm between scientists in different disciplines was even wider than any socially transmitted cultural problems. Scientists are not totally clueless about the importance of interpersonal relationships. They are as interested as anyone in learning how to get naturally reticent people to speak up or how to get naturally brash people to be quiet. But they tend to be very rigid in their thinking around their own discipline. For example, biologists are comfortable with the methodical use of trial and error; computer scientists consider it an inefficient way to design or debug a system. And all PhDs consider themselves experts in their field; they are not inclined to seek the advice of practitioners like clinicians who might be good doctors, but don't know the science.

But to produce new medicines, scientists in different disciplines not only had to get along, they needed to understand how each approaches and solves problems. Tadmor says the long-term solution to the challenge of building diverse research teams is to encourage the development of more interdisciplinary curricula at universities. "A growing number of universities are developing interdisciplinary education programs," she says. Meanwhile, in what she admits is a work in progress, Novartis has used a variety of approaches to build a more diverse and inclusive environment. It tries to pick R&D team leaders who have demonstrated an aptitude for collaborative work across disciplines. It has brought scientists into its labs from around the world to help broaden the perspective of its own staff. It has sent its own scientists on three-month-long "mini-sabbaticals" to work in Novartis labs in other countries. And it has assigned people from other disciplines to short-term projects in other offices and labs on what are jokingly called "nano-sabbaticals" lasting four to six weeks.

All these efforts are focused on creating widespread horizontal empathy across Novartis research laboratories, not only among scientists, but also among people in other disciplines. Functions such as law, marketing, finance, and software development are all driven by different cultures, yet they all have to work together seamlessly toward a common goal of developing new medicines in the shortest possible time frame. The efforts seem to be paying off: In 2010, the company won Food and Drug Administration (FDA) approval for four new drugs, and it has another fifty products in late-stage clinical trials, a large number for a pharmaceutical company of any size. According to one analyst, just one of the new drugs, the cancer medication Afinitor, could generate annual sales of $3 billion.

Bridging the gap between disciplines is proving critical to speeding innovation, lowering costs, and improving customer service in industries beyond pharma. Mansour Javidan of the Thunderbird School of Global Management reports that many companies seem to be concerned about this very issue, and at least one large European company has asked for Javidan's help in bridging the disciplinary divides within its own ranks. The proverbial silos that clutter the landscape of any large company are less the product of an organization chart run amuck than of cultural mindsets closely tied to people's functional discipline. People gravitate to the fields that are most compatible with their personalities and capabilities. Quants lean toward the sciences and engineering; poets, to the arts. Then they spend four to ten years in college, where that discipline's worldview is hammered into them, before graduating and joining a functional organization where it is further cemented. To call them "disciplines" is apt, because every function has unique and firm strictures on how that function is to be exercised. Functional myopia is a frequent side effect. Highly trained specialists make few close friends in other fields. Some functions are even traditional "enemies" of a sort. Their practitioners may not know each other as individuals, but they harbor certain prejudices about other functions. For example, engineers often assume that marketers are loose with the facts; people in marketing consider engineers anal-retentive nitpickers. Creating cross-functional teams might give everyone the same boss, but it won't change how they see the world. Yet an economy driven by innovation can't get into gear with a motley mix of allies, strangers, and enemies at the steering wheel. Breakthroughs like YouTube and Google, as well as Apple's iPhone and Nintendo's Wii, sprang from the marriage of art and technology. They are the product of right- and left-brain people working together, not sequentially.

But crossing the hermetic boundaries surrounding disciplines requires a trusted guide who knows the social and psychological territory—someone who understands how people in different disciplines think, act, and work, including the emotional values that guide them. Such leaders understand that some people approach problems methodically, while others prefer to brainstorm possible solutions. They know that some people derive personal satisfaction from the very process of solving a problem; others, only from the results. Such leaders broaden people's horizons by making the implicit explicit. In Tadmor's words, they unearth "the assumptions we bring with us that inhibit hearing good ideas or challenging stupid ideas."

Creating horizontal empathy doesn't have to be like an episode of *Dr. Phil* with all the attendant tears and group hugs. Nor does it require dangling team members off the face of a cliff until they trust each other. It starts with a leader who truly understands the value that each function brings to a common goal and the different approaches to realizing it. Such leaders forge agreement on a common method to achieve the goal at hand. Ideally, the new method melds elements of all the members' individual approaches, but at minimum it defines common principles, guidelines, and work patterns. And to keep team members out of the gravitational pull of their individual disciplines, such leaders put a premium on sharing information across disciplines and on celebrating team, rather than individual, achievements.

OtherWise managers have empathy not only for people in trouble, but also for the people they live and work beside day in and day out.

22

Practical Empathy

Ben Verwaayen has always had a subversive streak. In college, he organized the first student parliament in the Netherlands. As a recruit in the Dutch Army, of all places, he organized a union. And when his tour was up, he had a chance to serve on a government committee to reorganize the army, so he took a job that would give him plenty of free time.

That happened to be in the backwaters of an obscure subsidiary of ITT, and when someone bombed one of its facilities to protest the parent company's alleged role in overthrowing Salvador Allende's government in Chile, Verwaayen complained so loudly about the way the company was handling the fallout that he was made head of public relations for ITT's Dutch subsidiary, headquartered in The Hague. Over the next decade, he made so many friends in the Dutch government that he was appointed CEO of the state-owned phone company in 1988, and told to privatize it. He was all of thirty-six years old.

Some people might argue that only a subversive would have had sufficient reckless abandon to attempt the makeover of a sclerotic, public utility at such a young age. But Verwaayen had an edge that many of his seniors lacked. Practical empathy.

Practical empathy is more than feeling other people's pain. It is helping them figure out what to do about the situation in a way that motivates them to action. "What runs through my career is a skill in bringing people together," Verwaayen says. "One of my early PR assignments at ITT was to work with a guy who was negotiating a labor contract. He was still living in the 1950s—his attitude was 'I'm the boss because I'm the boss'—and he had absolutely no empathy for the workers, didn't have a clue what their life was like. So I negotiated a deal with the workers and then with headquarters."

"Building bridges," as Verwaayen puts it, is his stock in trade. "The story of my life is that of an outsider coming in but, from the moment I land, I slip into first-person plural—what *we* are going to do, what *we* are all about." Verwaayen has little patience for imperial CEOs who look at their companies as personal fiefdoms. He knows his limits and doesn't pretend to be a Swiss Army Knife CEO, capable of running every department better than the incumbent. According to Verwaayen:

> A CEO really has only three responsibilities. First, to put a dot on the horizon and give people a sense of where we're going; second, to set the tone for the organization; and third, to choose senior people who are capable of adopting the tone you've set.
>
> Putting a dot on the horizon sounds very simple, but it's not, because you have to make it a goal that is meaningful to everybody, from chairman to doorman. So if you have 80,000 people around the world and you say 'earnings per share is our goal,' you've lost 79,950 people already because EPS means nothing to them. Setting the tone is the boss's privilege and responsibility. If the boss looks for detail, everyone will become detail-oriented. If you're not interested in human beings, no one will be interested in human beings. The third thing is your choice of people. I can say I'm against bullying, but if I have a senior guy who gets great results, but is a bully, I've lost credibility. There's no clearer message than the people you choose.

Verwaayen may pay special attention to getting the right people in the top jobs, but he has no illusions about the utility of hierarchies.

"I hate hierarchies," he says with a passion that convinces you he means it. "They were great in a production model where the goal was duplication, but today, if you have a constructive dialogue with people and a clear decision moment, it will give you much more flexibility and speed." The people he's talking about are not on mahogany row in the executive offices, but the frontline workers at the other end of the organization chart.

For many of today's CEOs, those people are nearly complete strangers. The income gap between senior management and frontline workers has never been greater. Depending on how you value the fringe benefit, option, and restricted stock components of top management's compensation, CEOs make anywhere from 185 to 300 times more than their average employee. It's not hard for senior managers to lose touch with the rank and file when they encounter them only in structured business meetings or on plant tours. That's why Verwaayen spends a lot of time connecting with employees at all levels.

Vewaayen's second CEO job was at BT, the British equivalent of the Dutch phone company he had turned around, but much bigger and in much sorrier financial shape following a long series of expensive acquisitions. A year or so into the job, he was addressing an employee "town meeting" and decided to end it by challenging the crowd. "Tell me what internal obstacles are in your way," he cried, "and I'll get rid of them."

A hand went up in the back of the auditorium and a young manager stood, looked Verwaayen in the eye, and said, "You want to know about obstacles? You, you're an obstacle."

Verwaayen admits that he was taken aback. He asked the manager what he meant, if only to gain time to gather his thoughts. "If I get an idea, I give it to my boss, and she gives it to her boss who passes it up the line until—if I'm really lucky—it lands on your desk," the young man said. "But you're a middle-aged guy, and you probably have your own ideas, so you don't know what to make of my idea, so it dies." Verwaayen knew exactly what the young manager was saying, and he knew he was right. A CEO has the privilege and responsibility of putting a dot on the horizon, but if people don't feel that they have a say in where it goes, it is a random dot without purpose. That's when

Verwaayen started using two-way media, including e-mail and blogs, to communicate with employees. He did away with the executive dining room (as well as his private elevator) so that he and other senior managers would have more opportunity to interact with rank-and-file employees.

A few years later, when it came time to "put a dot on the horizon" for his third turnaround, this time at Alcatel-Lucent, he used social media to involve as many as 10,000 employees in thinking through where they should take the company and what they wanted it to stand for. He charged a group of up-and-coming young managers to coordinate and synthesize the input. And he told his senior team that they would be spending two or three hours every three weeks digesting and discussing this employee input. In the end, thousands of employees felt they had a hand in nailing that dot on the horizon, even if it didn't end up exactly where they would have put it. And a funny thing happened: Once everyone was looking at the same dot on the horizon, the "passport wars" that had come to define Alcatel-Lucent, ever since it was created in 2006 through the merger of French and American companies, began to subside. Greater internal cooperation allowed Verwaayen to make some big bets on new technologies his customers needed. So far, those bets seem to be paying off. In what *Bloomberg Businessweek* magazine called "one of the most startling turnarounds in tech," Alcatel-Lucent is winning billion-dollar contracts and holding its own in an industry that has yet to emerge from a nuclear winter.

When Verwaayen left BT, *Businessweek* called him "one of the best managers to run not just one, but two telecommunications companies in Europe." Just four years into his tenure at Alcatel-Lucent, the company is still a work in progress struggling to stay afloat in a sinking market, but the smart money says Verwaayen just might make it three out of three.

Part **Three**

Strange Times

23

Me, Us, and Them

"**N**ever before, perhaps, has a culture been so fragmented into groups, each full of its own virtue, each annoyed and irritated at the others." Historian Daniel J. Boorstin wrote those words in 1960. What would he make of us today?

On the political front, nearly two-thirds of Americans have a negative view of the federal government. Tea Partiers "want their country back." And a quarter million Texans have signed a petition to secede from the United States, an idea that the state's governor didn't think was particularly outrageous. On the social front, the cultural distance between people of different income levels and educational attainments has never been greater. They live in different worlds. They eat different foods, shop in different stores, watch different TV shows, vacation in different places, and seldom see each other except in the media.

They don't call, e-mail, Tweet, or Facebook one another. If they sat next to each other at a wedding reception, they'd probably have trouble striking up a conversation. And if one were forced on them, they'd probably need an interpreter

None of this would have surprised the Founding Fathers. James Madison, who was the principal author of the U.S. Constitution, believed that human nature itself "divided mankind into parties, inflamed them with mutual animosity, and rendered them much more disposed to vex and oppress each other than to cooperate for their common good." He believed that tendency was so strong that, when people couldn't find something substantial to divide themselves, "the most frivolous and fanciful distinctions have been sufficient to kindle their unfriendly passions and excite their most violent conflicts." And he worried that a small group of fanatics, "united and actuated by some common passion or interest," might trample the rights of other citizens. To keep these "factions'" hands off the tiller of state, Madison put the power to make laws in a legislature, elected by people in each of the individual states, rather than by a national popular vote. He thought the Bill O'Reillys and Keith Olbermanns of his day might be able to "kindle a flame within their particular States, but will be unable to spread a general conflagration through the other States."

Madison's theory worked when it took about a week for a newspaper to make it from Boston to Philadelphia. But geographical distance matters less in a world of instant communication, when a little-known Florida pastor can endanger U.S. troops half a world away by burning a copy of the Quran on his front lawn. Of course, Madison didn't put all his faith in geography. He also expected our elected representatives to possess "enlightened views and virtuous sentiments" that would "render them superior to local prejudices and schemes of injustice." In fact, Madison opposed a proposed addition to the Bill of Rights that would have compelled members of Congress to vote the way their constituents instructed them to. Madison would be sorely disappointed to learn that most of those representatives—on both sides of the aisle—are pandering to the very factions from which he expected them to protect us. Exploiting this or that faction has become the key to raising campaign money, winning the party's nomination, getting out the vote, and getting elected. And it has been that way ever since Thomas Jefferson ran against John Adams in 1796. Jefferson's camp accused Adams of being a secret monarchist; Adams's campaign tried to tie Jefferson to the violence of the French Revolution. And so it has gone ever since.

If sharp partisanship is not a new phenomenon in American elections, it has almost certainly reached a historic level. Keith T. Poole, a political scientist at the University of California, San Diego, says that ideological divergence in Congress is the highest it has been in at least 120 years. Political scientists think the seeds of this new strain of partisanship were sown in the 1970s, when conservative Southerners began abandoning the Democratic Party over civil rights issues, leaving a more consistently liberal party behind. At the same time, many moderate Republicans began to flee what was becoming a much more consistently conservative party, feeding on the counterculture's civil rights and Vietnam War protests. All that resorting resulted in two parties that were much more ideologically homogenous. And a seemingly endless cycle of campaigning helped move the ideological centers of both parties further apart.

Most political scientists agree that members of Congress have three main goals: first, to be reelected; second, to have influence within Congress; and third, to enact good public policy. Sadly, few politicians are that ambidextrous and, even if they were, they are one arm short. One of the goals has to get short shrift—and it's usually the third. Furthermore, all depends on the first goal—getting reelected— and that is increasingly a function of meeting some ideological litmus test. Former Congressman Lee Hamilton, who cochaired the 9/11 Commission, thinks he knows how we got into this situation. In part, it is because computers have given state legislatures the ability to draw congressional districts in a way that creates safely Democratic or Republican districts, capitalizing on people's tendencies to live among others of a similar political bent. "The result is that politicians running for the U.S. House don't have to appeal to the center to win," he says. "They need to appeal to the core of their parties' supporters." Not to mention the interest groups that fund them. Add to that a new tendency to use Congress's own procedural rules to partisan advantage, not to mention the endless games of "gotcha" that politicians play like kids with their first water gun. "The upshot," Hamilton says, "is that moderate Democrats and Republicans are the exception in office these days, not the rule." We have reached the point that the most conservative Democrat in Congress is likely to be more liberal than the most liberal Republican.

Of course, these ideological litmus tests have the convenient by-product of pigeonholing the candidates, which gives each side the advantage of shooting at a sitting target. Now the game is to twist every issue and event to political advantage so the gotcha game can continue. The national media, following politics the way they follow major league sports, but lacking any official scores until election night, fall over each other to declare winners and losers based on the gotcha sweepstakes and any polling data that might be available. The real issues get lost in the fog of polarized warfare.

Ironically, most surveys show that politicians and pundits are far more ideologically polarized than ordinary voters, who aren't required to have an opinion on every issue. "On individual issues or clusters of issues, Americans are not much more polarized now than thirty years ago," writes political scientist Andrew Gelman. "But as a nation, we have become much more polarized in our views of the major political parties, without there being much of a move to the extremes on the issues themselves." Because the parties are more polarized, it is easier for voters to sort themselves along ideological lines. Democrats are thought to be more liberal and Republicans more conservative. Voters arrange themselves accordingly. Republicans socialize mostly with Republicans; Democrats, with Democrats. But the actual positions they take on a range of issues are far less likely to be as extreme and uncompromising as their party's.

But the polarization that plagues our political institutions has other, more insidious effects. Some political scientists have concluded that ideological partisanship has produced gridlock not only in the corridors of power, but also in the very mechanisms by which people form their political opinions. One study found disturbing evidence that political polarization can actually affect how the public interprets and learns from new information that should objectively affect its opinions. In stark contrast to an analysis of survey data from the 1930s through the 1980s, the study found clear evidence that public opinion was no longer as responsive to changing events and new information as in the past. On the contrary, political partisanship along conservative/liberal lines has led to distortions in people's perceptions of reality and to biases in how they interpret the information on which they base their opinions.

Furthermore, people who are interested in politics are more likely to read blogs or subscribe to publications that specialize in political subjects. But research shows they turn primarily to sources that share their underlying ideology. And those sources link almost exclusively to other like-minded websites. As a consequence, people who are most interested in politics are the least exposed to alternative points of view. And when such people get together face-to-face, the process of reinforcement continues. A number of studies and experiments have shown that when like-minded people spend a lot of time together, they end up adopting a more extreme version of what they thought before they met. People who are worried about global climate change are even more worked up about it after meeting with others who share their perspective; similarly, those who think the whole climate change issue has been exaggerated become even less concerned after discussing the subject with other skeptics.

Chalk it up to the "folly of crowds." When individuals form an opinion, they usually recognize what they don't know about the issue or understand only imperfectly. When they join a group of like-minded people, though, they don't make mental adjustments for the possibility that the opinions expressed may have the same weaknesses—for example, they may be based on the same sources, reflect the same imperfect understanding, or be skewed to group expectations. As a result, existing opinions are corroborated and reinforced, and people's confidence in them rises. As their confidence rises, their views become even more extreme.

Very little can shake groups of like-minded people out of their complacent certainty. Another series of experiments has demonstrated fairly conclusively that when events contradict people's beliefs, instead of reconsidering their position, they crank up their advocacy on its behalf. So, for example, when the international banking system nearly collapsed, libertarians didn't ask for tighter or more effective government regulation; on the contrary, they doubled down on arguments for more unfettered free-market capitalism. It seems that people are hardwired to minimize doubts. And redoubling advocacy of one's beliefs banishes any lingering uncertainties.

Rounding out the danger of this folly, research also shows that people who hold an extreme position on any topic are far more likely to speak out on it if they think they are in the majority, even if that's a false assumption. So if a group of like-minded people are discussing a topic, not only do they reinforce their individual positions but the group members with the most extreme views leave the meeting assuming that everyone else shares their point of view, so they are more likely to share that viewpoint with still others. People who hear these extreme views on a regular basis start believing they are the norm. And so the cycle feeds on itself.

All of which argues for greater diversity. America's Founding Fathers had no idea just how diverse the country would become. Indeed, some of the Founding Fathers thought that anyone who was not English contributed to the land's diversity, and they counted the Irish as members of a different race. But as we have seen, they did recognize the value that diverse perspectives and opinions bring to civic life and governance. And they structured the legislative branch to be a diverse, deliberative body relatively free of the influence of special interests and the heat of parochial passions. That today's Congress falls short on both counts may explain its relative ineffectiveness and prove Madison's original theory correct.

As individuals, there is not much we can do about that, but there's plenty we can do to ensure that our own decision making is informed and protected from the folly of like-minded crowds. First, we can draw on the widest possible array of diverse perspectives, including those with which we don't agree. Our decisions shouldn't be the average of all the opinions in the room, but they should take them all into account. We can move sycophants to the side and surround ourselves with people unafraid to challenge our assumptions and our leanings. We can rightfully demand loyalty once a decision is made, but make it clear that no decision will be made without a full airing of all differences.

Finally, we can engage in what David Brooks terms "metacognition," or thinking about thinking. "Very few in public life habitually step back and think about the weakness in their own thinking and what they should do to compensate," he wrote. "A few people I interview do this regularly. But it is rare. The rigors of combat discourage it. Of the problems that afflict the country, this is the underlying one." The tendency to put our thoughts and opinions on autopilot is not limited to public officials. Business leaders at every level are guilty of the same thing. Jack Rowe, the former CEO of the Aetna health insurance company, was brought in from a highly successful career in the medical profession to turn the company around. In a meeting with stock analysts immediately after his appointment, the first question posed to him was more of a comment than a query. "You have had an illustrious medical career," the analyst said, "but you are not remotely qualified to hold this job." Rowe had to agree—he had a steep learning curve ahead of him. He was ultimately successful, and he claims that one of the things that sustained him was a lifelong habit of setting aside time in every workday to think. Not to do e-mail, not to make calls, not to meet with people, not to catch up on reading, but simply to think. As he remembers:

> When I was a young scientist, I published a peer-reviewed article in a highly respected journal every month for ten years. I had a very productive, successful scientific career as a tenured professor at Harvard, but about halfway through, I felt that I was on a treadmill. I was spending all my time either writing manuscripts or reviewing manuscripts and I didn't spend enough time thinking about the core questions. I realized how easy it is to get caught up in a self-propagating pattern in which your entire day is taken up with preprogrammed activities, but the creativity is in the interstices between those activities, not in the activities themselves. So I developed the habit of setting time aside every day just to think about what I was trying to do, what information did I need to make a decision, how would I get it. I'd question my most basic assumptions, alone or with one other person, and ask what if what I believe isn't true?

Rowe discovered that this "thinking about thinking" helped him focus his time and his efforts. It freed him from his inbox and from any preconceptions that sneaked into his day-to-day judgments. In fact, one of things he thought hard about was how to spend his time.

"I drew a chart of what I did every day," he says. "And I'd sit there at my desk and just look at it, asking myself if it was the right allocation."

Some psychologists believe that because conscious thought was such a recent evolutionary development, most of what we know about the world is acquired unconsciously. That accumulation of prejudices, stereotypes, and automatic responses is a mental guidance system that helps us navigate an often confusing and distracting world with a minimum of mental effort. It influences our behavior and our higher mental processes even when we think we're making considered decisions. Thinking about thinking ensures that this guidance system is kept in check, moderated, modulated, and even suppressed when necessary. Such thinking means confronting thoughts and feelings that might make us uncomfortable, and that's totally antithetical to today's culture. Why else would liberals have such difficulty admitting that George W. Bush's troop surge helped reduce sectarian violence in Iraq? Why else would conservatives have difficulty acknowledging that "Climategate" turned out to be a tempest in a teapot, and there is little evidence that the scientific data backing up climate change have been manufactured or exaggerated?

24

Sisyphus Had It Easy

It's the stuff of Greek myth. Like the poor guy condemned to roll a stone up a hill only to see it roll back down just as he reached the top, our ability to tap into events as they occur outstrips our capacity to understand them. By the 1960s, television had made "imagery" the dominant tool of communications and persuasion. In the last five years, the rise of social media has made "community" the new model. And the favored currency of every community is gossip and rumor.

One of the more unfortunate by-products of the information age is a steep rise in the rate and velocity of rumors. People have been gossiping about each other since Cain and Abel. And political rumors have an even richer history as a weapon of influence. Designed to reinforce the preexisting opinions of supporters, as well as to sow doubt among opponents, rumors herd people into camps of "us" and "them." Rumors bounce from computer to computer, eventually echoing through the so-called mainstream media, which are rapidly becoming a fun-house mirror of outrageous blog postings.

If anything, the volume of reckless e-mail is growing. During George W. Bush's eight-year presidency, the website Snopes.com

tracked forty-seven separate rumors about him. Twenty proved to be
true; four were partly true; seventeen were false; and six were neither
verified nor disproved. During the first two years of Barack Obama's
presidency, Snopes tracked *eighty-seven* rumors about him, only eight
of which have proved true. Of the rest, seventeen are partly true,
three were undetermined, and fifty-nine were false.

The most Rasputin-like of all these rumors was the accusation
that Obama is a Muslim. According to Pew Research, two years into
his presidency, nearly one out of five Americans said that Obama is a
Muslim and a plurality (43 percent) said they didn't know what religion he practiced. In fact, the percentage claiming he is Muslim had
grown by seven points since he had taken the oath of office, including
more than a third (34 percent) of Republicans.

The issue of Obama's religion came up early in his presidential
campaign, triggered in part by his father's Muslim faith, the years he
spent as a kid in Indonesia, his "funny" name, and some confusion
with the first Muslim congressman who took the oath of office with
his hand on the Quran. Obama's political opponents exploited all this
in an effort to make his religion an issue when he ran for president. It
didn't work then, and one would expect fewer people—not more—to
fall for it now. Except that Obama's outreach to the Muslim world,
his apparent support for a mosque near Ground Zero in downtown
Manhattan, and his family's decision not to join a Washington-area
church have created the impression that he is, at best, an agnostic
and, at worse, secretly a Muslim.

When Pew Research asks a question about Obama's faith, it
effectively gives people an opportunity to voice their disapproval of
the man himself, whether or not his religion plays a role in their attitudes. (In fact, they may not even be expressing an opinion about
Obama, but about their own economic situation.) Then, of course,
when the media report on the Pew Research, it puts the issue back
in play. People who weren't following the controversy all that closely
begin to think there's something to it. And at some point, of course,
something lands in their inbox that gives the rumor more currency.
For example, this e-mail was circulating widely in 2010:

> President Obama has directed the United States Postal
> Service to remember and honor the Eid Muslim holiday season
> with a new commemorative 44 cent first class holiday postage
> stamp.

In fact, it was President Bush's administration that first issued the Eid stamp in 2001 (when it cost only 34 cents). That admittedly was ten days before the September 11 attacks, but the post office has reissued it every year since (though in higher denominations). In first issuing the stamp, the U.S. Postal Service said it would "help us highlight the business, educational, and social contributions of the estimated six to seven million Muslims in this country whose cultural heritage has become an integral part of the fabric of this great nation." But to those who want to believe Obama is a secret Muslim, the Eid stamp is just one more piece of evidence. What makes this perplexing is that Obama's religion concerns a matter of fact, not opinion. It is one thing for increasing numbers of people to think Obama is a socialist, but doubting his professed religion is in a different category altogether. In our fragmented society, however, all facts are viewed through the narrow lens of our political persuasion, and we are quick to believe what tends to confirm what we already believe. Consider yet another e-mail that bounced from computer to computer in 2010 (its content is shortened here, in the interest of space):

> President Obama has decided to charge soldiers wounded in
> Iraq and Afghanistan for their medical treatment.

I chased this particular e-mail down and established that someone had taken a satirical essay, actually written to parody the attacks on Obama, and e-mailed it to his friends. They forwarded it on to other people, and it eventually landed in the inbox of someone willing to believe anything negative about Obama. He slapped a new subject line on it—"Most outrageous statement ever made by a public official"—and sent it to about ninety like-minded friends asking that they "please pass this on to every one including every vets [sic] and their families whom you know. How in the world did a person with this mind set become our leader?"

One might ask how rational people could believe that any commander in chief would try to charge the warriors under his command for the medical cost of treating their wounds. And yet many people did believe it, and with the certainty of any fact they had ever known. Conservative Republicans don't have a monopoly on falling for outrageous claims. In 2007, 42 percent of Democrats told pollsters that President Bush and Vice President Cheney either allowed the attacks of 9/11 to happen or deliberately caused them to occur.

None of this is a new phenomenon. As far back as the 1920s, columnist Walter Lippmann wrote in *Public Opinion* that "for the most part we do not first see, and then define, we define first and then see." The world is simply too complicated for us to react to every new experience as if we had never seen anything like it before; instead, we take the pragmatic approach of categorizing anything new with something already familiar. And we attach all the same feelings and associations to it, too. The phenomenon of baseless beliefs—whether "Obama is a Muslim" or "McCain is senile"—can be traced to our tendency to interpret (or deny) facts in a way that confirms our pre-existing beliefs and feelings. Psychologists call it "confirmation bias," and there's a mountain of research supporting the phenomenon. Simply put, it means that we see the world through a series of emotional filters we have built over our lifetimes. It's a mental shortcut that helps us make sense of the world. The Internet simply gives rumors and misinformation greater currency than ever before. But if the Internet makes it easy to spread rumors, it also makes it relatively easy to check their veracity. So why worry? Surely no one believes a rumor after it's been disproved.

Sadly, that's not how the human mind works. Misinformation is almost impossible to kill, particularly if it feeds a preexisting belief. For example, when John Roberts was nominated to the Supreme Court in 2005, an abortion-rights group ran a television ad attacking him for ruling in favor of a man on trial for bombing an abortion clinic. The ad was false. The case in which Roberts ruled had nothing to do with bombings; it was about the legality of blockades.

Roberts ruled that abortion clinics couldn't use an 1871 federal anti-discrimination statute against anti-abortion protesters who tried to blockade clinics because such blockades were already illegal under state law. A 6–3 majority of the U.S. Supreme Court agreed with him. The group that created the ad ultimately withdrew the commercial and admitted that it was inaccurate. What's interesting is how it affected the attitudes of people whose mind was already made up about Roberts. Before the ad ran, 56 percent of Democrats opposed the nomination of Roberts. After the ad ran, their opposition increased to 80 percent. But when the ad was withdrawn and repudiated by the very group that ran it, their opposition declined only to 70 percent, which was still a 25 percent increase from the original polling before the ad ran.

Liberals aren't the only ones whose opinions can be buttressed by demonstrably false information. After the invasion of Iraq, political scientists Brendan Nyhan and Jason Reifler provided two groups of volunteers with the Bush administration's prewar claims that Iraq had weapons of mass destruction. One of the groups was also given a refutation—the comprehensive 2004 Duelfer Report that concluded that Iraq did not have weapons of mass destruction before the United States invaded in 2003. Thirty-four percent of the group given only the prewar claims thought that Iraq had hidden or destroyed its weapons before the U.S. invasion, but 64 percent who heard both the claim and the refutation thought that Iraq had the weapons. Correcting the misinformation increased preexisting beliefs by 88 percent! The refutation actually made the misinformation worse. According to Nyhan, "People were so successful at bringing to mind reasons that the correction was wrong that they actually ended up being more convinced in the misperception than the people who didn't receive the correction. So the correction, in other words, was making things worse."

Big lesson learned? In the land of "us" and "them," emotion trumps reason every time. In the Roberts case, the emotional content of the initial misinformation persisted long after the rational content had been corrected. In the case of WMDs in Iraq, some people actually hardened their position when presented with information they considered contradictory to their long-held beliefs. As Churchill once said, "The desire to believe is much more persuasive than rational argument."

Recent research also reveals how even subtle appeals to group identity can influence our judgment and behavior. Spee Kosloff, a social psychologist at Michigan State University, and several of his colleagues tested two political smears circulating during the 2008 election: Obama is a Muslim and John McCain is senile. Not surprisingly, they discovered that people who are opposed to a candidate are inclined to believe the smear. Less expected is how relatively easy it is to persuade people who claim they hadn't made up their mind yet. It's simply a matter of getting them to think of ways in which the candidate is different from them. And even more surprising is how little it takes to get people to think of those differences. Simple demographic questions about race or age were enough to prompt subjects to draw subconscious distinctions between themselves and McCain or Obama. And those subconscious distinctions made subjects more likely to believe false smears about a candidate.

In one test conducted before the 2008 elections, the researchers concocted two phony editorials, one arguing that Obama is a Muslim, the other purporting that McCain is senile. Before reading the editorials, half of the test subjects were given a demographic questionnaire, asking their race and age. Among McCain supporters who were not asked the demographic questions, about half agreed with the editorial attacking Obama. But when asked about their race, about three-quarters of them did. Obama supporters who read the McCain editorial had similar results, depending on whether they were asked about their age. According to the study findings, "social category differences heighten smear acceptance, even if the salient category is semantically unrelated to the smearing label." In fact, in another study conducted about a year after the election, "the salience of race amplified belief that Obama is a socialist among undecided people and McCain supporters."

Those of us who would be OtherWise need to guard against accepting any "facts" that conveniently support our preexisting beliefs, especially if they appear to cinch an argument. But what about the whoppers other people swallow? Nyhan has come to the conclusion that it is virtually impossible to correct misinformation that people want to believe. For example, Nyhan pointed out that you get nowhere by simply saying "Obama is not a Muslim" because people tend to forget the "not" portion of the statement, and so the original claim, in all its glorious wrongness, is merely reinforced. Instead, Nyhan tested the approach of saying "I'm not a Muslim" against an alternative, "I'm a Christian." That would have been my advice, but Nyhan admitted that it worked only some of the time. And the reasons for that discrepancy are interesting in their own right. "When nonwhite students were interviewing respondents to the study, the message seemed to work, and in particular, with Republicans, the group most likely to hold the misperception," Nyhan said. "But when only white students [administered] the experiment, the correction appeared to actually make things worse." It seems that, when nonwhite students were present, people were giving responses that didn't line up with their unconscious associations of Obama (i.e., he's black). As Nyhan politely put it, using nonwhite interviewers "may have created an environment that people weren't comfortable saying what they really thought."

Is there is any way to correct misperceptions? Nyhan's advice is to take the battle to the source of these myths. "I think the most effective approach is to go after elites, to shame the people who are promoting these things, who are putting them out there," he has said. "At some point, people have to be cast out of polite society. You have to simply say, that is irresponsible and we're not going to give you our airtime, our print to make that sort of a claim. Politicians and talk radio hosts, they're going to push these things when it's in their interest to do so. It's a simple cost-benefit calculation. What I want to do is increase the cost."

People like Ann Coulter and Michael Moore are hard to shame, but it's worth trying. Sisyphus, move over.

25

Lost in a Loop

For centuries, new communications technologies have helped bring people together. Every innovation—from tribal drums to telephones—collapsed geography a little more, making the world smaller. Now it seems that the most powerful of those innovations—the Internet—is doing the exact opposite: Geography is actually folding in on itself, like a digital black hole from which nothing can escape. The Internet is enabling a decidedly unsocial network that isolates and divides.

Think of all the hateful e-mail, attacking one group or another, that fills your inbox every day. Or the websites designed to feed people's paranoia. Of course, all technological innovations have dark sides and unintended consequences. Socrates ranted that the invention of writing would corrupt the young. And I suppose some nineteenth-century dude figured out how to use the telegraph for prurient purposes. But it seems to me that we are on the threshold of something unprecedented.

The global village is fast becoming a series of tightly wound personal cocoons, tailored to their occupants' idiosyncratic tastes and opinions and connected only to others of like mind and passion. With the right filters, no one need fear being exposed to somebody else's thoughts or beliefs. That is exactly what's happening on every screen, whether on people's desks, in their pockets, or on their living room walls. Young people are spending inordinate amounts of time with the Swiss Army Knife of digital communications, their cell phones. But they seem to gravitate primarily to those functions that require the lowest level of synchronous engagement. On the latest models of smartphones they can choose between making a wireless voice call, initiating a video call, sending an e-mail, starting an instant message exchange, or texting. Texting is the feature they use the most. In her book *Alone Together,* MIT professor Sherry Turkle worries that we are raising an entire generation that will be "there but not there." Many kids have become texting zombies, incapable of making simple, direct connections with other human beings.

Back in the olden days—that is, the early 1990s—most Americans got their news from television broadcast networks. It was a fairly predictable, consistent news diet. For all its shortcomings, it fostered a collective intelligence and set the agenda for conversation around the dinner table and the watercooler. By the mid- to late 1990s, with the launch of new cable TV news networks, the rise in popularity of talk radio, and especially the Internet's availability to millions, that has all changed. Consider these statistics:

▨ In 1993, 60 percent of the American public reported watching network broadcast news on a regular basis, and the network news audience reflected the political makeup of the country nearly exactly.
▨ By 2004, only 34 percent of Americans watched network news broadcasts regularly. The three major TV networks have been losing viewers for decades, and the TV viewers that remain are now predominantly in their sixties.
▨ Meanwhile, regular news viewers have fled to cable, where the political makeup—and content—of news programs has become strikingly partisan. About a quarter of the American public regularly watches Fox News (23 percent) and CNN (24 percent). Yet about half (49 percent) of Fox News's audience leans Republican, and more than two-thirds (64 percent) of CNN's audience leans Democratic. MSNBC, which is viewed regularly by only about 15 percent of the

American public, has a similar partisan profile as CNN—60 percent of its viewers lean Democratic.

TV news audiences tend to trust the media outlet that presents the news in a way that agrees with their political ideology, which may be why the public trusts the cable news outlets CNN and Fox more than the broadcast networks. Cable attracts a largely partisan audience while the broadcast networks attract much larger audiences that broadly reflect the nation's overall political leanings.

According to an analysis by the Pew Research Center, behind these shifting audience numbers are major changes in the substance of news programming. Original reporting is in decline virtually everywhere; more than 80 percent of Internet news stories link back to the "old line" media they purport to replace, including the grayest of the media—newspapers. But most newspapers—after years of losing both circulation and advertising revenues—are laying off reporters and cutting their news hole to lower their cost structures. The only "old" news sector with growing audiences is cable, which spends the lion's share of its budget on opinionated hosts. In fact, in cable, radio, and social media (including blogs), passionate, outspoken opinion predominates. No wonder 72 percent of Americans feel most news sources are biased in their coverage and 70 percent feel overwhelmed rather than informed by the amount of news and information they see. If Americans once dined on a relatively thin diet of hard news, they are now gorging on their pet opinions and arguments. The side dish has become the main course in most American homes.

That's not the only way people's news consumption is changing. Few are passive diners anymore. They are sharing the feast with others of like mind by forwarding, commenting, tweeting, Facebooking, and otherwise sharing news with other people. "People use their social networks and social networking technology to filter, assess, and react to news," the Pew report says. A full 75 percent of online news consumers get news stories delivered via e-mail or social networking, and 52 percent of those people share news stories with others online. Even more intriguing, "72 percent of American news consumers say they follow the news because they enjoy talking with others about what is happening in the world." For example, Sarah Palin's accusation that the Obama administration's health-care bill would establish "death panels," authorized to ration end-of-life care to seniors, was not made in a television interview or in a speech, but in a comment on her Facebook page. Within minutes, it spread like wildfire through the blogosphere and into cable news programs, radio talk shows, and political town meetings. Though thoroughly debunked by most fact-checking organizations, it ultimately forced legislators to delete a provision that would have provided funding for end-of-life counseling as part of the Patient Protection and Affordable Health Care Act of 2010.

On a typical day, six in ten Americans (59 percent) get their news from a combination of online and offline sources. The Internet is now the second most popular news platform, behind television and ahead of newspapers and radio. News has become portable, personalized and participatory. One-third of us get the news over our cell phones. Young people use social networks to filter, assess, and react to news. What we used to call the "news" is becoming a lubricant of young people's social lives. And, as in all things social, the product is highly tailored to people's personal tastes and opinions. Sadly, this phenomenon is not limited to the electronic media. A study in the June 2009 issue of the journal *Communication Research* found that people spend 36 percent more time reading articles that agree with their point of view than those that challenge their opinions. Even when people read articles that counter their views, they almost always balance that by reading others that confirm their opinions.

Driven by page views, clicks, and ad revenue, nearly every website of significance—from Google and Yahoo to the *New York Times* and CNN—is experimenting with personalized content. Knowing that the amount of time you spend on a site (and especially the likelihood that you will return) increases with the personal relevance of their content, they track and analyze your web history to build a profile of your interests and preferences. Their goal is to show you what they think you want to see. Google, for example, already tailors search results to a user's past searches, among a host of other information it has captured and analyzed. Yahoo News users can set up their own filters; on other news websites, it's done automatically, without users even knowing. In both cases, the result can be a unique, personalized universe of information tailored to an individual's religious, political, or social beliefs.

This is a trend that troubles thinkers like Miroslav Volf. "What happens when technology allows you to ignore your interconnectedness with others?" Volf, a theologian, asks. "The world shrinks to your perspective on the world. But living in a community requires us to bump up against each other, to learn to deal with each other." Living in an echo chamber of one's own views reinforces a sense of separateness that makes it more difficult to trust others. On the contrary, it feeds social paranoia and resentment. "Notwithstanding all the access we have to media," Volf argues, "we know less about other people than our parents and grandparents did."

The new media environment has been blamed for everything from the decline of daily newspapers and book publishing to an increase in attention deficit syndrome and autism. But its biggest victim may have been the public's trust. In 1997, consumers claimed to trust more than half of all corporate and product brands in a major study; today, they trust only about one out of five. To be sure, people's faith in business and government has been severely rocked by a long series of betrayals, from accounting fraud in major companies and sexual scandals in our churches, to the discovery of salmonella in our peanut butter and human growth hormone in our baseball players. Partisanship in Congress produced more than gridlock; it fed the cynical conviction that our politicians are more interested in getting reelected than in serving the public interest.

Richard Hofstadter's 1964 essay, "The Paranoid Style in American Politics," could have been written about today's political scene. "American politics has often been an arena for angry minds," he wrote more than forty-five years ago. He calls the politics of angry minds "paranoid," not in the clinical sense, but because it is characterized by "heated exaggeration, suspiciousness, and conspiratorial fantasy." It is as if he was channeling Fox News, MSNBC, and just about any program on talk radio decades before they went on the air. Of course, Hofstadter—who died in 1970—couldn't have been writing about the Tea Party or the movement to occupy various streets and parks across America. But he seemed to anticipate the motivation underlying these protests, which he summed up just as neatly. "They feel dispossessed," he wrote. They believe that "America has been taken away from them and their kind." That sounds a lot like a Tea Party slogan seen on picket signs across America: TAKE OUR COUNTRY BACK, as well as the Occupiers' portrayal of themselves as the "99%" being exploited by the "1%." Tea Partiers want to take the country back from Big Government, while the Occupiers believe it was kidnapped by Big Business. In reality, although they generally hold each other in something approaching contempt, Tea Partiers and Occupiers are fighting different sides of the same machine—Big Business and Big Government working together to enrich themselves at everyone else's expense.

Tea Partiers believe "the old American virtues have already been eaten away by cosmopolitans and intellectuals," as Hofstadter wrote of an earlier generation's angry minds. For their part, the Occupiers believe "the old competitive capitalism" has fallen victim to a cabal of business and government cronies. If all that wasn't prescient enough, Hofstadter went on to warn that "the mass media" would enable modern political paranoids to make their villains "much more vivid than those of their paranoid predecessors, much better known to the public." And he was making this point well before cable TV and the Internet. To be fair, Hofstadter wasn't so much prescient as steeped in history. He could predict what would happen because he saw what had already occurred. Political paranoids were suspicious of Catholics in the nineteenth century; in the twenty-first century, they have refocused on Muslims. Yesteryear's plot by international bankers to take control of the world's money supply has morphed into a scheme by the U.N. to undermine Western capitalism. In the interests of fairness, I should add that Hofstadter didn't think the political right had a corner on paranoia. He saw signs of it among the Black Panthers as well. And angry minds are not limited to the political arena. Social issues are easily politicized; and politicians can easily co-opt them for their own purposes, aided in no small part by media that love a fight.

Even with the best of intentions, corporations can get on the wrong side of wedge politics. Target, for example, is a retailer widely admired for its ability to spot trends and capitalize on them by leveraging the creativity of a wide array of talented designers and manufacturers around the world. But even a company like Target can be politically tone deaf. In 2010, the company made a contribution to the political campaign of a candidate for governor of its home state of Minnesota because he was "business friendly." Reasonable people can argue about the appropriateness of corporate political donations, but it was legal and aboveboard. Unfortunately, the candidate it endorsed was strongly opposed to same-sex marriage, which was a hot issue in the campaign. Target—which had long provided domestic partner benefits to its gay and lesbian employees and was widely seen as a progressive company—appeared to be taking sides on the issue. Within days there were calls to boycott the retailer. "Flash mobs" descended on Target stores to perform musical skits attacking the company, often to the amusement of customers and embarrassment of management. At first, the company tried to defend its donation, pointing out that it did not oppose same-sex marriage. Eventually, though, the company's CEO felt it necessary to issue an apology and promise to review the process it uses for making political contributions. The boycott effort stopped for a while, but within months gay activists were combing through Federal Election Commission records to see whether the company was contributing to candidates with an "antigay agenda." Target had put its corporate reputation in the center of its own famous bull's-eye logo.

The big lesson to be drawn from Target's experience is not to shun controversy. Companies need to rigorously define their self-interest in terms of the values that are essential to their competitive success. They should support, and listen to, causes and groups that are aligned with those values. And they should be ready to go the distance on that small number of issues where they are threatened. One might question, however, Target's calculation that a candidate's pro-business stance outweighs his position on gay rights. To compete in an industry whose principal engine is human creativity, Target must attract and keep the best talent available without regard to race, gender, disability, religion, sexual orientation, or any other irrelevant circumstance.

Trying to walk down the middle of the road on that issue left it vulnerable to both sides.

In an age of angry minds and single-issue politics, no institution can afford to underestimate the power of small groups with big interests. They cannot be bought off or outspent because they do not run on money. They get their power from the righteousness of their cause and the people who are drawn to it. Companies should never allow themselves to be dragged into a fight with true believers unless the stakes are so high that the only realistic alternative is to win. However, they should be prepared to go the distance for that small number of issues that are central to corporate values.

Even paranoids have enemies, it's said. These days, it has become obvious that they have plenty of company, too.

26

Voting with Your Feet

If digital media companies have contributed to the fragmentation of American society, they have had potent allies in Mayflower Moving, National Van Lines, and the Seven Santini Brothers.

Journalist Bill Bishop analyzed zip code data going back four decades and discovered that people are not only expressing their political opinions in election booths, they are also voting with their feet. What Bishop uncovered was a stark change in American migration patterns. Starting in the 1970s, people moved for very different reasons as compared with earlier migrations. The great movement of blacks from the South to the industrial North following World War II was motivated by economic hardship and opportunity. But in the last four decades, people have moved for more personal, idiosyncratic reasons. Young people moved from rural areas to the cities, where they would find others with the same tastes and interest. Wealthier people moved to more prosperous neighborhoods. Blacks moved to cities with large African-American populations, like Atlanta and Washington, D.C. Gay couples congregated in cities where they would find like-minded people and a compatible social life. People in creative professions moved to communities with job opportunities in their field.

These new migration patterns stimulated economic growth in some communities and drained it from others. The impact was enormous. About 5 percent of Americans relocate from one county to another every year. (From 2009 to 2010, about 10.5 million Americans changed counties, or about 3.5 percent of the population. That is actually the lowest percentage since 1947, probably reflecting the lingering impact of the 2007–2009 recession.) As an overall trend, "more people were moving from one county to another in a single year than new population was added nationally in four years," Bishop noted. And as he described in his bestselling book, *The Big Sort,* the political impact was just as big.

Americans don't choose where to live on the basis of their political preferences, but as Bishop points out, they do like to be around people with the same level of education, similar jobs, and compatible lifestyles, including the kind of foods they like, the music they listen to, the sports teams they follow, and the spiritual beliefs they hold. They want to live among like-minded people. That's the Big Sort. Party affiliation and political leanings are only the tail on a mixed breed dog, although Bishop showed that tail does wag furiously during elections.

The trend is most obvious when looking at county election returns in presidential elections. In 1976, just 27 percent of the nation's voters lived in counties where the winning presidential candidate had a margin of at least 20 points, indicating that most voters lived in counties that were pretty evenly divided politically. But then the Big Sort began and the country started to segregate itself politically. In the presidential elections of both 2004 and 2008, nearly half of voters lived in such counties. Despite what was generally considered a massive movement of independent voters to Obama in 2008, only 12 percent of the nation's counties switched party allegiance between 2004 and 2008. The historically Republican counties were a little less vibrantly red; the Democratic counties, a brighter and deeper blue.

Politicians have learned to exploit these tribal sentiments, whether through gerrymandering or campaign sloganeering. In fact, by many measures, political segregation—though largely self-imposed—is even greater in most communities than racial segregation, though the latter is still a lot worse than we like to admit. The paradox of American politics is that, while most people are pretty close to the center on specific issues, those who have aligned themselves with one political party rather than another, or lean in that direction, do so because they have widely diverging economic, social, and cultural values. Over the last thirty years or so, people have increasingly sought the company of like-minded friends.

Ed Block, a wise friend who ran public relations at AT&T in its monopoly days, when the job was like being secretary of state for a small country, put his finger on the core issue. "Most of us live in a giant feedback loop," he told me, "an echo chamber, hearing only our own thoughts about what's right or wrong reflected back to us by the TV shows we watch, the newspapers and books we read, the blogs we visit online, the sermons we hear, and the neighborhoods we live in." That self-isolation, by itself, would be bad enough, but it seems to have led to one of the greatest ironies of the so-called information age. "We've become a country of tribes," Block says. "Our best and our brightest seem intent on recreating a primitive tribal society in which people who don't look like us, talk like us, or think like us must be regarded as hopeless misfits to be avoided or enemies to be eliminated."

Bishop, too, says that "the country seems divided because that's the way we've made it. That's the way we think and that's the way we move." Bishop's observation appears to be buttressed by reams of social research documenting the so-called *homophily principle,* which says that like associates with like or, to paraphrase James Joyce, "Like likes to like like." However, a 2010 study by three scientists at Yahoo Research suggests that partisan ghettos are not as tightly confined as they appear. The homophily principle has a trapdoor corollary along the lines of "Like is not always like like." It seems that we tend to *overestimate* just how much our friends agree with us. In fact, knowing that they are like us on one issue, we tend to assume that they agree on all issues when in reality, we are probably surrounded by a greater diversity of opinions than we realize. The Yahoo researchers asked 2,504 people about their attitudes on a range of issues, and then asked what they thought their friends' opinions were on the same topics.

Although the study revealed significant areas of agreement between friends, there was a lot more disagreement than people realized.

Even though many people in the study claimed to talk about politics with their friends, the researchers discovered that those discussions were relatively superficial. Most of what people claimed to "know" about their friends appeared to have been inferred from indirect evidence, rather than from actual discussions about the issues themselves. As a result, even relatively good friends who said they talked about politics were typically unaware of each other's views on matters like immigration, tax policy, or the Iraq War. So it turns out that even in a solidly blue or red community, the "Other" could be the neighbors with the same political bumper sticker on their car. Yet, not everyone who likes Sarah Palin shares every one of her views, just as not all Barack Obama supporters have been totally behind him on every issue.

Back in the 1920s, the Pulitzer Prize–winning columnist Walter Lippmann observed that most of us experience the world as "pictures in our heads," rather than through personal experience. The pictures in our heads, of course, are seldom-perfect representations of reality. Our attention spans are too short, our vocabulary too inadequate, and our brain's storage capacity too limited for that. Furthermore, a constant stream of incoming pictures is colored by the images we have already stored—what Lippmann called the "stereotypes" through which we interpret the world and which direct the play of our attention. Over time, the pictures in our heads fade or sharpen, condense and combine, until we have made them our own. At that point, we have such an emotional stake in those "pictures," they form part of our identity. But in reality, most of our ideas are really hairballs of accepted wisdom caught in the lint traps of our own brains.

Even when stereotypes seem positive—as in "Asians are hard-working"—they're literally "de-meaning" because they rob people of their individuality and uniqueness. Yet, it's amazing how powerful those "pictures in our head" can be. "Those pictures which are acted upon by groups of people," Lippmann wrote, "are Public Opinion with capital letters." To Lippmann's mind, public opinion doesn't arise from the careful consideration of a group of facts. On the contrary, public opinion is the screen through which we *see* the facts. So when the late Democratic Senator Daniel Patrick Moynihan quipped that everyone is entitled to his own opinions but not his own facts, he actually had things a bit reversed. Public opinion is not coolly rational and analytic. It is highly emotional. "Opinions are not in continual and pungent contact with the facts they profess to treat," Lippmann wrote. "But the feelings attached to those opinions can be even more intense than the original ideas that provoked them." In other words, over time people know what they feel without being entirely sure why they feel it.

Of all the pictures in our head, the most loaded are those dealing with home, country, and God. Our stereotypes and prejudices are not coolly analytical; they are vestigial emotions that our prehistoric ancestors developed to avoid trouble. All the "isms" that divide us—racism, sexism, ageism—are not a form of criticism; they are predispositions. The key to being OtherWise is learning to control those predispositions by recognizing their existence and their power.

We think the people we like are like us because it is easier than finding out who they really are. Can it be that the people we don't like are more like us than we think?

27

Free-Floating Anger

John Gilfeather is a professional reader of tea leaves. He's not the kind tea-leaf reader who occupies a narrow storefront with crystal balls stenciled onto the plate glass, but the kind who feeds survey data into a mainframe and sorts it to find meaningful patterns.

Gilfeather has been doing market research for more than four decades and has worked with some of the world's leading companies. In the summer of 2010, he helped design and test a research instrument that probed people's feelings about companies in the context of the political and social issues roiling the country. Instead of asking about the presence or absence of the usual favorable attitudes—such as whether companies are "well managed," "trustworthy," "caring," and the like—the questionnaire intentionally confronted the negative attitudes that everyone knew were on people's minds. For example, the survey asked, "Does this company have executives who are more concerned about how much money they make than the long-term health of their company?" It went so far as to probe for negative attributes, using terms such as "greedy," "arrogant," and "secretive" to characterize companies and their executives. And, in a last-minute, "what the hell" moment of inspiration, Gilfeather even added "idiots" to the list.

The survey examined fifty-four companies through 10,800 online interviews. The companies tested were a mix of those that demonstrated sterling reputations in other surveys— Johnson & Johnson and Kraft, as examples—and those that Gilfeather likes to call "the villains du jour," represented by Halliburton, Goldman Sachs, and BP. The results were unlike anything Gilfeather had seen in more than forty years of plumbing the public's psyche. Of course, the data reconfirmed what he already knew, such as the axiom that people who are more familiar with a company are more likely to think favorably of it. But there were plenty of unexpected results, too. For example, when respondents' opinions were averaged across all fifty-four companies, nearly a third of those surveyed agreed that executives were more interested in their personal compensation than their companies' long-term health. Nearly a third said the companies were "greedy." More than a quarter said they were "arrogant" and "secretive." And one out of five said they were "idiots."

Naturally, the villains had more negatives. More than half of respondents agreed that BP's executives were only looking out for themselves. But even the heroes had tarnished crowns. Nearly one out of five felt the same way about Kraft and J&J, which were the companies people held in highest esteem. This wasn't simply a factor of a few outliers bringing the average down for everyone. "I've never seen so much free-floating anger," Gilfeather said. "And it appears that it will attach itself to any company, even those that have had great reputations in the past. It's not just an erosion of positives; it's a rise in distinct negatives. Companies aren't dealing with neutral audiences anymore."

That free-floating anger is attaching itself to more than Big Business. Another 2010 survey, this one by the Gallup organization, showed that a majority of Americans have confidence in only three institutions: the military, small businesses, and the police. (One might assume it is a coincidence that two out three carry guns.) Less than a quarter of people expressed confidence in institutions ranging from newspapers, banks, television news, organized labor, large corporations, health insurers, and—big surprise —Congress. Even organized religion, the medical system, and the U.S. Supreme Court failed to inspire confidence in a majority of Americans. Trust in all institutions has never been lower.

Interestingly, whites expressed greater alienation than minorities, even though, by most measures, the economic downturn has been tougher on people of color. Ron Brownstein of the *National Journal* noted that a number of national surveys showed that whites "have been more likely than minorities to say that they did not expect their children to match their own standard of living." As if to drive the implications of the situation home, Brownstein speculated that "if polls existed just before the French Revolution, they might have returned results such as these."

Even Peggy Noonan, who was a speechwriter for Ronald Reagan, arguably one of our most optimistic presidents, worries that the country suffers from unprecedented pessimism. "The biggest political change in my lifetime is that Americans no longer assume that their children will have it better than they did," Noonan wrote in the *Wall Street Journal*. Noonan sees this development as a big deal, because it is a sharp break with the assumptions that shaped us as a nation.

As it turns out, the public's pessimistic assumptions have some basis in reality. A host of studies on "intergenerational mobility," the technical term for what we know as the American Dream, showed that "if you are born into poverty in the U.S., you are actually more likely to remain in poverty than in other countries—in Europe, the Nordic countries, even Canada, which you would think would not be that different [from the United States]." Furthermore, it is no longer certain that each generation does better than the last. In the United States today, men in their thirties earn 12 percent less than their fathers did at the same age. For many people, the American Dream has become a fantasy, a cheery story that few expect to come true. And that disillusionment may be feeding people's deep alienation toward America's private and public leadership. As Brownstein puts it, there is "a widely shared conviction that the country's public and private leadership is protecting its own interest at the expense of average (and even comfortable) Americans."

Indeed, a lot of the nativist, Islamophobic, and Tea Partying rhetoric in the media and in the streets may have its roots in this sense of alienation. It may reflect a search for certainty in an uncertain world, familiarity amid change, and the comfort of precisely identifying your enemy against a backdrop of endless indignities. Arguably, Republicans seem to have done a better job of identifying with the white middle class, while Democrats seem to be champions of those the middle class fears most—the social-experimenting elite who would upend their way of life in the name of some new theory. The Tea Party has vowed to take America back from the New York, Washington, and Hollywood elites who have reframed, repurposed, and redecorated it. Meanwhile, the elites deride members of the Tea Party as bible-thumping, knuckle-dragging hillbillies.

One doesn't really understand the other. Worse, they think they do.

28

Mind the Gap

Fear of immigrants. Racial differences. Culture wars. Political polarization. These issues appear to be what divides us. Pundits on both sides of the right-left divide proclaim, bemoan, and celebrate their favorite "fragmentation" thesis. To the left, we are polarized economically, with the rich getting richer and middle-class incomes stagnating. To the right, we are polarized culturally, with godless sybarites on the two coasts and God-fearing, respectable people in the heartland. Both see a yawning divide between two Americas, separated by irreconcilable differences. The even more toxic theory holds that America is shattering along deep fault lines into tiny worlds that occasionally touch but never mix.

But, as we have seen, most Americans are pretty close to the center on specific social issues, with a relatively small number at the vocal fringes. As compared with many other countries or even previous periods of our own history, a smaller percentage of the U.S. population was born elsewhere. And the largest political faction in the United States is the majority that doesn't vote at all, followed by independents, who are just as likely to vote for one party as the other, depending on macroeconomic factors that are beyond the influence of any politician. Still, people seem to be stumbling over fracture lines right and left. Just listen to the nonstop bloviating on talk radio or cable TV news, segueing from gotcha moment to ad hominem attack.

Claude Fischer is the sociological equivalent of a geologist, mapping the fault lines in human society. He is also, by his own admission, a professional skeptic. "Sociology is, by its nature, a debunking discipline," he has said, "It searches for the reality behind official interpretations of society." As coauthor of *Century of Difference: How America Changed in the Last One Hundred Years,* Fischer has little patience with all that talk of fissures, fractures and fragments. He thinks the notion that the United States is polarized and conflict-ridden misses something important: historical context. "If one compares the 2000s to the 1960s, the 1930s, the late-nineteenth century, or the 1860s, today's battles seem like snowball fights," he writes. "Consider the struggles over immigration: Our arguments can be tense and unpleasant, but we have not experienced the viciousness of the nineteenth-century anti-Catholic and anti-Asian struggles, which included bloody street riots and lynchings."

Obviously, Fischer has a point. He also has decades of data to back it up. Fischer and his coauthor, Michael Hout, used the General Social Survey to analyze public opinion on a range of social issues over several decades. They discovered a consistent pattern on every issue. When a question—for example, "Should married women work outside the home?"—is first asked, the percentage agreeing is relatively low. For example, in 1938, only about 20 percent of American adults believed married women should work outside the home. In subsequent years, the proportion agreeing with this notion slowly increased and, after a while, the pace picked up as more and more people got comfortable with the idea. Then it slowed down as the only people left were those who were strongly opposed to the idea. In this case, that was a hard-core 20 percent of adults in 1998—the last time the question was asked. Plotted on a graph, the changing levels of agreement over time scribe a curve that looks like a stretched-out S. Fischer and his colleagues ran the data on about a dozen different "cultural" questions, ranging from "the ideal size of a family" to "the conditions under which the respondents would allow abortion." Opinion on almost all questions followed the same pattern when plotted over time—what mathematicians call a "logistic function" or "S curve" (see Figure 2). The proportion agreeing tended to increase over time—which is not what one would expect if people were truly polarized around the issue.

There were demographic differences in rates of adoption, however. For example, on the question of voting for a Jewish presidential candidate, respondents in the South were much slower to agree than people of other regions, creating a gap that widened from the 1930s to the 1950s before narrowing and essentially disappearing in the 1990s. Similar group differences waxed and waned on other cultural issues over the roughly sixty-year period that Fischer examined. "In general, younger, Northern, more educated, and more urban Americans typically adopted new positions first," Fischer notes. "Older, Southern, less educated, and less-urban Americans did so later." And the peak of the battle—the period when the gap between early and late adopters was widest—seemed to be from the late 1950s through the early 1970s.

In general, then, early adopters accept a new idea sooner than late adopters.

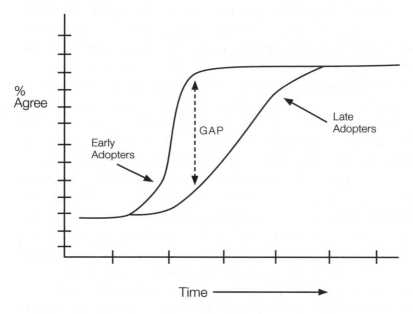

Figure 2. The acceptance of new ideas follows a characteristic "S curve" pattern.

At any given time, there may be a substantial gap between the two groups, although they will ultimately end up in the same place.

It is also clear from Fischer's studies that new cultural issues are constantly arising. For example, when the General Social Survey asked people in 1972 whether premarital sex between unmarried adults was wrong, only about a quarter (28 percent) said they saw nothing wrong with it; by 2006, nearly half (46 percent) felt that way. The change in attitude springs from two countervailing factors. On the one hand, people get more sexually conservative as they get older. But then, when they die, they are replaced by younger, more liberal-thinking people.

In the end, Fischer makes a compelling case that most of the big cultural issues—like racial and gender equality—have been settled, at least in theory if not always in practice. "Abortion is the only truly polarizing topic in the last quarter of the [twentieth] century," he says. Even on that third-rail issue, he points out that the period of greatest division was between 1975 and 1980, not today. Other issues—like same-sex marriage—will arise as new cultural possibilities emerge and spread, but we are far from experiencing the multiple-front battles of the 1960s. As Fischer puts it, "One might say the culture wars are a reality, but a reality of much longer ago." That doesn't mean Fischer thinks American society is free of fault lines. On the contrary, he sees at least three big ones. Two are relatively obvious and, as already discussed, may be related: race and immigration.

Despite great progress over the last forty years, America still shows troubling signs of a black/white divide. On average, African Americans today have better-paying jobs than they did four decades ago; they have access to better housing; their children are better educated; and they have gained greater acceptance almost everywhere. But compared to whites, they still lag on almost every measure. In mid-2011, the unemployment rate for black men (16.7 percent) was twice that for white men (8 percent). The poverty rate among African Americans is almost twice that of non-Hispanic white Americans (10 percent). And while intermarriage between blacks and whites has grown in recent years, it is still at very low levels.

Many recent immigrants are also people of color who suffer

from the same prejudice in terms of access to well-paying jobs, safe housing, and good schools for their children. Unemployment rates for black (12.4 percent) and Hispanic (11.3 percent) immigrants are significantly higher than for those who are white (7.4 percent). Ironically, Fischer and other scholars worry that as Asians and Hispanics acculturate and intermarry with the majority, a new racial divide will arise between blacks and nonblacks. "The big split," Fischer says, "will be between the descendants of American slaves and the rest." No one can predict the exact course of their acculturation, or the persistence of racial prejudice. In 2000, at the turn of the twenty-first century, who would have predicted the election of an African-American president before the new century's first decade was completed?

The third fault line runs even deeper and gets relatively little attention. It is the split between the college-educated and others. Education is the biggest contributor to the components of class distinction since the better educated get better jobs, earn more, and accumulate more wealth than the less educated. They are also more likely to hang on to their jobs in tough economic times. During the Great Recession of 2007–2009, the under- and unemployment rate for college graduates was about 7 percent, but it was 35 percent for high school dropouts.

"Education and economic inequality represent a classic chicken-and-egg problem," Fischer told me. "The children of wealthier people get better educations and the people with better educations get wealthier." And the divisions run even deeper: The better educated are more likely to get married, are less likely to divorce, and if they do divorce, are more likely to remarry. They are more likely to have high-paying jobs and to get a sense of satisfaction from them, and more likely to keep those jobs. They live in better neighborhoods, have more free time, and are less politically alienated. Along with financial resources, they give their children certain cultural advantages, such as exposure to the arts and foreign travel. "In these various ways," Fischer says, "the material and social divisions by levels of education are growing wider." If, as W. E. B. DuBois said, "The problem of the twentieth century is the problem of the color-line," then the problem of the twenty-first century may be the line between those who are college educated and those who are not.

The proportion of Americans with a college degree has nearly tripled in the last forty years, rising from 10.5 percent in 1972 to nearly 30 percent in 2006. Even so, there is increasing evidence that educational opportunities can be handed down from one generation to another, just like the family silver. The cost of higher education is well beyond the financial capabilities of many lower-income and middle-class families. And it turns out that the best predictor of earning a college degree isn't race, income, or even what your parents do for a living. It's how much education your parents received.

About half of Americans between the ages of 25 and 44 have only a high school diploma. Eight out of ten of them are white, but their employment potential is grim because they don't have the educational credentials for better-paying managerial or professional jobs. They are less likely to marry, but even *more* likely to have kids.

The most significant difference, though, between the college-educated and others is something sociologists have noted since the 1950s. College-educated people take a broader view of social relationships. They are less likely to consider differences threatening. And they are more likely to participate in social institutions. In fact, Fischer's analysis of all those data-runs establishes that people's educational attainment is a stronger predictor of their feelings and opinions than the tried-and-true distinctions of gender and geography.

Education may be the principal fault line in American society. And it may prove as difficult as any to bridge.

29

The Chicken Soup
of Social Life

"Trust is the chicken soup of social life," according to University of Maryland political scientist Eric Uslaner. By that, he means it's good for what ails us, operates rather mysteriously, and is somewhat oversold as a cure-all.

Not that he doubts the importance of trust. Trust is an essential element of cooperative behavior. Jill won't go up the hill with Jack if she doesn't trust him to help carry the pail of water on the way down. Similarly, President Reagan wouldn't blindly trust Prime Minister Gorbachev to cut the Soviet Union's stockpile of weapons. What Jill and Reagan were exercising was *strategic* trust, based on their individual assessments of their counterpart's sincerity and competence to, respectively, fetch the pail of water and junk some nukes. Their assessments might have been based on previous experience or perhaps reflect their calculations of sophisticated game theory.

But Uslaner argues that there is another, even more important kind of trust, based not on experience but on a moral belief that you can count on people, even in the absence of supporting evidence. Trust in government, business, and other institutions is based on performance, so it changes all the time, reflecting our own uncertainty. Trust in other people, on the other hand, is a value we learn early in life, based on experience with our closest caregivers. It is relatively resistant to experience, good or bad. Good experiences confirm our preexisting belief; an occasional bad experience is chalked up as an exception to the general rule. Uslaner calls this *moralistic* trust. Initially, people trust others like themselves—members of their family, clan, or ethnic group—more than outsiders. But this rather restricted level of trust can broaden into more generalized trust through meaningful contact with others, particularly at a young age. And that more inclusive trust, which binds us to the larger community, is what's really important.

So it's a little disconcerting to discover that Americans not only mistrust institutions of all kinds, but they aren't too sure about each other anymore, either. In 1960, when national surveys first began asking whether "most people can be trusted," nearly two-thirds of Americans said yes. In 2008, less than a third agreed with that statement. Not surprisingly, social scientists across the country fired up their computers to figure out what was going on. For the most part, their computer data-runs all pointed in the same direction, showing a remarkable link between people's levels of trust and something totally unanticipated: income inequality.

Their statistical analyses revealed a tight correlation between trust and relative levels of income. "America in the 1950s and 1960s was more egalitarian than it had been in more than a century," sociologist Robert Putnam of Harvard University wrote. "Those same decades were also the high point of social connectedness and civic engagement. Conversely, the last third of the twentieth century was a time of growing inequality and eroding social capital." Sometime in the late 1960s, Putnam thought, America reversed course: Income inequality began increasing and social connections began fraying.

Indeed, Uslaner's own analysis indicates that "the level of economic equality is *the strongest determinant* of trust." He found a strong causal link between the two, not only in the United States but also in other countries. For example, the countries that tend to have the highest levels of trust in the World Values Survey—namely, the Nordic countries, the Netherlands, and Canada—also rank highest on economic equality. The same holds true *within* the United States. Trust is generally higher in states with greater income equality, although levels of trust in the country overall have declined as inequality has risen over time.

Uslaner theorizes that moralistic trust rests on an optimistic view of the world and one's ability to control it. Equality leads to greater optimism and stronger bonds between different groups in society. When there isn't a large gap between the incomes of different groups, people are more optimistic about their chances of moving from one side to the other. They have an easier time imagining that people on both sides of the income gap share values and beliefs and have the same goals in life. Conversely, inequality breeds resentment, suspicion, and fear. "As inequality grows," he writes, "the perception that people have a common stake in society's well-being withers." There is no longer a basis for trust when others don't seem to be part of one's moral community. "Trust cannot thrive in an unequal world, Uslaner writes. "Those at the top can enforce their will against people who have less. And those at the bottom have little reason to believe that they will get a fair shake."

The Fourteenth Congressional District of New York, which includes most of Manhattan's Upper East Side and parts of Queens, is five subway stops away from the Sixteenth Congressional District in the South Bronx. That's about two miles. But in terms of income, education, and life expectancy, the two districts are seventy years apart. New York's Fourteenth Congressional District is the wealthiest, best educated, and healthiest in the country; the Sixteenth is dead last in earnings and fourth from the bottom overall. In terms of human development, it's stuck in the 1940s. The contrast between those two New York City neighborhoods is stark, but it is not unique. There are equally wide variations within states and between states.

According to economist Emmanuel Saez, the income gap in America hasn't been this wide since the 1920s. Between 1993 and 2008, the average annual incomes of 99 percent of Americans grew at three-quarters of a percent (0.75%) in real terms. Meanwhile, the incomes of the top one percent of the population grew nearly 4 percent a year in the same period. That means the top one percent captured more than half of the overall economic growth in the period.

In the 1960s and 1970s, it seemed that those in the lowest economic classes might revolt to get a greater share of the nation's wealth. In the 1980s and 1990s, some thought the middle class might join that struggle. These days, the charge might be led by what author Matt Miller calls "the lower upper class"—doctors, lawyers, accountants, engineers, and all those company executives who report to the CEO. Nine out of ten Americans would count them lucky. But the "lower uppers" can't help noticing that there are lots of people with credentials no better than theirs who live in "Gatsby-like splendor." As Miller points out, "If people no smarter or better than you are making $10 million or $50 million or $100 million in a single year, while you're working yourself ragged to scrape by on a million or two—or, God forbid, $300,000—then something must be wrong."

Something *is* wrong, and it is contributing to the increasing fragmentation of society. As Miller points out, many people don't see the success of the super-rich as a product of the free market, but of "rigged systems that are as likely to reward failure as success." CEOs who preside over years of tumbling stock prices—or even the very dissolution of their companies—walk away with "separation packages" worth tens of millions of dollars; hedge fund managers collect as much for barely beating the S&P and avoid paying taxes at ordinary rates, to boot; investment bankers pocket millions in fees regardless of whether the deals they engineer work out.

Meanwhile, nearly a third of people in the poorest 19 percent of households were unemployed at the end of the 2007–2009 Great Recession, a higher rate than during the worse year of the Great Depression. Among families with household incomes of at least $150,000, unemployment was just 3 percent, which most economists consider "full employment." Nearly two-thirds of Americans fortunate enough to have a job in 2009 lived paycheck to paycheck, up from 43 percent in 2007. Over 1.5 million Americans filed for personal bankruptcy in 2010, a 14 percent increase over 2009. For the first time in history, more than 44 million Americans are on food stamps.

America has always had economic classes, but they used to be relatively porous. People weren't confined to them for their lifetimes. They could climb out through education and hard work. In fact, the

American Dream has always been about ladders. Even if you were born poor, in America, you could work your way up the economic ladder. Admittedly, for more than a hundred years, the taller ladders were not available to people of color. But the American ideal was still a meritocracy, where hard work paid off for everyone. Today, though, for many people it seems that some ladders go in only one direction.

Uslaner believes that such inequality causes people to particularize their natural tendency to trust others. Instead of feeling that everyone is in the same boat, people at one end of the economic scale begin to think that they have little in common with people at the other end. They tend to trust only those who share their economic lot because they assume only they have the same values and beliefs. As inequality rises, the lives of the haves and the have-nots intersect less and less frequently and, when they do, it only reinforces their differences. The *favelas* of Brazil, for example, are often built on hillsides, just below the mansions and condo complexes of the wealthy. But the urban poor who live in the shantytowns seldom leave their crowded alleys and staircases. Their lives seldom intersect with their rich neighbors' at the top of the hill. The United States has always had tenement slums and poor neighborhoods, and in the most dire of economic times, tent cities have cropped up in open spaces like parks and highway underpasses. But the dramatic increase in the number of gated communities is perhaps one of the clearest signs of the growing chasm between rich and poor in America.

In 1970, there were about 10,000 such private communities in the United States, housing about 2 million people. In 2010, nearly 62 million Americans lived in about 310,000 gated communities with an estimated value approaching $4 trillion, almost 20 percent of the value of all U.S. residential real estate. Whether they were established to preserve real estate values, to deter crime, or to create a haven for like-minded people, gated communities represent a separate world from the larger society. They provide many of their own services, such as security and trash collection, control access to public spaces, and set their own rules. Their residents tend to focus on life within the gates rather than on issues within the larger city or town. And gated communities have, almost by definition, an aura of "exclusiveness" that exaggerates differences between residents and nonresidents. In separating themselves from the larger community, they send a signal to others that they are "different," implicitly "better," and certainly on a different social and economic track.

People on different sides of the gate have fewer interactions with each other, which inevitably reduces trust to the lowest common in-group denominator. If we trust only people who are just like us, we will associate only with our own kind, which will make us even more suspicious of others. And round and round we will go in a vicious circle. Trust that makes no room for the Other is no trust at all. It's symptomatic of a society on the verge of a nervous breakdown. And no amount of chicken soup can cure that.

30

People Are Crazy

In becoming OtherWise, it helps to remember that other people are just as rational as we are. Which isn't saying much. Psychologists (not to mention ministers and bartenders) have accumulated impressive evidence that the most sober and deliberate of us can be dependably irrational in some of the most important aspects of our lives.

For example, the American economy was built on a three-part explanation of human behavior: (1) People are rational; (2) they always act in their own self-interest; and (3) the good of society is based on people acting in their own self-interest. But Barry Schwartz, who has spent his career studying the intersection of economics and psychology, doesn't think human nature is quite that simple. "The reductive appeal to self-interest as the master human motive," he says, "is a false description of human nature."

Worse, appeals to self-interest can have perverse consequences. For example, when the Swiss government asked people if they would allow a nuclear waste site to be built in their neighborhood, people who were offered financial compensation were half as likely to agree as those who weren't. Apparently, introducing the idea of financial incentives causes people to ask "What's in it for me?" and crowds out other considerations, such as civic duty. And when a day-care center started fining parents who were late picking up their children, late pickups *increased*. When parents knew they would be paying for leaving their kids past closing time, they felt less guilty about being late; the day-care center, on the other hand, couldn't allocate its resources efficiently because it never knew how many kids would be staying late. So a bunch of individuals acting in their own self-interest doesn't always add up to a net benefit for the larger community.

Furthermore, people aren't always clear about what constitutes their own self-interest. What they say and what they do are often very different. Eugene Caruso, a professor of behavioral science at the University of Chicago, gave participants in a trivia game the option of choosing partners based on traits that were relevant to success (such as IQ) or else traits irrelevant to success (such as weight). Although participants said that weight was "the single least important factor in their choice," a clear preference for thin partners emerged. In fact, participants sacrificed between ten and twelve IQ points to work with the thinner teammate. In another study, participants were willing to accept a 20 percent lower salary to work for a man, instead of a woman. Leaving IQ points or money on the table, especially when one explicitly reports that weight and gender don't matter, is hardly rational.

The dot.com and housing bubbles put a stake through *Homo economicus*'s undeserved reputation for making financial decisions based only on the best use of the best available information. Neither of those financial fiascos can be explained without reference to investor psychology. Housing prices rose to stratospheric heights, for example, because they had always gone up and people just assumed that their inexorable trend upward would continue indefinitely. In psychological terms, they suffered from a toxic muddle of cognitive deficiencies that cause us to give greater weight to the most recent data we saw (recency and anchoring) or to the data that is easiest to get (availability bias), or that agrees with our preexisting opinion (confirmation bias), or that confirms what everyone else is doing (bandwagon effect), or, failing all else, allows us to simply assume that things will continue to go the way they've been going (disregard of regression toward the mean).

Compounding the problem, normalcy in the housing market depends not only on dramatic price reductions, but also on overcoming cognitive biases in the opposite direction. And getting more data won't necessarily help. Functional MRI (fMRI) research has demonstrated that the part of people's brains involved in rational decision making and controlling emotions actually switches off when presented with too much information. All of these cognitive deficiencies have been observed, studied, and validated. And yet they persist and continue to be ignored. Two cognitive scientists have even suggested that our capacity to reason is not designed to make better decisions, but rather to win arguments over the decisions we've made.

Furthermore, a long litany of psychological experiments demonstrates that our behavior is easily influenced by external events outside our consciousness. One study, done back when phone booths were a lot more ubiquitous, showed that if someone dropped papers outside a phone booth, people were more willing to help if they had just found money in the coin-return slot. Another study showed that someone standing outside a bakery with the smell of fresh bread in the air is more likely to help a stranger than someone standing outside a "neutral-smelling dry goods store." A third study indicated that someone asked to read sentences containing words like *honor* and *respect* is more polite, minutes later, than someone who read words like *obnoxious* and *bluntly*. And psychologists have amply demonstrated an ability to manipulate perfectly average, ethical people to do terrible things, just by configuring situations in a certain way.

Finally, experiments have demonstrated that as soon as humans bunch together in groups, we start to copy other members of our group, favor members of our own group over others, look for a leader to worship, and eagerly fight anyone not in the group. And it takes very little to corral people into herds. In one famous experiment, psychologist Henri Tajfel assigned teenage boys to different groups based solely on their preferences for paintings by Klee and Kandinsky. The boys never met each other and had no idea what significance their group assignment had. Each boy was then taken into a cubicle and asked to distribute money to the members of both groups. The only information they were given was a code indicating each boy and his group membership. With no more than that to go on, the boys distributed more money to the members of their own group than to the other. The boys displayed classic in-group behavior even though it didn't seem they had anything to gain from it.

In reality, they did have something to gain—something that they realized unconsciously. Tajfel argues that people build their own identities from their group memberships. Part of who we are depends on the group we are part of. The boys in the experiment were boosting their own identities by making their own group look better. Tajfel's experiment has been replicated many times, using symbols instead of money and changing the rules to tease out different motivations, but the results are always the same—people always find a way to favor their own group even though they have been members for only minutes, have no idea who else is in it, and don't really understand what their membership signifies. Such is the power of group membership.

If part of our personal identity comes from the group memberships that are important to us—that is, the people we associate with—another way we define ourselves is by what sets us apart from others. People in the so-called "developed world" have a long history of setting themselves "above" others by stressing differences and by finding (or, if necessary, manufacturing) ways to highlight those dissimilarities. Some of our ancestors made African Americans into cultural Others through the use of minstrel shows in blackface; they also invented archetypes like Sambo and Aunt Jemima, and separatist policies like the Jim Crow laws.

Anyone of a different race, ethnicity, sexual orientation, religion, or culture is potentially Other, and we derive some sense of who we are from our differences. Sometimes the Other is quite exotic—someone who lives in a distant land, who speaks a strange language, and follows unusual customs. Ironically, it's not too hard to accept those Others. We may visit them, marvel at their differences, and take lots of photos to show the folks back home. But the Other on the next block, at the next table, or next in line is another matter entirely. The Other who lives nearby is a potential source of tension and conflict. He may even be a member of one of the many groups with which we have affiliated ourselves; groups come and go like ripples on the surface of a pond, after all. But if the differences between us touch on those areas that are closest to our sense of who we are, it's very hard to see beyond them.

Miroslav Volf, who as we have seen has more reason than many to feel prejudice against certain classes of people, suggests that an alternate way to construe identity is to think of it as *including* the Other. "We are defined not simply by what distinguishes us from others," he writes, "but also by what we have in common with others. We need the Other in order to know ourselves." You can't understand the Other until you understand yourself, and especially all the different lenses through which you see the Other.

This may sound like the philosophical musings of a mystic, but it's rooted in scientific observation. Australian psychologist Cordelia Fine writes that "the boundary of self-concept is permeable to other people's conceptions of you (or somewhat more accurately, your perception of their perception of you)." We are all many people. For example, many men are simultaneously husband, father, son, boss, subordinate; many women have comparable identities. Which person we are at any particular moment is a function of the context in which we find ourselves. Indeed, the Spanish philosopher José Ortega y Gasset coined the maxim, "I am I and my circumstances." When our environment makes a particular aspect of our personality salient, associative memories and learned expectations ripple through our mind and into our behavior. We literally become the role we are playing under those circumstances. Other people relate to us within that context, and we respond in kind, reinforcing our mutual perceptions.

Most of us think that, if we know anything, we know ourselves. But there was a reason the Greeks inscribed "Know Thyself" on Apollo's Temple at Delphi. The self most of us know is an idealized self, the self we would like to be, and probably the self that only our mother would ever recognize. Most of us get a true understanding of ourselves only when we see ourselves through the eyes of others. And in the process, if we are open enough, we will gain a better understanding of the Other as well.

As we have seen, there is evidence that adopting an outsider's perspective reduces prejudice toward that person's group. On that score, the same evolutionary processes that hardwired prejudice into us have given us the tools to surmount it. We humans have an amazing capacity to understand what's on the minds of others and to actually experience their feelings as our own. Of course, some people have more empathy than others. Some people never seem to develop the capacity to understand others. And others seem to lose it at a certain point in their lives.

Jonah Lehrer is a brilliant, thirtysomething neuroscientist who may have figured out why so many powerful people seem to act so hypocritically. He suggests it may be because "power makes us less sensitive to the needs and feelings of others—it silences our empathy—and so we only think about our own motivations and needs." Social scientists have long suspected that our sense of fairness is rooted in feelings of empathy. It seems logical, then, that people who are isolated from others because of their "special status" would be less able to put themselves in the other person's place.

How do executives pulling down six- or seven-figure salaries relate to the ordinary people they'd like to have as customers? And how do they relate to the disadvantaged people to whom they have a civic responsibility? One way is to get them out of their corner offices and encourage them to mix it up with people who deal with hunger, homelessness, blight, and despair every day. That's an approach that Roger Crockett calls "heading to the 'hood." Crockett is an African-American journalist, and he's not talking about touring the inner city from an executive coach or doing a little glad-handing at the local soup kitchen. He means actually "shedding your suit jacket and sitting side by side with people in the inner city, helping them administer programs, raise money, and develop skills." It's not such a pie-in-the-sky idea. Crockett points out that hard-nosed accounting giant Ernst & Young has embraced this approach. "Nearly 50 percent of its 1,200 top leaders serve on community boards," he says, "and each year the firm invests 115,000 hours of employee time, valued at $17.25 million, toward volunteer community work." That level of involvement raises what the company calls the "inclusiveness competence" of Ernst & Young executives. It could help bridge the cultural gap between them and their communities. It could help them better understand the Other.

Stepping outside the comfort of our routine to interact more directly with people unlike ourselves can pay great benefits. At minimum, we can learn that people we once considered "Other" are really not all that different from ourselves. And that, of course, means that those Others are creatures of logic and emotion, the handiwork of heritage and personal experience, who navigate the world guided by both facts and feelings. To some extent, their self-concept and even their behavior are a function of their perception of *our* perception of *them*. As in all of us, when faced with a threat or a difficult decision, instinct and habit exert a strong pull. But reason and values weigh in too, and in a supportive environment, where people are recognized as individuals of worth, those higher level powers can prevail.

31

Fluent Listening

When the chairman of Aetna invited Jack Rowe to dinner, the president of the Mount Sinai Medical Center assumed it was to dissuade him from joining more than 700,000 practitioners in a class-action suit against the insurance industry. Instead, the Aetna chairman asked Rowe if he'd consider becoming the company's CEO.

Rowe had been a physician for nearly thirty years at that point and CEO of Mount Sinai for the last twelve of those years. His specialty was gerontology, and he was fast approaching the point in his life when his own need for the service would interfere with his return to studying it. But something about the challenge of turning Aetna around intrigued him. Aetna was a mess. Both doctors and patients hated its bureaucracy, its interfering ways, its dubious billing practices, and its unresponsiveness. Plus, Aetna was losing money and had gone through three CEOs in the last three years. Rowe knew that there were plenty of turnaround experts who could restore the company to financial health, at least in the short term, by slashing costs. But he believed it would take someone who really understood the health-care field to figure out how to keep Aetna financially viable and perhaps even attain growth in an era of escalating medical costs.

Rowe took the job and, brushing off the stock market's less-than-enthusiastic endorsement, went on a listening tour of Aetna's employees and customers. To cynics and skeptics, it must have seemed like something he pulled from the standard ninety-day playbook for new CEOs: Spend your early days "listening" to employees, while the finance department draws up a list of potential targets to be slashed and burned.

Although it is a physical impossibility, most of us listen with our ears half-closed. Rowe, however, is a fluent listener. Walk into his office and you won't see a sheet of paper on the surface of his desk. Sit down across from him and he won't be fiddling with his cell phone or pager. Start talking and he will listen, asking questions when you pause if he doesn't understand something, repeating what you said in his own words to check—and demonstrate—that he does understand.

One of the by-products of working at people's bedsides for so many years (Rowe even did monthly medical rounds with residents when he was president of Mount Sinai) is that he is very adept at reading expressions. On his way to the hospital room of New York City's grand rabbi, he saw two burly Hasidic men outside the door and, as he approached, he noticed one of them peer at his hospital ID. Anticipating the man's question, he said, "I'm Irish Catholic." Perhaps surprised to see a Catholic running a Jewish hospital, the Hasidic man replied, "You must be very smart."

No surprise, he is. And he knew that, before he was done at Aetna, there would be blood up to his ankles, swelling at times to his knees. He laid off 15,000 employees and replaced all but three senior executives—the heads of communications, human resources, and law. Of course, much of that is exactly what any turnaround whiz would have done. The hard part would be growing the company again. Rowe concentrated on two sources of growth: doctors and employees. He believed that Aetna's ultimate customers are the people whose health it insures, but their doctors and his own employees were his primary vehicle for reaching them, along with the employers who ultimately foot the bill. Priority number one was to repair relations with the doctors who treated the people Aetna insured. To do that, Rowe changed the policies that doctors and patients considered so intrusive and burdensome. So the company began giving patients more say in their care, requiring fewer permissions for basic procedures. And to put the past completely behind him, Rowe also became the first insurer to settle the class-action suit that many physicians had filed against the industry. As part of the $170 million cash settlement, the company contributed $20 million to establish a foundation to study issues such as childhood obesity, end-of-life care, and racial disparities in health care.

Regaining employee confidence would be a tougher nut to crack. Most of the employees who were left had been there for decades, and as a result of his employee listening tour, Rowe knew they were understandably demoralized and scared. The heads of communications and human resources had been trying to gather employee survey data for years, but every time they broached the subject, someone would tell them it was the wrong time. It was either too close to earnings, or too close to bonuses, or too close to the holidays to try to get employees to complete a survey. Initially, Rowe felt the same way, but eventually the need for specific data outweighed those concerns. "I needed specific data on how people felt so I could address their concerns," Rowe recalls. When the survey data came in, he began analyzing it just as he would have analyzed clinical data in his research days nearly three decades earlier. His diagnosis was simple: Aetna's employees had lost their pride in the company. They no longer knew what the company stood for beyond making money. And it wasn't even good at that.

So Rowe started some medical initiatives designed in part to demonstrate to employees that Aetna was going in a different direction, shifting its focus to caring for patients' health. Even though Rowe's decisions caused the actuaries and lawyers to wring their hands in anxiety, the company began a series of programs to address racial disparities in health care, to teach patients how to better manage depression, and to provide better end-of-life care. Not coincidentally, many of these initiatives were also of great interest to the doctors the company served.

"I wanted to show our employees that Aetna had a pulse," Rowe says, "that the referee might have reached a nine in his count, but we could still get up and finish the bout. That we were doing something forward-looking they could be excited about." Later surveys showed that the initiatives were working, but for Rowe, the real proof came in another in the series of employee meetings that he had never really abandoned. During the question and answer period, a woman got up, stated she had been an employee for twenty-two years, and asked, "Dr. Rowe, what are all these charts about? What exactly are you trying to do here?" Rowe paused for a moment, gathering his thoughts. Then he looked her in the eye and said, "This is about restoring pride in this once-great company." The room exploded in applause.

Pride turned out to be a key driver of Aetna employee attitudes. While 46 percent of employees said they were proud of the company in 2002, that number had jumped to 69 percent in 2006, thanks to Rowe's efforts, and continued to increase in subsequent years to an unprecedented 84 percent in 2010. Among the company's top 200 executives, 199 rated the company 5 on a five-point scale. Rowe, the lone holdout, gave it a 4. The man has high standards, but a thirty-second elevator ride with a thirty-year Aetna employee almost caused even him to reconsider his rating. Rowe didn't know the employee who got in the elevator with him one day. She obviously recognized him, though, because she said, "Dr. Rowe, I want to thank you for two things—my new dining room set and for saving Aetna." Who would have guessed that listening to employees could result in such a powerful mix of tangible and emotional rewards.

Not everyone is a Jack Rowe, but anyone can become a better listener. The biggest obstacle is a natural tendency to evaluate what people are saying while they are saying it. We are all judgmental by nature, and doubly so when emotions are running high. That characteristic probably once helped save our species from hidden or unfamiliar threats. But, in modern days, we usually manage to control our fight-or-flight instincts and just keep right on talking past each other. Fluent listening, on the other hand, requires a sharp ear, a keen eye, and lots of concentration. It means listening to people's emotional tone as well as their words, and watching the other person's body language and posture for cues. It means listening for ideas and patterns, not just for facts, and stifling the urge to judge or even evaluate what is being said. And it requires that we demonstrate attention by maintaining eye contact, leaning forward, and nodding occasionally, but otherwise staying still, not fiddling with anything or trying to take notes. Finally, it means repeating what the other person said and waiting for positive feedback before asking open-ended questions.

This kind of listening is very different from the typical approach managers are advised to use in addressing large groups. In those cases, anybody who asks a question is essentially a springboard for the message the manager wants to deliver. The manager speaks to the entire group rather than the individual who asked the question. And one never follows up by asking, "Did that answer your question?" for fear that it didn't. That's not really listening; it's public speaking with a semiscripted interlocutor. In a typical Q&A session, questioners might as well be ventriloquist dummies because they are merely props.

Real listening happens only between two people who, for the moment, are equals. They aren't trying to win a debate; they are trying to gain understanding.

32

Presence

Bob Selander, the chairman and former CEO of Master-Card International, says one of the things he looks for in managers is "an ability to see things from others' point of view." He calls that talent "presence," but as he explains it, it is clear he's talking about a particular application of empathy. "Presence is being able to deal with different constituencies in an appropriate way," he says. "It's not just the ability to capture an audience's attention, but the ability to get the right results."

Selander is an easygoing though demanding and no-nonsense executive; he is hard to rattle (even when, in the middle of a board meeting, he gets a phone call from his doctor telling him he has prostate cancer). The local paper where he lives once wrote that "with mature good looks . . . [Selander] could probably moonlight as a model for a clothing catalog, stacking firewood or patting a golden retriever." But Selander admits that he didn't always have "presence."

"Earlier in my career, I was comfortable dealing [with people] one-on-one or in small groups," he remembers, "but when I got up in front of an audience of, say, 500 people, it was a real challenge." But then the bank he had joined just out of college began a serious push into markets outside the United States. Over the next twenty years, that bank would become Citigroup, and Selander would find himself living and working in five countries on three continents. And as the bank grew, he not only lived in different places, he worked in a broad range of jobs, from overseeing the bank's consumer banking and retail brokerages, to running its credit card business and leading the development of new banking technologies. Besides discovering that jet lag was a big part of his job, he gained insight into the ways different people think.

Salespeople have long realized that meeting their quota often depended on understanding customers emotionally, as well as intellectually. Knowing what really motivates a customer—including outside interests, personal history, and family—can give a salesperson a real edge. The same principle applies to all managers: As they progress in their careers, they have to interact with a larger circle of stakeholders, from customers and shareowners to suppliers, employees, community leaders, and members of Congress—not to mention all the people on the organization chart above, below, and to the sides of them who can influence their success.

In the course of his career, Selander has learned that each of these people responds to the same facts and data in different ways. "Presence means being able to take that into account," he says. "It's a combination of not only how you convey things, but *what* you convey. Presence is learning to deal with different people in a way that allows them to get what they need out of the interaction, while getting the results that you'd like."

Dwight Eisenhower is supposed to have said that "leadership is the art of getting someone else to do something you want done because he wants to do it." Presence would seem to be a prerequisite for that kind of leadership, whether you are planning the D-Day invasion or leading a company that processes 22 billion transactions worth more than $2 trillion every year.

To know what matters to people, you have to be present in the sense of being attentive. Attentiveness is about more than being a good listener or being able to read body language, though those skills are also critical. It is being able to put yourself in other people's positions, to feel what they feel, to make an emotional connection. It doesn't mean adopting other people's emotions as your own and trying to please everybody. That would be a formula for gridlock or mushy decisions. But it does mean giving appropriate weight to other people's feelings in your decision making, realizing that people's feelings are often the source of their motivation.

Interestingly, the ad campaign that MasterCard launched not long after Selander became CEO demonstrated all those qualities. Selander wanted to distinguish MasterCard globally from its arch rivals, the much larger Visa credit card system and the more exclusive American Express card. Research in the United Kingdom, Brazil, Germany, Japan, and the United States suggested that the self-indulgent *Bonfire of the Vanities* culture of the 1990s was losing steam. "We discovered that people weren't buying a fifty-inch plasma TV simply to one-up their next-door neighbor," Selander recalls. "They were looking for a way to have a fun, family evening on a Friday night. Watching something on the big screen in the comfort of their own home was something they could do together." Discovering that emotional linkage, which resonated with people around the world, ultimately led to the strategy of positioning MasterCard as the best way to pay for those purchases that matter most. And the execution of that strategy was the company's long-running "Priceless" campaign.

The research underlying MasterCard's ad campaign was undoubtedly expensive, but it ultimately proved priceless in its own right. And that points up another important aspect of presence. Don't try to wing it. "I don't think it's smart to walk into a room where the facts and data are not known," Selander cautions, "so it's important to get to that basis quickly by asking questions," and especially if you suspect that you won't like the answers. Selander once used his own brush with prostate cancer as an example. "I would have preferred that it never happened. But you know what? It was a reminder that things can go bad, but also that the stuff you don't know can hurt you. And when you find out about it, it gives you a chance to do something about it." That's presence.

33

Congruence

Reynold Levy, fresh from a five-year term as president of the International Rescue Committee, didn't become the obvious candidate to be president of Lincoln Center for the Performing Arts until his final interview with its search committee. Someone asked him what unique qualities and experience he would bring to the job. "Well, from what I've seen so far," he said, "you could use a U.N. peacekeeping force."

The committee members were struck by his understatement. Lincoln Center is unique among cultural organizations. It is not a singular institution, but a confederation of twelve artistic organizations, including the Metropolitan Opera, the New York Philharmonic, Jazz at Lincoln Center, the Julliard School, the School of American Ballet, and the Film Society of Lincoln Center, among others. Each of those organizations has its own administration and board of directors. Lincoln Center for the Performing Arts is merely one of twelve constituent groups that mounts its own productions and happens to be the other groups' "landlord."

In 2002, when Levy was interviewed for the job, relations between these constituent "tenants" and their "landlord" were about as fractious as those in New York City as a whole, which actually has an insurgent "Rent Is Too Damn High" political party. Many of Lincoln Center's constituent groups were in high dudgeon over renovation plans drawn up by Levy's predecessors. Not only did they not like the plans themselves—which included erecting a giant glass dome over the central plaza—they were especially incensed by what they anticipated would be a raid on their respective donors. Much of the associated *Sturm und Drang* played out in soap opera tones in the city's paper of record, the *New York Times,* causing many ticket buyers and donors to question what was going on.

In that situation, it wasn't Levy's love of the arts, nor even his prodigious fund-raising skills, that made him a natural candidate for the Lincoln Center job. It was his innate ability—honed to an incisive edge through his experience in a range of settings, from the richly paneled executive offices of AT&T to the gritty corridors of the 92nd Street Y and the tent cities of the International Rescue Committee—to find congruence where others see only conflict. It may be one of the keys to being OtherWise. "It's basic Adam Smith," Levy says. "People are driven by their interests. If you can find a congruence of interests, you're likely to find a very productive relationship."

Finding congruence is more than a search for the overlaps in intersecting circles and sorting Venn diagrams. By that measure, General George A. Custer and the Sioux people had several points of congruence—they were human beings, rode horses, and settled their differences at the Little Bighorn River. They also had common interests—among them, to live in peace and freedom on the great prairies. Unfortunately, no one ever figured out a way to reconcile their differences in a way that satisfied their mutual interests. Levy was in a similar situation at Lincoln Center, and his immediate predecessor had already played the role of Custer after just nine months in the job. "Generally, most institutions run away from challenges that threaten their very existence—or they attack them on the margins," he observed. "Lincoln Center was no different. From the outside, we seemed to be in total disarray; on the inside, it was business as usual. I decided to treat it as a crisis because key stakeholders—patrons and donors—were losing faith in Lincoln Center and voting with their feet."

One of Levy's advantages is that he has never been totally absorbed by the organizations for which he worked. No one was more dedicated or put in longer hours. Levy's father used to joke that his son was determined to never earn more than $10 an hour, no matter what his total compensation was. But he was never dependent on the institution to which he was dedicating all those hours for his personal identity or sense of worth. He considers that liberating because it affords him an unusual degree of objectivity, along with the freedom to fail. So he saw all the backbiting and sniping for what it was—the constituent groups' perfectly understandable efforts to pursue their own interests as they saw them. "I saw my task as finding congruence, to figure out a way to serve their interests while moving us all to higher ground," he has said. In this case, higher ground meant finding a way to fund the repair and reconstruction of the Center's forty-year-old physical structure. The travertine cladding the buildings was stained and cracking. The mechanical systems were in dire need of modernization. And the Center itself was criticized for standing aloof from the city around it on a pile of limestone surrounded by multiple lanes of traffic.

No one seriously disagreed that decades of deferred maintenance had to be addressed, but no one wanted to get stuck with the bill. "All the conversation was about cannibalization," Levy recalls. "They were each afraid we'd go after their donors." As Levy saw it, Lincoln Center's challenge was not wringing more money out of existing contributors, but attracting new donors. "The real challenge was persuading people who didn't care about opera, didn't care about dance, didn't care about all these art forms," he said. "And we would only bring them in if we could interpret Lincoln Center in a way that addressed their interests—as say, an important civic institution, an engine of economic development, a source of civic pride, a tourist attraction, a way to attract and retain employees." But that meant doing something about the Center's aloofness from the city in which it sat, like a haughty but threadbare dowager.

When he arrived, Lincoln Center had only a $240 million commitment in principle from New York City and another $15 million from an anonymous donor (later revealed to be the city's billionaire mayor, Michael Bloomberg). But the city commitment was subject to everyone agreeing on a common plan, and that seemed even less likely than resolving the problems in the Middle East. For example, Joseph Volpe, who rose from apprentice carpenter to general manager of the Metropolitan Opera, sniped at the redevelopment plan from its earliest stages, accusing the people in charge of being "evasive," "high-handed," and intent on turning Lincoln Center into "a shopping mall." At one point, Volpe loudly pulled the Met out of the entire effort, trying to take its 30 percent share of the city's promised money with it. He eventually came back to the table, after securing a veto over any aspect of the master plan he didn't like, and up to the day he retired in 2006, there was still plenty that rankled him: He opposed erecting a new home for the City Opera in the city-owned park adjacent to the Met, and he didn't want changes in a parking lot entrance he considered the "Met's principal drop-off point." Both ideas were dropped. Levy knew, however, that what continued to rankle the Met, as well as the other constituents who might, for the moment, be less vociferous, was the prospect that finding nearly a billion dollars to pay for all the redevelopment would inevitably eat into their own fund-raising.

So Levy took a leap into the unknown. He proposed that, as landlord, Lincoln Center for the Performing Arts would pay for all capital improvements, including a total upgrade of the aged mechanical systems. In an unprecedented move, he offered to share the central development office's resources, including its donor lists, for the constituents' own fund-raising campaigns. And finally, he pledged to match whatever the constituents raised for their own artistic projects, 20 cents on the dollar of the first $25 million raised, 15 cents on the dollar above that, making Lincoln Center the largest single donor to all these constituencies. It was an artistic and civic trifecta—for Lincoln Center, for its constituent artistic companies, and, in the end, for the people of New York City.

New York Times architecture critic Nicolai Ouroussoff had a decidedly mixed reaction to the redeveloped campus. After praising the architects' respectful restraint and the way they managed to connect the "famously aloof complex to its surroundings," the *Times's* critic hankered for an even bolder, more coordinated plan. "[The] architecture is too subdued in some places, pointlessly gimmicky at others," he wrote. "Worse, the spaces don't flow together in a way that might have given the center the internal coherence that it sorely needs." All in all, he considered the reconstruction an "apt metaphor for Lincoln Center's history of institutional discord." Perhaps. But considering the depth of that discord when the project was first launched, some were understandably impressed that the redevelopment was ever even completed.

The reaction of the *Times* music critic Anthony Tommasini was probably closer to the average New Yorker's. "I am delighted and surprised that the center has been able to make itself so much more inviting, to blend into the neighborhood," he wrote. "There used to be something oppressive about Lincoln Center. For me that is no longer so." Indeed, the American Institute of Architects recognized the Center's redevelopment for "reinvigorating what was already a creative, inspiring public place with a new life for the 21st century." As if to prove the point, the plaza is almost always crowded with people who aren't just there to see a performance, but to be part of the show that is New York City.

And it didn't take a contingent of blue-helmeted U.N. soldiers to make it happen once everyone's common interests were uncovered and served.

Conclusion

How to Be OtherWise

Everybody is somebody's Other. But it is amazing how many of us are "OtherDumb" or "OtherDim." Whether it stems from fear, anger, or sheer laziness, whether the product of our upbringing, our schooling, or our experience, whether reflecting our religious, political, or social beliefs, or simply the vestige of some evolutionary adaptation that lost its usefulness long ago, few people would argue that we Americans are OtherWise.

We are widely known for knowing little about the rest of the world geographically, politically, culturally, religiously, or historically. When times get tough, our inclination is to close the blinds, lock the doors, and blame our troubles on all the foreigners—here and abroad—who are stealing our jobs. The Germans may have a word for the fear of foreign things and people—*überfremdung*—but Americans have turned it into a political and social art.

America has a long history of "otherizing" people. Blacks were slaves until 1865 and didn't get a guarantee of full citizenship rights until 1965. Asians were barred from immigrating to the United States by a 1917 law that was amended and turned into a narrow quota in 1924, and was not completely overturned until 1965. Women couldn't vote until 1920 and didn't win the right to equal pay until 1963. The miscegenation laws of thirty-eight states weren't declared unconstitutional until 1967. The last state laws prohibiting sex between consenting adults of the same gender were not abolished until 2003. It was only as recent as 2010 that gay citizens won the right to fight our wars without hiding their true sexual identity. And even today gays are struggling for the right to marry with the same benefits as heterosexuals.

Meanwhile, America is cleaving into two castes—the roughly 25 percent who graduated from college; married; had children; and live comfortable, affluent lives totally segregated from the roughly 30 percent of their fellow citizens who are less likely to marry; more likely to have kids out of wedlock; more likely to be obese; and less likely to participate in civic life. These two castes know little of each other's life experience; they live in self-absorbed isolation, geographically and culturally. Worse of all, the one caste essentially runs all the institutions on which the other depends. As political scientist Charles Murray has written, "It's not a problem if truck drivers can't empathize with the priorities of a Yale law professor. It is a problem if Yale law professors, or producers of nightly news, or CEOs of great corporations, or the President's advisors, cannot empathize with the priorities of truck drivers."

This is not to suggest that Americans are worse than people in other cultures, but our founding documents held us to a higher standard, even if actual practice fell woefully short before the ink on the Declaration of Independence had dried. A more charitable view would suggest that American history since then has been a series of dogged efforts to correct injustices and perfect our national character. And there is no question that we have made progress, just as few people would disagree that we still have a long way to go.

Contributing to our zigzag progress toward a more OtherWise society, political and cultural partisans, like old soldiers, always seem to be fighting their last war to some sense of completion. Conservatives continue to battle the it's-okay-as-long-as-it-feels-good, "anything goes," sexual excesses and self-absorption of the 1960s. Liberals remain obsessed with the "greed is good" acquisitive excesses of the 1980s. Those of us in the middle would like to reconcile the two—being liberal on some issues, conservative on others—but we can't get a word in edgewise.

Perhaps that's because so many of our differences stem from deeply held beliefs about right and wrong.

In *The Wealth of Nations,* Adam Smith observed that "two different schemes or systems of morality" seem to prevail in all civilized societies, and "one may be called the strict or austere; the other the liberal, or, if you will, the loose system." Historian and social conservative Gertrude Himmelfarb is a big fan of Smith and believes he could have been describing America, although when he wrote those words, the nation didn't yet exist. She sees two Americas: one that is religious, family-centered, and conformist, and another that is secular, hedonistic, and tolerant. One America believes safe sex is more harmful than smoking. The other believes sex is just another form of recreation and wants the government to stay out of people's pants.

In today's America, fissures based on sexual orientation, education, and income crisscross the traditional fracture lines of religion, race, and ethnicity. Dealing with people across these fractures is a long trek through prickly emotional underbrush. And in the case of religion, politics, and sex, it almost always leaves scars.

The traditional solution in most pluralistic societies—and certainly within the business community—is the cultivation of tolerance. But tolerance is the cheapest virtue, if it is a virtue at all. At best, it is a ceasefire that allows each side to retain, and even cement, its hostile attitudes. One party can agree to put up with the Other and still look down on him. Keeping one party at a distance nearly always fosters misunderstanding and suspicion. Tolerance may promise noninterference and facilitate peaceful coexistence, but it doesn't lead to understanding. On the contrary, it is built on a willful ignorance that leaves the Other unknown. Productive societies need more than what one philosopher called a "benign indifference to difference." Tolerance is only the first—and arguably lowest—step in becoming Other-Wise. Sometimes, it may be all that is attainable; but it should never be a satisfactory goal.

The opposite of "intolerance" is not tolerance but "hospitality." Hospitality requires us to welcome and to make room for the Other, without any judgment beyond recognizing our common humanity. It is about seeing the Other as a person and not simply as a totem of difference.

It is engaging that person in conversation, fueled not only by curiosity, but also by the conviction that the other person can teach us something of value. It is sharing that person's experience emotionally as well as intellectually. That doesn't mean we have to set aside our own beliefs in favor of cultural and political relativism. But such an encounter forces us to surface and examine our own preconceptions and biases.

As we have seen, much of our behavior and many of our inclinations reflect adaptations to circumstances that changed long ago. Many of our beliefs have roots deep below our consciousness. And threats to our self-esteem or group identity can increase our feelings of prejudice. Psychologists at Northwestern University have discovered through a series of experiments that "feeling good about oneself can lead an individual to feel good about others, even stereotyped and stigmatized out-groups." In fact, the very act of trying to assume someone else's perspective activates our self-concept and causes us to see more of ourselves in the Other. It shakes us free from thoughtless conformity and passivity. And it enables us to find what the philosopher Hans-Georg Gadamer called "a fusion of horizons," which is the key to being OtherWise.

Whenever two people engage in conversation, what each person says reflects a personal perspective, or how each person sees the world. Their separate perspectives are the product of their unique intellectual and emotional capabilities, life experience, unconscious biases, and unexpressed hopes and dreams. No two people have exactly the same perspective. We are each embedded in the particular history and culture that shaped us. Gadamer would say we all have different "horizons." To be OtherWise is to share "horizons," if only long enough to truly understand each other. This doesn't mean we will necessarily agree with each other, but our respective meanings will be clearer, permitting us to find the common ground of mutual interests, which can be the basis for continuing engagement and inclusion.

The importance of sharing horizons is critical even in the absence of overt disagreements, if there is a yawning gap between personal experiences. One striking example is the case of transracial adoptions. Over the last several decades, thousands of white American families adopted children from various Asian countries. They had the best of intentions, but many of these families didn't have a clue about the difficulties that transracial adoptees face. Adopting a colorblind attitude and ignoring an uncomfortable discussion about race, they inadvertently communicated the message that their adopted child was an "honorary white." When told about racial taunting at school, they brushed away their child's tears and told her to ignore the teasing. They made special effort to acquaint the child with what they considered Asian culture, perhaps taking her to Asian restaurants or sending her to Asian culture camp in the summer, not realizing that some adoptive children are uncomfortable around other Asians, particularly if they are with their adoptive parents. Raised in an overwhelmingly white home, the adopted child couldn't help but be confused about her own identity, exacerbating the feelings of abandonment that haunt many adopted children.

The experience of Asian adoptees is unique in many respects, but it is also emblematic of the challenges in relating to people who are different, even if one's intention is rooted in love and compassion. Whether someone is an adoptee, a child of mixed heritage, an immigrant of the first, second, or third generation, or someone who has little idea of his ancestors or the circumstances of their arrival, to be OtherWise is to respect people as individuals—not as exemplars of an entire culture, race, ethnicity, or color—and to validate their personal experience.

Being OtherWise means treating others as individuals, with their own unique story. Paradoxically, it requires keen *self*-awareness. Only then can we be free of our preconceptions and unspoken fears. Thus unencumbered, we can discover all the ways we are the same—in our interests and our destiny, if not in our experience and our ancestry.

Of course, that all sounds somewhat philosophical. And philosophers seldom, if ever, have to execute the triple play of meeting a payroll, investor expectations, and customer demands. Why bother to acquire the wisdom of relating to the Other? Not because it's the nice—or even right—thing to do, but in order to be more effective in our increasingly diverse and global society. Becoming OtherWise is a critical management requirement of the twenty-first century. And it entails intellectual, as well as emotional, development, along the lines we've already discussed:

- Expanding our worldview to include news of other countries
- Increasing our cultural literacy of other people
- Increasing our religious literacy of other faiths
- Challenging our biases and assumptions about the "Others" in our lives
- Educating our emotions and developing our sense of empathy
- Engaging with people outside our immediate circle in meaningful ways

In the 1950s, sociologist David Riesman introduced the term *other-directed* to describe the tenor of the times. People were obsessed with "others" but only as fellow consumers. Anxious to keep up with the proverbial Joneses, the "other-directed" were obsessed with status. Other-directed people found their identity and self-worth in reference to others—in how much they make, what they consume, and what they possess. If anything, they were "other-bound."

To be OtherWise is to be open to others and to see them not as consumers or the source of comparative status, but as fellow human beings of dignity and worth. It is to be knowledgeable about differences but, even more, eager to learn. It is to hear their story and to share our own story with them. It is appreciating their differences while finding in them common interests and values. The OtherWise are not naive and gullible. They realize that some people would take advantage of them, even do them harm. But they try not to make such judgments based on stereotypes and, instead, evaluate people as individuals. And they don't paper over real disagreements; they confront differences of opinion honestly without thinking less of the person who holds a different view. They try to find a way to respect the perspective of other people, even if they can't share it.

To be OtherWise is to see ourselves as others see us and to see ourselves in the Other. It is to understand the hidden forces that shape the Other's behavior, as well as our own. Only then will we see the Other, not as something apart, but as some*one* who is part of our world and our life. Only then, will we be OtherWise.

Acknowledgments

I have already acknowledged Marilyn Laurie's role in inspiring this book, but I should also thank her husband, Bob, for his generosity in allowing me to quote so extensively from my private conversations with her.

This book also benefited from my conversations with a number of people who shared their experiences and studies. In alphabetical order, they are Mark Addicks, chief marketing officer of General Mills; Mark Beckwith, Episcopal bishop of the Diocese of Newark; Ed Block, former senior vice president of public relations at AT&T; Roger Bolton, former chief communications officer of Aetna Healthcare; Brenda Colatrella, executive director of the Merck office of corporate responsibility; Debra Elam, chief diversity officer of General Electric; Claude Fischer, professor of sociology at the Berkeley campus of the University of California; Peter Francese, author and demographics trends analyst; John Gilfeather, executive vice president of Koski Research; Richard Haass, president of the Council on Foreign Relations; William Helms, my insightful and diplomatic editor at AMACOM; Mansour Javidan, dean of research at Thunderbird School of Global Management; Reynold Levy, president of Lincoln Center; Esther Novak, founder and CEO of VanguardComm; Marian

Prio-Odio, Miami-based psychotherapist; Rudy Rodriguez, director of multicultural marketing at General Mills; John Rowe, former CEO of Aetna Healthcare; Bob Selander, chair and former CEO of Master-Card International; Esther Silver-Parker, former senior vice president of corporate affairs at Walmart; Brigitta Tadmor, global head of diversity, inclusion, and health policy at Novartis Institutes for BioMedical Research; Dr. Beverly Daniel Tatum, president of Spelman College; Ben Verwaayen, CEO of Alcatel-Lucent; Miroslav Volf, professor of systematic theology at Yale Divinity School; Kip Williams, professor of psychological sciences at Purdue University; and Jeff Yang, writer and business/media consultant. I want to thank them for allowing me to quote them in these pages. Any mistakes of interpretation are entirely my own.

I profited from the comments and suggestions of several friends who read and commented on early drafts, especially Michael Goodman, director of Baruch College's master's program in communications; Beadle Moore, retired from the political science department of the University of Arkansas; and Lucien Richard, theologian and retired fellow of university professors at Boston University.

I am also grateful to Jonathan Haidt, of the University of Virginia, for the chart displaying the foundations of morality in Chapter Twelve. I would like to thank John Felstiner of Stanford University for permission to quote his translation of Paul Celan's poem, "Death Fugue" in Chapter Ten. And, of course, I am indebted to Richard Wiseman of the University of Hertfordshire in the United Kingdom for permission to quote some of the world's funniest jokes.

I also received help from the following people, who were generous with their time and advice: Adele Ambrose, chief communications officer of Merck; Ed Bligh, vice president and editorial director at the International Rescue Committee; Tomika DePriest of Spelman College; Rebecca Edwards, director of employee communications at General Electric; Kathy Fitzgerald, retired head of communications for KPMG; Maerenn Jepsen, of General Mills corporate public relations; George Kupczak, of the AT&T Archives; Jeff Lockwood, global head of communications at Novartis Institutes for BioMedical Research; Wilma Mathews, retired director of communications for

Arizona State University; Tim McClimon, president of the American Express Foundation; Tom Miller, former vice president of Business for Diplomatic Action; Mike Paul, president of MGP & Associates; Gary Sheffer, corporate vice president of communications at General Electric; Jennifer Stalzer, corporate communications at MasterCard International; Dave Sullivan; and Betsy Vorce, vice president of communications at Lincoln Center.

And finally I'd like to acknowledge the advice, love, and support of my wife, Ginny, and my children, Chris, Liz, and Juli, all of whom constantly show me what it looks like when someone is truly OtherWise.

                                            Dick Martin

Notes

Much of this book flowed from conversations with people in a wide range of fields, including religion, politics, sociology, business, and the arts. In all such cases, I have made my sources clear in the text. In other instances, I have benefited from the writings and research of experts and academics. Usually, I would include the specific citations as a footnote in the printed text. I have deviated from that practice here for several reasons.

First, in all honesty, writers don't like footnotes—with the possible exception of those who worry treatises out of keyboards. Tiny superscript numbers are the typeface equivalent of a stage whisper or, worse, a sharp elbow in the side. They are distracting and interrupt the flow of thought. At best, footnotes provide evidence that the writer isn't simply making things up, though they leave open the possibility that the sources cited might have, or that they might have been the victims of near-criminal misinterpretation. However, if only for the latter reason, some readers appreciate the opportunity to review for themselves the material a writer quotes. Other readers would like to delve more deeply into topics of particular interest.

So the chapter notes that follow refer interested readers to the sources for the quotes in this book, as well as for factual information that is not self-evident. Questions or comments can be addressed to the author at DickMartinBooks@aol.com.

Chapter 1: Who Is "Other"?

2   *Categorical thinking*: For more on the subject of categorical thinking, see C. Neil Macrae and Galen V. Bodenhausen, "Social Cognition: Categorical Person Perception," *British Journal of Psychology* 92 (2001), pp. 239–255, available at http://othr.ws/categorical-thinking.

3   *new middle class*: McKinsey & Company projects that the purchasing power of the rising middle class in emerging markets may reach $20 trillion over the next decade—twice the current level of consumption in the United States. The four biggest emerging economies—Brazil, Russia, India, and China—are large producers and consumers of goods and services, and will also be important in shaping the pace, direction, and sustainability of global economic growth; see http://othr.ws/world-middleclass.

3   *is fast becoming a minority-majority*: According to an analysis of census data by the Pew Research Center, 92 percent of the country's population growth between 2000 and 2010 was due to growth in minority populations, whether by births or immigration. Hawaii, California, Texas, and New Mexico have minority-majority populations. The non-Hispanic white populations of another eight states are very close to falling below 50 percent. For more details, see http://othr.ws/pew-pop-growth.

6   *Krippner has said, "Humanity is entangled"*: Stanley Krippner, a professor of psychology at Saybrook University, made these remarks during a video interview at a conference of the Common Bond Institute in 2008; see http://othr.ws/youtube-krippner.

Chapter 2: Strangers Climbing in the Window

11   *instinctual suspicion of people*: See, for example, "Social Development and Human Evolution: Managing the Ingroup Boundary," by Michael Lovaglia, Chana Barron, and Jeffrey Houser, theory workshop presentation, January 31, 2003, available at http://othr.ws/suspect-strangers. Evolutionary scientists differ on the precise period in which social groups began to include outsiders without kin relationships, but many arrive at an estimate of about 50,000 to 150,000 years before the present time. See, for example, C. S. Henshilwood and B. Dubreuil, "Reading the Artifacts: Gleaning Language Skills from the Middle Stone Age in Southern Africa" in R. Botha and C. Knight (eds.), *The Cradle of Language*. (Oxford: Oxford University Press, 2009), pp. 41–61.

11   *principal source of conflict in American society*: In the summer of 2009, the Pew Research Center asked people about different sources of social conflict. Of those surveyed, 55 percent said there are "strong or very strong" conflicts between immigrants and people born in the United States, followed by 47 percent citing conflicts between rich and poor people, 39 percent citing conflicts between blacks and whites, and 26 percent noting conflicts between young and old. For more details, see Rich Morin, "Black-White Conflict Isn't Society's Largest," Pew Research Center, September 24, 2009, at http://

othr.ws/pew-conflict. A 2012 survey showed similar results, though tensions between rich and poor replaced immigration as the greatest source of conflict, 66 percent versus 62 percent, a difference close to the margin of error. For more information, see Rich Morin, "Rising Share of Americans See Conflict Between Rich and Poor," Pew Research Center, January 11, 2012, at http://othr.ws/pew-conflict-2012.

12 *immigration tsunami:* According to a report by the Pew Research Hispanic Center ("Unauthorized Immigrant Population: National and State Trends," February 2011), the states with the largest proportion of illegal immigrants to population were Nevada (190,000 or 7.2 percent), California (2,550,000 or 6.8 percent), Texas (1,650,000 or 6.7 percent), New Jersey (550,000 or 6.2 percent), and Arizona (400,000 or 6 percent). Overall, Pew estimated there were 11,200,000 undocumented immigrants in the United States, or 3.7 percent of the population. Also, the states with the largest share of unauthorized immigrants in the workforce were Nevada (10 percent), California (9.7 percent), Texas (9 percent), New Jersey (8.6 percent), and Arizona (7.4 percent). Nationwide, undocumented immigrants represent 5.2 percent of the workforce. See http://othr.ws/pew-undoc-immigrants.

12 *news reports:* Brian Ross of ABC News made the claim that Phoenix is "the kidnapping capital of America" during a report on the network's *Nightline* program on February 11, 2009. See http://othr.ws/abc-kidnap. The *Los Angeles Times* quoted Mark Spencer of the Phoenix Law Enforcement Association as saying "It may be safer in Beirut than Phoenix"; see Michael Truelsen, "Crime Argument Used on Both Sides of Immigration Debate," *TucsonSentinel.com,* May 4, 2010; see http://othr.ws/phoenix-beirut.

12 *Arizona's restrictive immigration laws:* The most notorious of these laws is the "Support Our Law Enforcement and Safe Neighborhoods Act," which makes it a state crime to lack immigration papers and requires police to determine the immigration status of anyone they arrest. It also requires the police to determine the immigration status of anyone they stop if they reasonably suspect them of being illegal aliens and if it is practical to do so. (The full text of the law, otherwise known as Arizona State Senate Bill 1070, is available at: http://othr.ws/az-immigration-law.) A U.S. District Court judge issued an injunction against the Arizona law's most controversial provisions, on the grounds that they interfered with the federal government's authority over immigration and could lead to the harassment of legal residents. Arizona appealed, and the case is destined for Supreme Court review. Meanwhile, in 2011, Arizona considered even more restrictive laws to deny any form of state license—driving, marriage, business, whatever—to undocumented immigrants. The legislature dropped the idea under pressure from a business community still reeling from the job losses, sales declines, and cancelled contracts resulting from the earlier law.

12 *drain on state budgets:* In 2007, the nonpartisan Congressional Budget Office concluded that unauthorized immigrants imposed costs on state governments that were small relative to the states' overall budgets and were essentially offset by increased tax revenue and federal aid. See "The Impact of Unauthorized

Immigrants on the Budgets of State and Local Governments" (Washington, DC: CBO, December 2007); http://othr.ws/cbo-financial-impact. A 2008 study by the Udall Center for Studies in Public Policy at Arizona State University estimated that Arizona collected $2.4 billion in taxes from immigrant workers (about $860 million from naturalized citizens plus about $1.5 billion from noncitizens). The study estimated this was about $940 million more than immigrants cost the state for education, health care, and law enforcement. For more, see Judith Gans, *Immigrants in Arizona: Fiscal and Economic Impacts*, Udall Center for Studies in Public Policy, The University of Arizona, 2008, at http://othr.ws/arizona-immigrants.

12   *demand for goods and services:* Harry Holzer summarizes the consensus view of most economists in "Immigration Policy and Less-Skilled Workers in the United States," (Washington, DC: Migration Policy Institute, January 2011); see http://othr.ws/immigration-economic-impact.

13   *crimes committed by undocumented immigrants:* In 2005, the Federal Reserve Bank of Chicago issued a report, "Why Are Immigrants' Incarceration Rates So Low?" by Kristin F. Butcher and Anne Morrison Piehl. The authors concluded that those who self-selected to immigrate were less inclined to commit crimes than others. See http://othr.ws/illegals-crime.

13   *violent crimes in Arizona:* According to the Department of Justice's Bureau of Justice Statistics, the violent crime rate in Arizona was lower in 2006, 2007, and 2008—the most recent years for which data are available—than any year since 1983. The property crime rate in Arizona was lower in 2006, 2007, and 2008 than any year since 1968. Overall, Arizona's violent crime rate dropped by 19.5 percent between 2002 and 2008, more than twice the U.S. average of 7.9 percent during the same time period. See: http://othr.ws/az-crime-rate.

13   *opportunities in Mexico:* Damien Cave, "Better Lives for Mexicans Cut Allure of Going North," *New York Times*, July 6, 2001; see http://othr.ws/nyt-immigration-decline.

13   *approve of Arizona's tough immigration laws:* In a 2011 survey, Pew Research found that six in ten Americans (61 percent) expressed approval of Arizona's tough new immigration law. Nearly half (46 percent) said that dealing with illegal immigration is a top policy priority. See "Public Favors Tougher Border Controls and Path to Citizenship," Pew Research Center for the People and the Press, February 24, 2011, at http://othr.ws/pew-attitudes-illegal-immigration.

13   *limit the number of immigrants:* A 2009 CNN poll showed that 73 percent of Americans want to see a decrease in illegal immigration, while only 3 percent believe there should be an increase. (See http://othr.ws/cnn-attitudes-immigration.) Americans have a complicated and nuanced attitude toward immigration. According to Gallup, 57 percent believe immigration is good for the country overall, but significant numbers want it decreased (54 percent of Republicans, 44 percent of Independents, and 39 percent of Democrats). See Lymari Morales, "Amid Immigration Debate, Americans' Views Ease Slightly," Gallup, July 27, 2010; at http://othr.ws/gallup-immigration.

Chapter 3: Strangers Making Themselves at Home

15 *international migrants:* The United Nations tracks the so-called international migrant stock and issues periodic reports. Its data tables are available online at http://othr.ws/un-migration.

15 *about 12.5 percent of the U.S. population:* See "U.S. Foreign-Born Population: How Much Change From 2009 to 2010?" published on January 9, 2012, and available at http://othr.ws/us-foreign-born. For the most up-to-date U.S. Census data on immigration, go to http://othr.ws/census-foreign-born.

15 *foreign-born populations of other countries:* The Organization for Economic Cooperation and Development (OECD) shows the foreign-born population of selected countries to be: the Netherlands (10.7 percent), the United Kingdom (10.2 percent), Germany (12.3 percent in 2003), Belgium (13 percent), Spain (13.4 percent), Sweden (13.4 percent), United States (13.6 percent), Austria (14.2 percent), Ireland (15.7 percent), Canada (20.1 percent), New Zealand (21.6 percent), Switzerland (24.9 percent), and Australia (25 percent). For the latest data, see http://othr.ws/oecd-library and select "Factbook."

15 *public reaction to the rising tide of immigrants:* A forty-seven nation Pew Global Attitudes Survey from 2007, titled "World Publics Welcome Global Trade— But Not Immigration," showed that large majorities in forty-four countries believe that "we should further control and restrict immigration." (See http://othr.ws/pew-attitudes-immigration.) A 2009 CNN poll showed that 73 percent of Americans want to see a decrease in illegal immigration, while only 3 percent believe there should be an increase. (See http://othr.ws/cnn-attitudes-immigration.) For more on Americans' attitudes toward immigration, see Lymari Morales, "Amid Immigration Debate, Americans' Views Ease Slightly," Gallup, July 27, 2010; at http://othr.ws/gallup-immigration.

15 *the United States, France, and Germany:* See Joel Fetzer, *Public Attitudes Toward Immigration in the United States, France, and Germany* (New York: Cambridge University Press, 2000). Fetzer is a political scientist at Pepperdine University and a recognized expert on immigration. His examination of survey data and immigration patterns going back to the end of the nineteenth-century finds that despite the vast differences among these three countries, the decisive factor in attitudes toward immigrants is resentment against cultural outsiders.

16 *"swamped by people of a different culture":* Prime Minister Margaret Thatcher of Great Britain was quoted by Julian Simon in *The Economic Consequences of Immigration* (Ann Arbor: University of Michigan Press, 1999), p. 11. Three decades later, during his 2010 reelection campaign, U.K. Prime Minister Gordon Brown was caught speaking into an open microphone calling a constituent, who was essentially repeating Thatcher's opinions, a "bigoted woman." See http://othr.ws/brown-youtube.

16 *Americans have been wary of newcomers:* Many observers believe America's historical suspicion of immigrants was rooted in racism. For example, see Kevin R. Johnson, "Race, the Immigration Laws and Domestic Race Relations: A Magic Mirror into the Heart of Darkness," *Indiana Law Journal* 73 (Fall 1998). For excerpts, see http://othr.ws/race-history.

16   *European stock:* Hans-Jürgen Grabbe, "European Immigration to the United
      States in the Early National Period, 1783–1820," *Proceedings of the American
      Philosophical Society* 133 (1989): pp. 190–214. And U.S. Immigration and Nat-
      uralization Service data is available in the *Statistical Yearbook of the Immigra-
      tion and Naturalization Service* (Washington, DC: U.S. Government Printing
      Office), various years of publication.

17   *benefits of this immigration boom:* See Duke University, Pratt School of Engi-
      neering study, "Skilled, Educated Immigrants Contribute Significantly to
      U.S. Economy," January 4, 2007, at http://othr.ws/duke-imm-impct. See also
      William Kerr and William Lincoln, "The Supply Side of Innovation" (working
      paper, Harvard Business School, December 2008), at http://othr.ws/hvd-inn.

17   *altering the demographic course:* For the various projections of U.S. ethnic and
      racial makeup, see the U.S. Census Bureau report on "Race and Hispanic Ori-
      gin of the Foreign-Born Population in the United States: 2007," at http://othr.
      ws/census-proj.

17   *"competitive breeding":* The Federation for American Immigration Reform
      (FAIR) is probably the best known, best funded, and most vocal of anti-immi-
      gration groups. In 1997, Dan Stein, then president of FAIR, was quoted by
      Tucker Carlson in the *Wall Street Journal* accusing immigrants of "competitive
      breeding." (For a copy of the October 2, 1997 op-ed, "The Intellectual Roots of
      Nativism," as entered in the *Congressional Record,* see http://othr.ws/wsj-fair).
      The Southern Poverty Law Center tracks the activities of the most vocal anti-
      immigration groups; see http://othr.ws/anti-imm.

18   *"make more babies":* As reported by *Time* magazine, on May 11, 2006, John
      Gibson of Fox News implored viewers to "Do your duty. Make more babies
      . . . half of the kids in this country under five years old are minorities. By far
      the greatest number are Hispanic. You know what that means? Twenty-five
      years and the majority of the population is Hispanic. Why is that? Well, the
      Hispanics are having more kids than others. Notably, the ones Hispanics call
      gabachos, white people, are having fewer." See Massimo Calabresi, "Is Rac-
      ism Fueling the Immigration Debate?" *Time,* May 17, 2006; see http://othr.ws/
      make-more-babies.

18   *the great "melting pot":* The "melting pot" metaphor originated in a 1908 play
      of the same name by Israel Zangwill. "There she lies, the great Melting-Pot—
      Listen! Can't you hear the roaring and the bubbling? . . . Ah, what a stirring
      and a seething! Celt and Latin, Slav and Teuton, Greek and Syrian, black and
      yellow . . . Jew and Gentile . . . East and West, and North and South, the palm
      and the pine, the pole and the equator, the crescent and the cross—how the
      great Alchemist melts and fuses them with his purifying flame!" The complete
      script for the play is available at http://othr.ws/melting-pot-play.

Chapter 4: Bouillabaisse or Consommé?

19   Democracy in America: Tocqueville's most famous book is available online,
      courtesy of the University of Virginia, at http://othr.ws/democracy-in-america.

19   *Peter Salins:* Salins is a professor of urban affairs at Hunter College, former

editor-in-chief of the *City Journal,* and author of *Assimilation American Style* (New York: Basic Books, 1997). He believes that in America, unlike in other countries, assimilation does not require immigrants to abandon the culture of the country of their birth. On the contrary, America's basic values allow them to keep as much of it as they like, as long as they accept some minimal requirements.

20   Beyond the Melting Pot: Daniel Patrick Moynihan and Nathan Glazer, *Beyond the Melting Pot,* 2nd ed. (Cambridge, MA: MIT Press, 1970). Moynihan and Glazer did not believe that assimilation was as complete as the metaphor—and popular opinion—might suggest. "The point about the melting pot," they wrote, "is that it did not happen." Moynihan was interviewed by the *New York Times* on the occasion of the book's twentieth anniversary. See Jane Perlez, "Beyond 'Beyond the Melting Pot,' Moynihan and Glazer Feel Vindicated," *New York Times,* December 3, 1983, available at http://othr.ws/nyt-20th.

21   *second thoughts:* Glazer first expressed his frustrations with the pace of African-American assimilation in "Is Assimilation Dead?" *Annals of the American Academy of Political and Social Science* 530, no. 1 (November 1993), pp. 122–136; see http://othr.ws/assimilation-glazer. It was a theme he returned to in *We Are All Multiculturalists Now* (Cambridge, MA: Harvard University Press, 1997), which suggested many people of color thought the only alternative to assimilation was a kind of ethnocentric multiculturalism that celebrated differences rather than commonalities.

21   One Nation, After All: Alan Wolfe's *One Nation, After All* (New York: Penguin, 1999) was a study of middle-class America that came to the conclusion that we basically agree on most social issues. He discovered that people were opposed to multiculturalism if they thought it meant "forced bilingual education." (See, for example, pp. 154–163.) When described as "teaching people respect for other cultures," most of the people he interviewed—black and white—were enthusiastic about it.

22   *new, more nuanced theory:* Alejandro Portes, of Princeton University, and Min Zhou, of UCLA, introduced the concept of "segmented assimilation" in "The New Second Generation: Segmented Assimilation and its Variants," *Annals of the American Academy of Political and Social Science* 530, no. 1 (November 1993), pp. 74–96.

22   *change their name:* a 2010 *New York Times* review of court records revealed that, unlike earlier generations, few of today's immigrants change their name to facilitate assimilation. New York City has a greater foreign-born population than any other city in the United States. Yet, out of 500 applications for name changes before the New York Civil Court in June 2010, only about half a dozen seemed directed at Anglicizing or abbreviating "foreign-sounding" surnames. See Sam Roberts, "New Life in U.S. No Longer Means New Name," *New York Times,* August 25, 2010, at http://othr.ws/nyt-namechange.

23   *in-language media:* The U.S. Hispanic community is served by thirty-seven daily and 385 weekly Spanish-language newspapers, more than 100 Spanish-language television stations, hundreds of cable affiliates, and more than 900 Spanish-language radio stations. The Asian-American community has many more lan-

guages, but major U.S.–based newspapers serve Chinese, Korean, Vietnamese, Japanese, Filipino, Asian Indian, Pakistani, Cambodian, Thai, and Laotian readers in their own language. Most of the United States now has access to Asian-language television through satellite and local cable systems. Cities with large Asian populations, such as New York, Los Angeles, and San Francisco, even have multilingual or language-specific radio and television stations.

23   *interracial and interethnic marriage:* For more information on intermarriage, see Paul Taylor et al., "The Rising Rate of Intermarriage," Pew Research Center, February 16, 2012, available at http://othr.ws/pew-intermarriage-rise.

24   *"way of life needs to be protected":* Americans are not unique in fearing the effect of foreign influence on their culture. See Chapter 5 of "Views of a Changing World 2003," published by the Pew Research Center, June 3, 2003, available at http://othr.ws/foreign-influence.

24   *"some facility" in English:* See U.S. Census Bureau's 2009 American Community Survey at http://othr.ws/census-languages.

25   *"muscular liberalism":* British Prime Minister David Cameron gave a speech at the annual Munich Security Conference on February 5, 2011, in which he echoed previous declarations by Germany's Angela Merkel that "multiculturalism has failed." For a copy of the complete speech, see http://othr.ws/cameron-spch.

25   *prime age workforce:* David Ellwood, "Grow Together Faster or Grow Slowly Apart," The Aspen Institute, Domestic Strategy Group report, January 2002. See http://othr.ws/aspen-wrkfrc.

Chapter 5: A New America

28   *multigenerational country:* The era of the baby boomers is pretty well accepted to be 1946 to 1964, but the duration (and even the names) of subsequent generations varies widely. The segmentation used here is taken from Kenneth Gronbach, *The Age Curve* (New York: AMACOM, 2008), which was also the principal source of many of the observations about each generation's characteristics and values.

29   *the developing boom in older consumers:* Ken Dychtwald, CEO of AgeWave, a management consultancy specializing in the "mature" marketplace, coined the term *middlescence* to describe the baby boomers in old age. For more information, see http://othr.ws/agewave. SymphonyIRI Group is another marketing consultancy that has identified the baby boomer generation as an emerging marketing opportunity, though cautioning against a one-size-fits-all approach. For its July 2009 study, "The Baby Boomers II Report," see http://othr.ws/boom-2.

Chapter 6: It's the Culture, Stupid!

34   *increasingly diverse:* According to an analysis of census data by Pew's Hispanic Research Center, 92 percent of the country's population growth between 2000 and 2010 was due to growth in minority populations, whether by births or immigration. For more information, see http://othr.ws/pew-pop-growth.

34   *so-called multicultural communities:* The Selig Center for Economic Growth
     at the University of Georgia produces a comprehensive report of consumer
     buying power in the United States. See Jeffrey M. Humphreys, "The Multi-
     cultural Economy 2009," *Georgia Business and Economic Conditions* 69, no. 3
     (3rd quarter 2009), at http://othr.ws/selig-est.

35   *on beauty products:* The P&G research on black women's spending for beauty
     products was reported by "She-conomy," a website that bills itself as "a guy's
     guide on marketing to women." For more, see http://othr.ws/she-con.

35   *throwback to America of the 1950s:* The median age of U.S. Hispanics (27.5) is
     about where the whole country was in the 1950s; they are thirteen years younger
     than non-Hispanics. Hispanics mirror the United States of the 1950s in other
     ways, too. More than a third of Hispanic households (35 percent) consist of
     a married couple with children, versus only about a fifth (21 percent) of non-
     Hispanic households. The average Hispanic family has 3.4 members, versus 2.4
     for non-Hispanics. Hispanic families spend 9 percent more than non-Hispanics
     on meals at home and 6 percent less on meals away from home. Almost half of
     Hispanics live in the suburbs of major metro areas, and that's expected to grow
     to 60 percent during the next five to ten years. For more, see Peter Francese,
     "Hispanic America 2010," *Ad Age Insights,* July 26, 2010, p. 6.

40   *"leading with ethnic insights":* McDonald's U.S. marketing chief spoke to *Bloom-
     berg Businessweek's* Burt Helm for his story, "Ethnic Marketing: McDonald's
     Is Lovin' It," July 8, 2010; see http://othr.ws/bw-mcd.

Chapter 7: Race Matters

42   *race is not real:* The anthropologist Ashley Montagu always put the word "race"
     within quotation marks to signal that it not only has no biological meaning,
     but is laden with social implications. He thoroughly debunked the concept
     of race in his 1941 book, *Man's Most Dangerous Myth: The Fallacy of Race*
     (Walnut Creek, CA: Altamira Press, 6th ed., 1997). Law professor Ian Haney
     Lopez wrote a brilliant essay on the meaning of race in which he observes,
     "Race is neither an essence nor an illusion, but rather an ongoing, contradic-
     tory, self-reinforcing process subject to the macro forces of social and political
     struggle and the micro effects of daily decisions." See Ian F. Haney Lopez,
     "The Social Construction of Race: Some Observations on Illusion, Fabrica-
     tion, and Choice," *Harvard Civil Rights–Civil Liberties Law Review* 29 (Winter
     1994), at http://othr.ws/haney-race.

42   *Race matters:* A number of books and articles have been written about the
     history and social significance of race. One of the most accessible books, from
     which I drew significant insights, is Richard J. Payne, *Getting Beyond Race:
     The Changing American Culture* (Boulder: Westview Press, 1998.) For a more
     recent treatment, see Joshua Glasgow, *A Theory of Race* (New York: Routledge,
     2008). See also Natalie Angier, "Do Races Differ? Not Really, Genes Show,"
     New York Times, August 22, 2000, at http://othr.ws/nyt-race-genes,

42   *ways to categorize races:* Jared Diamond, among others, has shown that catego-
     rizing human beings by skin color is no more valid than grouping people by

other genetic traits, such as lactose-tolerance or the presence of antimalarial genes. Under the former scheme, Swedes would be grouped with the Fulanis of Africa, while most other African "blacks," Japanese, and American Indians would be grouped together. Under the latter system, Swedes would be grouped with the Xhosas of Africa but not with Italians or Greeks. And most other peoples usually viewed as black Africans would be grouped with Arabia's "whites." For a full explanation, see Jared Diamond, "Race Without Color," *Discover*, November 1994, http://othr.ws/race-color.

43   *colorism:* See Evelyn Nakano Glenn, ed., *Shades of Difference: Why Skin Color Matters* (Stanford, CA: Stanford University Press, 2009). For a briefer survey, see Taunya Lovell Banks, "Colorism: A Darker Shade of Pale," *UCLA Law Review* (2000), pp. 1705–1746, http://othr.ws/banks-colorism.

43   *"crazy aunt in the attic of racism":* DeNeen Brown, "The Legacy of Colorism Reflects Wounds of Racism That Are More Than Skin Deep," *Washington Post,* July 12, 2009; see http://othr.ws/crazy-aunt.

43   *elections:* Jennifer L. Hochschild and Vesla Weaver, "The Skin Color Paradox and the American Racial Order," *Social Forces* 86, no. 2 (December 2007); see http://othr.ws/color-paradox.

43   *earnings:* Using data from the U.S. Census Bureau's New Immigrant Survey in 2003, an economics and law professor at Vanderbilt University found that immigrants with the lightest skin color earn on average 16 percent to 23 percent more than comparable immigrants with the darkest skin color. These estimates control for years of legal permanent residence in the United States, education, English language proficiency, occupation in source country, ethnicity, race, country of birth, as well as for extensive current labor market characteristics that may be themselves influenced by discrimination. Furthermore, the skin color penalty does not diminish over time. See Joni Hersch, "The Persistence of Skin Color Discrimination for Immigrants," *Social Science Research* 40, no. 5 (September 2011), pp. 1337–1349. Available at http://othr.ws/color-income.

44   *drug charges:* See Human Rights Watch, "Decades of Disparity: Drug Arrests and Race in the United States," March 2009, available at http://othr.ws/drug-charges. According to the study, "the higher rates of black drug arrests do not reflect higher rates of black drug offending." Indeed, a prior Human Rights Watch study (*Targeting Blacks: Drug Law Enforcement and Race in the United States,* May 2008) established that blacks and whites engage in drug offenses—possession and sales—at roughly comparable rates. But because black drug offenders are the principal targets in the "war on drugs," the burden of drug arrests and incarceration falls disproportionately on black men and women, their families, and neighborhoods.

44   *capital offense:* Jennifer Eberhardt et al., "Looking Deathworthy: Perceived Stereotypicality of Black Defendants Predicts Capital-Sentencing Outcomes," paper 41, *Cornell Law Review* (2006), http://othr.ws/deathworthy.

44   *colorism* within *a community of color:* See Christina Gómez, "Brown Outs: The Role of Skin Color and Latinas," at http://othr.ws/Hispanic-colorism.

44 *implicit bias:* For more than a decade, researchers at Harvard University have compiled data on the implicit biases of millions of people worldwide. They have measured unconscious prejudice on factors such as age, race, skin tone, disability, gender, and sexual orientation. Bias is assessed on the basis of individual responses to rapid word association tests administered on the website. Nearly 80 percent of everyone who has taken the test—including blacks, non-blacks, Hispanics, and Asians—have had "pro-white" biases. To take the test yourself, see http://othr.ws/harvard-test.

44 *Asians and Asian Americans:* See Achel Mehra. "Fair and Ugly: Indian Americans and Skin Color," paper delivered at the 2004 Meeting of the Latin American Studies Association, Las Vegas, October 7–9, 2004; see http://othr.ws/Asian-colorism.

44 *skin-whitening products:* According to a report by Global Industry Analysts, the global skin-lightening market will reach $10 billion by 2015, driven by new markets in the West and sustained growth in the Asia-Pacific region. See http://othr.ws/skin-lightening.

44 *stereotyping:* Franklin Ng's *Asian American Interethnic Relations and Politics* (New York: Routledge, 1998) is a bit dated in terms of demographic information, but the issues it addresses so insightfully are enduring, from the "model minority" stereotype to interethnic conflicts with other groups.

45 *Harris poll:* Harris Interactive completed 1,427 interviews among the general adult population of the United States in January 2009. See http://othr.ws/harris-asians.

45 *Richard Thompson Ford:* Ford is a law professor at Stanford University and an expert on civil rights. His article, "The End of Civil Rights," appeared in the *Boston Globe,* May 17, 2009. See http://othr.ws/globe-ford.

46 *Hurricane Katrina:* Richard Thompson Ford, *The Race Card: How Bluffing About Bias Makes Race Relations Worse* (New York: Macmillan Picador, 2009), p. 57.

46 *racial injustices:* Richard Thompson Ford, "Why the Poor Stay Poor," review of *More Than Just Race: Being Black and Poor in the Inner City,* by William Julius Wilson, *New York Times,* March 6, 2009, Book Review; see http://othr.ws/nyt-poor.

47 *"shopping while black":* According to an ABC News "What Would You Do?" segment, some surveys show that 60 percent of blacks have had the experience of being "shadowed" while shopping. See http://othr.ws/abc-bias. Psychologists at Manhattanville College wrote a paper examining the issue from a number of angles; see George E. Schreer, Saundra Smith, and Kirsten Thomas, "Shopping While Black: Examining Racial Discrimination in a Retail Setting," *Journal of Applied Social Psychology* 39, no. 6 (June 2009), pp. 1432–1444.

47 *don't talk to their kids about race:* A 2007 study in the *Journal of Marriage and Family* found that nonwhite parents of kindergarteners are about three times more likely to discuss race than white parents. See Tony Brown et al., "Child, Parent, and Situational Correlates of Familial Ethnic/Race Socialization," *Journal of Marriage and Family* (February 2007).

48   *racism as a zero-sum game:* See, for example, Michael I. Norton and Samuel R. Sommers, "Whites See Racism as a Zero-Sum Game They Are Now Losing," *Perspectives on Psychological Science*, May, 2011, available at http://othr.ws/race-zero-sum-game.

48   *feelings of anxiety:* Lee Sigelman et al., "Making Contact? Black-White Social Interaction in an Urban Setting," *American Journal of Sociology* (March 1996), pp. 1306–1332. Numerous other studies have identified intergroup contact as a potential source of anxiety. See, for example, Ashby Plant and Patricia Devine, "The Antecedents and Implications for Interracial Anxiety," *Personality and Social Psychology Bulletin* 29, no. 6 (2003).

48   *"invisible knapsack of white privilege":* Peggy McIntosh's essay "White Privilege: Unpacking the Invisible Knapsack" originally appeared in as a working paper in 1988 and has been reprinted many times since. It is available online at http://othr.ws/mcintosh-privilege."

49   *"implicit social cognition":* Two psychologists—Anthony Greenwald of the University of Washington and Mahzarin Banaji of Yale University—wrote a more technical overview of implicit social cognition for the *Psychological Review.* It describes the basic concepts and the science behind the unconscious assumptions people make about other people; it is available online at http://othr.ws/social-cognition. UCLA law professor Jeffrey Kang has written a highly accessible primer on implicit bias for the courts. He discusses the implications for our system of justice, but it has readily obvious application to everyday life. The primer is available at http://othr.ws/bias-primer.

49   *height:* See Steve Landsberg, "Short Changed," *Slate*, March 25, 2002, at http://othr.ws/short-changed.

49   *"beautiful" or "handsome":* See Daniel Hamermesh and Jeff Biddle, "Beauty and the Labor Market," National Bureau of Economic Research, working paper, November 1993. See http://othr.ws/beauty-bias.

50   *other primates:* Yale University researchers found in a series of experiments that monkeys treat monkeys from outside their groups with the same suspicion and dislike as their human cousins tend to treat outsiders. See Neha Mahajan et. al., "The Evolution of Intergroup Bias: Perception and Attitudes in Rhesus Macaques," *Journal of Personality and Social Psychology* 100, no. 3 (March 2011), pp. 387–405. Available at http://othr.ws/bias-evolution.

50   *prospective employers:* See Marianne Bertrand and Sendhil Mullainathan, "Are Emily and Greg More Employable Than Lakisha and Jamal? A Field Experiment on Labor Market Discrimination," *American Economics Review* (2004), p. 998. In 2007, Dan-Olof Rooth, of Kalmar University in Sweden, writing on "Implicit Discrimination in Hiring: Real World Evidence," replicated their research. See http://othr.ws/name-bias.

50   *Public officials:* Daniel M. Butler and David E. Broockman, "Do Politicians Racially Discriminate?" published online April 27, 2011; see http://othr.ws/bias-public-officials. Researchers sent a letter requesting information on voter registration to 4,859 legislators in forty-four states. The letters signed with a "white" name—"Jake Mueller"—received responses 60.5 percent of the time;

those with a "black" name—"DeShawn Jackson—were answered only 55.3 percent of the time. The results were the same when correcting for political affiliation.

50 *doctors:* Alexander R. Green et al., "Implicit Bias Among Physicians and Its Prediction of Thrombolysis Decisions for Black and White Patients," *Journal of General Internal Medicine* 22, no. 9 (2007). Given an Implicit Bias Test, doctors in Atlanta and Boston were found to have implicit bias in favor of white patients and an unconscious attitude that black patients tended to be less cooperative. See http://othr.ws/dr-bias.

50 *empathy:* "Racial Bias Clouds Ability to Feel Others' Pain, Study Finds," posted to Annals Articles page, *Annals of the American Psychotherapy Association,* May 27, 2010. European researchers used functional MRI (fMRI) imaging to show that empathy is diminished when people see pain inflicted on those of another race. See http://othr.ws/empathy-bias.

50 *basketball referees:* Joseph Price and Justin Wolfers, "Racial Discrimination Among NBA Referees," *Quarterly Journal of Economics* (November 2010). Economists at the Wharton School and Cornell University studied the statistics for NBA basketball games from 1991 to 2004. They found that more personal fouls were awarded against players when they were officiated by opposite-race referees than when officiated by referees of the same race as the players. See http://othr.ws/ref-bias.

50 *"have a mind of their own":* Jon Hanson, "Why Race May Influence Us Even When We 'Know' It Doesn't," posted to "The Situationist," February 19, 2009. See http://othr.ws/race-inf.

Chapter 8: The Cost of Diversity

52 Bowling Alone: Robert Putnam's book was based on an article, "Bowling Alone: America's Declining Social Capital," which was published in the *Journal of Democracy's* January 1995 issue. An online version of the original article is available at http://othr.ws/bowling-alone. The book, with a lot of new research, as well as a new subtitle—*Bowling Alone: The Collapse and Revival of American Community*—was published by Simon & Schuster in 2000.

53 *research on diversity:* Robert Putnam's paper, "E Pluribus Unum: Diversity and Community in the Twenty-First Century," was published in the June 2007 issue of the *Scandinavian Political Journal.* An online version, from which the quotes in the text are taken, is available at http://othr.ws/diversity-cost.

54 *Pat Buchanan:* During the immigration debate that raged in the months leading up to the 2008 election, Buchanan referenced Putnam's research and article in a column entitled, "Dr. Putnam's Bunker-Buster." The entire column is available at http://othr.ws/pat-bust.

54 *"It's a benefit":* This quote on the benefits of diversity is from an interview with Putnam by National Public Radio host Michel Martin on August 15, 2007. For a transcript of the interview, see http://othr.ws/npr-diversity.

54 *makes people more creative:* Angela Ka-yee Leung, William Maddux, Adam Galinsky, and Chi-yue Chiu, "Multicultural Experience Enhances Creativ-

ity: The When and How," *American Psychologist* (April 2008), pp. 169–181; to download a Word document of the article, see http://othr.ws/diversity-and-creativity. See also Katherine Phillips, Katie Liljenquist, and Margaret Neale, "Better Decisions Through Diversity," Kellogg Insight, October 2010, available at http://othr.ws/white-diversity.

55   A 2012 *Pew Research Center report*: See Paul Taylor et al., "The Rising Rate of Intermarriage," Pew Research Center, February 16, 2012, available at http://othr.ws/pew-intermarriage-rise. To be fair, and perhaps to temper our sense of optimism, there are stark differences between people of different races and even between different genders within the same race. For example, some 24 percent of all black male newlyweds in 2010 married outside their race, compared with just 9 percent of black females. Among Asians, the gender pattern runs the opposite way. Some 36 percent of Asian female newlyweds in 2010 married outside their race, compared with just 17 percent of Asian males. The disparity between the intermarriage rates of Asian men and women seems to be a function of cultural stereotypes. Besides the fetishization of Asian women, Asian men seem to suffer a cultural penalty in the realm of dating and romance. In a study of online dating, MIT economists discovered that white women would only consider dating men of color if they earned more than a comparable white man. Hispanic American men had to earn $77,000 more to be on an equal footing; African Americans, $154,000 more; and Asian Americans, $246,000 more. Günter J. Hitsch, Ali Hortaçsu, and Dan Ariel, "What Makes You Click? Mate Preferences and Matching Outcomes in Online Dating," MIT Sloan working paper 4603-06, February 2006. For the complete study, see http://othr.ws/mit-asian-marr.

56   *senior leadership ranks*: According to the Equal Employment Opportunity Commission, although "minority" employees accounted for about a third of the workforce at U.S. companies in 2008, only about 12 percent of all executive and senior managers were minorities. For updated EEOC statistics, see http://othr.ws/eeoc-asian.

56   Human Resource Executive Online: Putnam was interviewed by Scott Flander for *Human Resource Executive Online* on the topic of diversity's effect in the workplace. A copy is available at http://othr.ws/hrexec-putnam.

57   *colorblindness*: For an excellent survey of research on the nature and consequences of colorblindness, see Evan P. Apfelbaum et al., "Racial Colorblindness: Emergence, Practice, and Implications," awaiting publication in *Current Directions in Psychological Science*. Available at http://othr.ws/racial-colorblindness.

57   *"employee affinity groups"*: This is a topic Dr. Beverly Daniel Tatum has explored as author of *Why Are All the Black Kids Sitting Together in the Cafeteria?* rev. 5th anniversary ed. (New York: Basic Books, 2003).

58   *Diversity in their personal networks*: See David Thomas and John Gabarro, *Breaking Through: The Making of Minority Executives in Corporate America* (Boston: Harvard Business Press, 1999).

Chapter 9: Queerness

61   *"Queer theory"*: It is exceedingly difficult to find a generally accepted definition of Queer theory because its various proponents resist being nailed down. Indeed, the person who is often credited with coining the term in 1990—film critic and social theorist Teresa de Lauretis—abandoned it just three years later because the mainstream media had made it a synonym for "gay and lesbian studies." De Lauretis thought this made "queer" just another pigeonhole within the framework of identity politics, which was the very structure of "normative thinking" she opposed. She rejected the whole idea of categorizing people based on their gender, genitalia, or sexual desires. On the contrary, she wanted the word *queer* to be an anti-identity, recognizing that people's gender and sexuality was fluid and capable of constant change. For a comprehensive website that includes book reviews, articles, and a general introduction to the field, see http://othr.ws/queer-theory.

62   *"preferred gender pronouns"*: For an excellent summary of the issue, see Jennifer Conlin, "The Freedom to Choose Your Pronoun," *New York Times*, September 30, 2011, http://othr.ws/nyt-pgp.

62   *Pastor Fred Phelps*: Pastor Phelps makes no effort to disguise his hateful messages. On the contrary, he maintains a website that makes all his sermons widely available. Go to http://othr.ws/westboro-church. His right to picket the funerals of fallen soldiers was challenged all the way to the Supreme Court, which ruled in his favor on free speech grounds.

63   *textual evidence in the Bible*: Among the Bible verses Phelps references in his condemnation of homosexuality are the following: Sodomites are wicked and sinners before the Lord exceedingly (Genesis 13:13), are violent and doom nations (Genesis 19:1–25; Judgments 19), are abominable to God (Leviticus 18:22), are worthy of death for their vile sex practices (Leviticus 20:13; Romans 1:32). Needless to say, many biblical scholars disagree with Phelps and liken his interpretation of these passages to prior efforts to justify slavery by quoting Leviticus 25:44 or Exodus 21:7.

63   *"between two adults of the same sex"*: When the question was last asked on the General Social Survey in 2006, 56.2 percent of U.S. adults said it was "always wrong" for two adults of the same sex to have sexual relations; 4.9 percent said it was "almost always wrong," 6.7 percent said it was "sometimes wrong," and 32.3 percent said it was not wrong at all. In the same survey, 51 percent opposed same-sex marriage. See http://othr.ws/gss-homosexual-sex.

63   *hate crimes*: According to the FBI, in 2010, there were 160 hate crimes directed at Muslims versus 887 directed at Jews, 534 directed at Hispanics, 1,230 directed at homosexuals, and 2,201 directed at blacks. See the FBI Uniform Crime Reports at http://othr.ws/fbi-crime.

66   *"less likely to cause injury"*: Frank Bruni, "Genetic or Not, Gay Won't Go Away," *New York Times*, January 29, 2011. See http://othr.ws/nyt-bruni.

67   *on the issue of same-sex marriage*: According to a 2009 Gallup survey, opposition to same-sex marriage is strongest among people who do not know

someone who is gay, with 72 percent opposing it. Attitudes among those who know someone who is gay are more evenly split, with 49 percent in favor and 47 percent opposed. See a summary of the full report at http://othr.ws/gallup-gay-marriage.

67   *generation gap:* This data is from the General Social Survey and is well summarized in the online "DemoMemo" of April 9, 2011, available at http://othr.ws/demo-memo.

67   *gay men and lesbian women in society:* This data is from the General Social Survey subject index under "Gays and Lesbians," "Civil Liberties of." Go to: http://othr.ws/general-social-survey.

Chapter 10: Strangers with a Strange God

69   *irony was said to have died:* Smoke was still rising from the fallen Twin Towers when Graydon Carter, editor of *Vanity Fair,* told an entertainment website what it all meant. "It's the end of the age of irony," he said. From that moment forward, no one could hide behind apparent contradictions. Everything would be as it seemed. (Carter was quoted by Seth Moonkin, "In Disaster's Aftermath, Once-Cocky Media Culture Disses the Age of Irony," *Inside.com,* September 18, 2001.) For a fuller dissertation on the meaning of irony, see Alex Steiner's 2004 essay, "The End of Irony or the Irony of Ends," at http://othr.ws/end-of-irony.

69   *"we shovel a grave in the air":* Taken from the English translation of "Death Fugue" by John Felstiner, *Selected Poems and Prose of Paul Celan* (New York: W. W. Norton, 2001). Used by permission.

69   *"rivers of blood have flowed":* "From Exclusion to Embrace: Reflections on Reconciliation," message given at the Sixteenth Annual International Prayer Breakfast at the United Nations, September 11, 2001. The full text of Volf's prayer breakfast remarks, from which this quote is taken, are available at http://othr.ws/volf-un.

69   *on the strength of a book:* The book was *Exclusion and Embrace: A Theological Exploration of Identity, Otherness, and Reconciliation* (Nashville: Abingdon Press, 1996).

70   *"Can I embrace a cetnik":* Volf was quoted by Mark Oppenheimer, "Miroslav Volf Spans Conflicting Worlds," *Christian Century,* January 11, 2003.

71   *the great "Clash of Civilizations":* See Samuel Huntington, "The Clash of Civilizations?" *Foreign Affairs,* Summer 1993. Huntington wrote the article after the collapse of the Soviet Union. He believed that the source of future conflicts would be cultural as the three most historically important civilizations—the Western, the Muslim, and the Confucian—struggled for dominance. See http://othr.ws/clash-civilizations.

72   *religion is under attack:* In late 2006 and early 2007, WorldPublicOpinion.org conducted an in-depth study of public opinion in Egypt, Morocco, Pakistan, and Indonesia. On average, 79 percent believed America's foreign policy goal is to weaken and divide Islam. See: http://othr.ws/muslim-opinion. Informed

by these and other polls, political psychologist Steven Kull conducted focus groups in six Muslim-majority nations to better understand how Muslims see America. His findings, published in *Feeling Betrayed: The Roots of Muslim Anger Toward America* (Washington, D.C.: Brookings Institute Press, 2011), confirm that Muslims' anger toward the United States is rooted in a fear that America will overwhelm and destroy their traditional Islamic culture, in contradiction with its stated values and intentions. Kull had conducted focus groups across the Islamic world to better understand Muslims' attitudes toward America. He found evidence that Muslims "tend to view current events through the lens of a long-standing historical narrative" in which, going back as far as the Middle Ages, "Christian forces from the West have persistently sought to break the grip of Islam on its people." See "Why Muslims Are Still Mad at America," *WorldPublicOpinion.org*, September 9, 2011, originally published on CNN's Global Public Square on September 5, 2011; available at http://othr.ws/muslim-narrative.

72   *Glenn Beck:* Glenn Beck made this assertion in his book *The Real America* (New York: Gallery Books, 2005, p. 138) and repeated it on his radio show on December 6, 2010.

72   *Franklin Graham:* Reverend Graham made these comments to CNN's John King on August 19, 2010. See http://othr.ws/cnn-graham.

72   *Newt Gingrich:* At the "Value Voters Summit" in Washington, D.C., on September 18, 2010, Newt Gingrich said, "We should have a federal law that says under no circumstance, in any jurisdiction in the United States, will sharia be used in any court to apply to any judgment made about American law." See http://othr.ws/cnn-gingrich.

72   *2009 Pew survey described American Muslims:* In its December 2009 report, the Pew Research Center, as part of its Global Attitudes Project, found "little support for terrorism among American Muslims," who it characterized as "middle class" and "mainstream." See http://othr.ws/pew-us-muslims.

72   increased *with their religiosity:* The Muslim American Public Opinion Survey interviewed 1,410 Muslim American respondents on issues of religion, civic engagement, and public policy in the United States. See "National Survey of American Muslims Finds Mosques Help Muslims Integrate into American Political Life," news release, March 8, 2011, at http://othr.ws/muslim-civic.

73   *Europe:* Pew estimates there are about 2.5 million Muslims in the States. By contrast, more than 13 million Muslims live in the European Union. The largest concentrations of Muslims are in France (about 5 million), Germany (around 3 million), and Britain (about 2 million). Spain, the Netherlands, and Bulgaria have just around a million each. To put these numbers in context, if the French Muslim population were proportionately reproduced in the United States, there would be 24 million American Muslims.

73   *religious behavior:* Michèle Tribalat's study was quoted by Jytte Klausen in *The Islamic Challenge: Politics and Religion in Western Europe* (Oxford: Oxford University Press, 2005), p. 140.

73   *values of Muslims living in Western societies:* See Ronald Inglehart and Norris

Pippa, "Muslim Integration into Western Cultures: Between Origins and Destinations." Harvard Kennedy School (HKS) Faculty Research Working Paper Series RWP09-007, 2009; see http://othr.ws/muslim-values.

74 *Americans told the Gallup organization:* According to a 2010 Gallup Survey, Americans are more prejudiced toward Muslims than toward people of any other religion—43 percent admit to at least "a little" prejudice toward Muslims contrasted with only 18 percent who feel that way toward Christians, 15 percent toward Jews, and 14 percent toward Buddhists. See http://othr.ws/gallup-muslims.

74 *nearly half of Americans:* A 2011 Pew Research Center survey indicates that 40 percent of all Americans believe Islam is more violent than other religions, while 42 percent disagree. See "Continuing Divide in Views of Islam and Violence," Pew Research Center, March 9, 2011, at http://othr.ws/pew-muslims.

74 *"band of Others":* Kerem Ozan Kalkan, Geoffrey C. Layman, and Eric M. Uslaner. "'Bands of Others'? Attitudes Toward Muslims in Contemporary American Society," *Journal of Politics* 71 (2009), pp. 847–862; see http://othr.ws/bands-others. The "'Bands of Others'" study includes an analysis of data from the 2004 American National Election Survey, which asked voters to rate different groups on a "feeling thermometer" with a scale of zero to 100. A reading of "0" indicates that the respondent has a "very cold or unfavorable feeling" toward the group, while a reading of "50" would indicate "no feeling at all" and "100" would be "a very warm or favorable feeling." In the 2004 survey, for example, the mean of white respondents' ratings of all groups was 62.8. Whites' mean ratings of Jews (68.1), Asian Americans (67.6), Hispanics (66.6), and blacks (69.2) were all above that overall mean, while their ratings of illegal immigrants (38.7), gays and lesbians (48.5), Muslims (52.2), welfare recipients (54.6), and feminists (55.1) all fell below it. Note that, in addition to Muslims, *all* of the groups that fall below the mean on the feeling thermometer are people who differ from the mainstream principally in their behavior and values. This is significant because, although racial and religious minorities have not had an easy time in American society, they have almost always been more popular than cultural "out groups." In fact, only one of the cultural out-groups—gays and lesbians—is viewed more favorably today than it was thirty years ago, and the group's rating on the feeling thermometer is still nearly 15 points lower than the overall mean. That suggests that Muslim prejudice is unlikely to change quickly. But there is also reason for optimism. Hispanics and Asian Americans had similarly low ratings in the 1970s and 1980s. And only a quarter of Muslims say they have ever suffered discrimination. In 2008, the FBI tracked only 105 anti-Muslim incidents, compared with 1,013 against Jews, who rate more positively on the feeling thermometer. Furthermore, most Muslims report having many non-Muslim friends, and we know that personal ties lessen even unconscious feelings of prejudice. An increase in religious literacy wouldn't hurt, either. "The key," according to the 'Bands of Others' study, "is whether Americans will come to see Muslims as part of the American melting pot, as they do with other racial and religious minorities,

or continue to see them as a suspicious Other, as they do with other cultural minorities."

74   *practiced in very different contexts:* See Mohammed Ayoob, *The Many Faces of Political Islam* (Ann Arbor: University of Michigan Press, 2007).

74   *Muslim among their friends:* The Council on American-Islamic Relations surveyed attitudes toward Islam and Muslims in 2004 and 2005 and found, on average, that only one-fifth of respondents reported having Muslim colleagues or friends. In other words, most Americans lack personal experience with Muslims. See http://othr.ws/muslim-friend.

74   *"the Quran is a vast, vague book":* Quotes from Fareed Zakaria, "The Politics of Rage: Why Do They Hate Us?" *Newsweek,* July 18, 2008; see http://othr.ws/politics-rage.

75   *"a common belief in one God":* Quote from Miroslav Volf, *Allah: A Christian Response* (New York: HarperOne, 2011), p. 35.

76   *"hostile to Islam":* The entire report, "History of Islam in Iowa," is at http://othr.ws/islam-in-iowa. An even more extensive survey—"A Century of Islam in America" by Dr. Yvonne Y. Haddad—is available at http://othr.ws/islam-in-america.

76   *Christian broadcasters:* Reverend Franklin Graham called Islam "wicked" and "evil" on ABC's "This Week" on October 10, 2010. He went on to profess his love for "the Muslim people," but said he has "great difficulty with the religion, especially with sharia law and what it does for women—toward women, toward nonbelievers, the violence that is given in—under sharia law." See http://othr.ws/cnn-graham.

76   *Pope Benedict:* In a speech at the University of Regensburg, on September 12, 2006, the pope quoted the Byzantine emperor Manuel II Paleologus as saying, "Show me just what Mohammed brought that was new and there you will find things only evil and inhuman, such as his command to spread by the sword the faith he preached." For a full copy of Pope Benedict XVI's lecture, see http://othr.ws/pope-lecture. For a thorough summary of the reaction, see http://othr.ws/wiki-reaction.

76   *"Only when we see both":* Volf expressed these views in a guest commentary for Reuters on President Obama's June 2009 speech to the Muslim world from Cairo University. See Miroslav Volf, "Guestview: Obama Speech Not Historic, but Could Become So," Reuters FaithWorld (blog), June 4, 2009, at http://othr.ws/reuters-volf.

77   *moderate Muslims are ready:* This view was eloquently expressed by Irshad Manji, "Islam Needs Reformists, Not Moderates," *Wall Street Journal,* May 7, 2011. See http://othr.ws/islam-reform.

77   *the Good Book:* This verse is from the Quran, chapter 49, verse 13. For a full explanation, see "We Have Made You Nations and Tribes: A Qur'anically Based Vision of Multiculturalism and Inter-Religious Relations," by Dr. Aisha Musa, assistant professor of Islamic Studies, Department of Religious Studies, Florida International University. See http://othr.ws/quran-nations.

Chapter 11: World Values

78   *World Values Survey:* For more background on the World Values Survey, see http://othr.ws/world-values-survey.

78   *opportunities for self-expression:* In 2009, the Pew Research Center asked people in a number of countries, to choose which of Franklin Roosevelt's famous "four freedoms" is most important to them personally—free speech, freedom of religion, freedom from hunger and poverty, or freedom from crime and violence. By and large, middle-class people said that being able to speak freely in public was most important to them. Lower-income respondents, on the other hand, were more likely to value being free from hunger and poverty. For a copy of the full Global Attitudes report, see http://othr.ws/pew-4freedoms.

79   *become less religious:* For an accessible summary of this finding, see Ronald Inglehart and Christian Welzel, *Modernization, Cultural Change, and Democracy: The Human Development Sequence* (New York: Cambridge University Press, 2005).

80   *highly religious:* This data is from Robert Putnam and David Campbell, *Amazing Grace: How Religion Divides and Unites Us* (New York: Simon & Schuster, 2010), pp. 7–8. These statistics and others discussed in this chapter are from the Faith Matters surveys on which their book is based. The statistics on belief in God were derived from the following question: "Are you absolutely sure (80 percent), somewhat sure (9.4 percent), not quite sure (4.6 percent), not at all sure (2.2 percent) you believe in God or are you sure (3.6 percent) you do not believe in God?" The role of religion in political party allegiance is discussed on page 320 of *American Grace.*

83   *personal values:* Michael Robinson wrote what he termed "a contrarian view" of U.S. public opinion trends and American values for the Pew Research Center in September 2010. In an extensive review of twenty years of survey data, Robinson came to the conclusion that, despite all the partisan sniping on both sides, American values are actually quite traditional and static in terms of how Americans describe themselves. See http://othr.ws/pew-contrary.

Chapter 12: Gut Values

84   *morality:* Haidt initially built his "Moral Foundations Theory" on a system of five innate emotional mechanisms. However, he reformulated the theory in 2011 as he was writing his latest book, *The Righteous Mind* (New York: Pantheon, 2012). The revised theory expanded the list of emotional mechanisms to six and slightly changed the nomenclature and definitions. The revised list is "care/harm, fairness/cheating, loyalty/betrayal, authority/subversion, sanctity/degradation, and liberty/oppression" The most significant change was the addition of "liberty/oppression," which he described as "the feelings of reactance and resentment people feel toward those who dominate them" and which he acknowledged was in some tension with the emotional mechanism of authority. He also clarified the concept of "fairness," which

in his original conception, emphasized "equality," a concept more strongly endorsed by political liberals. The new description now emphasizes "proportionality," which he believes "is endorsed by everyone, but is more strongly endorsed by conservatives." For a fuller explanation, see the website Haidt built for other researchers to test the theory, available at http://othr.ws/haidt-homepage.

85   *innate emotional mechanisms*: Haidt built his Moral Foundations Theory on this system of five innate emotional mechanisms, and he has written about it broadly in technical as well as popular publications. The best source for more information is the website he built for other researchers to test the theory, available at http://othr.ws/haidt-homepage.

85   *"quick gut feelings"*: From Jonathan Haidt, "What the Tea Partiers Really Want," *Wall Street Journal,* October 16, 2010; see http://othr.ws/wsj-haidt.

86   *"as inappropriate as smoking"*: Haidt made this observation in a discussion with journalist Bill Moyers on PBS's *Moyers & Company,* February 3, 2012. A full transcript is available at http://othr.ws/moyers-haidt."

86   *"disgusted by things like dog poop"*: From Paul Bloom, "Do Liberals and Conservatives Think Differently?" a panel discussion video recorded on February 25, 2011, at the Connecticut Forum. Available at http://othr.ws/youtube-bloom. Other scientists, such as Joshua Tybur of VU University in Amsterdam, suggest that conservatives' heightened feelings of disgust were more pronounced for sexual topics, but were similar to liberals in the areas of disease avoidance and moral judgment. See http://othr.ws/disgust-conservatives.

87   *"the normal human condition"*: See "When Morality Opposes Justice: Conservatives Have Moral Intuitions That Liberals May Not Recognize," *Social Justice Research* 20, no. 1 (2007), pp. 98–116. Available at http://othr.ws/haidt-conservatives.

Chapter 13: Second That Emotion

89   *"emotional intelligence"*: Daniel Goleman, "What Makes a Leader?" *Harvard Business Review* (November–December 1998). Goleman had written two books about emotional intelligence by the time his *HBR* article appeared. The article itself became so popular that it was updated and reprinted in January 2004.

89   *animals need emotions to survive*: Darwin wrote a book on the subject in 1872, thirteen years after *On the Origin of Species. The Expression of the Emotions in Man and Animals* is widely considered his most significant contribution to psychology. The full text is available online at http://othr.ws/darwin-emotion.

90   *six primary emotions*: There are many competing lists of primary emotions. This one was developed by Paul Ekman in 1972 based on research among tribesmen who had no exposure to modern society. Although Ekman expanded the list in later years, there is little question that his initial list is biologically universal. For more, see http://othr.ws/primary-emotions.

90   *facial muscles*: Dr. Paul Ekman, a psychologist and an expert on body language,

has developed the Facial Action Coding System (FACS) for deciphering which of the forty-three muscles in the face are working at any given moment, even when an emotion is so fleeting that the person experiencing it may not be conscious of it. The CIA, the FBI, and many Hollywood studios are among the organizations that have sought his counsel. Ekman maintains a lively and interesting website on his work. See http://othr.ws/ekman-homepage.

Chapter 14: Feeling What Others Feel

92   *Kip Williams:* Kip Williams is now a professor of psychology at Purdue University, where he has established a lab to study ostracism and exclusion. He developed a free downloadable program called "Cyberball" that can be used in research on ostracism, social exclusion, rejection, bullying, and discrimination. It is available at http://othr.ws/williams-cyberball. For a paper on the measurement of the pain of social rejection, see Naomi I. Eisenberger, Matthew D. Lieberman, and Kipling D. Williams, "Does Rejection Hurt? An fMRI Study of Social Exclusion," *Science* (October 10, 2003).

93   *"possible reactions to social ostracism":* Kip Williams, "Ostracism," *Annual Review of Psychology* 48 (January 2007); available at http://othr.ws/ostracism-williams.

94   *campaign speech:* The full text of President Obama's 2008 presidential campaign speech, "A More Perfect Union," was reprinted in a number of newspapers. See, for example, the *Wall Street Journal,* at http://othr.ws/wsj-obama.

94   *complaining:* Fresh from a tour through rural Pennsylvania, Obama was trying to explain working-class culture to some wealthy Californians. Here is the full text of his remarks: "You go into some of these small towns in Pennsylvania, and like a lot of small towns in the Midwest, the jobs have been gone now for twenty-five years and nothing's replaced them. And they fell through the Clinton administration, and the Bush administration, and each successive administration has said that somehow these communities are gonna regenerate and they have not. And it's not surprising, then, they get bitter, they cling to guns or religion, or antipathy to people who aren't like them, or anti-immigrant sentiment or anti-trade sentiment as a way to explain their frustrations." See Mayhill Fowler, "Obama: No Surprise That Hard-Pressed Pennsylvanians Turn Bitter," *Huffington Post,* April 11, 2008, at http://othr.ws/huffpost-obama.

95   *"perspective taking":* See, for example, A. R. Todd et al., "Perspective Taking Combats Automatic Expressions of Racial Bias," *Journal of Personality and Social Psychology,* June 2011. Abstract available at http://othr.ws/perspective-taking-prejudice. Also see Adam Galinsky, "Creating and Reducing Intergroup Conflict: The Role of Perspective-Taking in Affecting Outgroup Evaluations," in N. M. A. Mannix, E. A. Mannix, and H. Sondak, eds., *Toward Phenomenology of Groups and Group Membership* (Bingley, UK: Emerald Group Publishing, 2002), 4: 85–113.

96   *a less-threatening suggestion:* Elizabeth Lesser's talk at the 2011 TED (Technology, Entertainment, Design) Conference is online at http://othr.ws/youtube-lesser.

97   *empathy is in sharp decline:* See the news release issued by the University of Michigan, "Empathy: College Students Don't Have as Much as They Used To," issued on May 27, 2010, and available at http://othr.ws/um-empathy.

97   *"bad biology":* Frans de Waal challenged the "survival of the fittest" school of economics in a 2009 essay written for *RSA Journal,* a publication of the Royal Society for the Encouragement of Arts, Manufacture, and Commerce. See "How Bad Biology Killed the Economy," available at http://othr.ws/bad-biology.

97   *self-interest:* This theory, known as Social Darwinism, is often attributed to Herbert Spencer (1820–1903), who coined the phrase "survival of the fittest." The theory was actually popularized by Richard Hofstadter in his 1944 book *Social Darwinism in American Life.* Some scholars, notably Princeton economist Thomas Leonard, believe that Hofstadter mischaracterized Spencer's actual beliefs, which were much closer to Adam Smith's theory of free-market economics and made ample allowances for charity and altruism. See Thomas Leonard, "Origins of the Myth of Social Darwinism," *Journal of Economic Behavior and Organization* 71 (March 6, 2009), at http://othr.ws/social-darwin.

98   *"of others were all that mattered":* From de Waal, "How Bad Biology Killed the Economy," http://othr.ws/bad-biology.

98   *"Empathy for 'other people'":* From Frans de Waal, *The Age of Empathy* (New York: Harmony Books, 2009), p. 204.

Chapter 15: Strange Places

101   New York Times *opinion piece:* From Theodore Levitt, "Yes. Throw Money at Problems," *New York Times,* April 28, 1978; see http://othr.ws/nyt-levitt.

102   globalization: There is some controversy about the origins of the term *globalization.* Two history professors—Harold James at Princeton and Matteo Albanese at the European University Institute—claim that the radical left-wing Italian underground periodical *Sinistra Proletaria* carried an article in 1970 entitled "The Process of Globalization of Capitalist Society," which purported to describe IBM. The article was in Italian and *globalization* was actually rendered as *mondializzazione.* Be that as it may, Levitt's was certainly the first usage of the term in English—or in any other language—to attract much attention.

102   *long-distance phone call:* International calling rates are from FCC International Traffic Data (http://othr.ws/international-calls).

102   *cost of shipping goods internationally:* Shipping rates from Marc Levinson, *The Box: How the Shipping Container Made the World Smaller and the World Economy Bigger* (Princeton, NJ: Princeton University Press, 2006), which quotes economists Edward L. Glaeser and Janet E. Kohlhase on the economics of containerized shipping: "It is better to assume that moving goods is essentially costless than to assume that moving goods is an important component of the production process" (p. 8).

102   *"multinational":* The McKinsey Global Institute reported on the impact of multinational companies on U.S. global competitiveness in 2010. See http://othr.ws/mckinsey-comp.

104 *"the alleviation of life's burdens"*: From Theodore Levitt, "The Globalization of Markets," *Harvard Business Review*, May/June 1983.

104 *"glocalization"*: Roland Robertson, "Comments on the Global Triad and Glocalization, Globalization, and Indigenous Culture," given at the Institute for Japanese Culture and Classics, Kokugakuin University, Tokyo, 1997. For the full text of the speech, see http://othr.ws/glocalization.

Chapter 16: Roots, Not Branches

110 *Edelman's annual "Trust Barometer"*: Edelman is the world's largest independent public relations agency. It conducts an annual survey of adults in twenty-three countries that it terms the "Edelman Trust Barometer." The first survey, in 2001, revealed that nongovernmental organizations (NGOs) were growing in influence. By 2011, NGOs were the most trusted institutions to do "what is right." Nearly two-thirds of the respondents (61 percent) trusted NGOs, compared to only about half (56 percent) who trusted businesses. For more on the 2011 Edelman Trust Barometer findings, see http://othr.ws/edelman-trust.

112 *Environmental Defense Fund*: For more on the Environmental Defense Fund's business partners, see http://othr.ws/edf-business.

112 *river blindness*: For more on Merck's campaign to eradicate river blindness, see http://othr.ws/river-blindness.

113 *"If you [as an NGO] are not talking to business"*: Randall Hayes of the Rainforest Action Network was quoted in "The 21st Century NGO: In the Market for Change," *SustainAbility Report* (June 26, 2003), p. 30.

113 *Sebastian Mallaby's book*: Sebastian Mallaby, *The World's Banker* (New York: Penguin Press, 2005).

Chapter 17: Political Attunement

114 *phone tapped*: One of Vice President Cheney's national security assistants monitored National Security Agency intercepts of Haass's telephone calls when he was traveling in the Middle East. This episode is described in Barton Gellman's book on the Cheney vice presidency, *Angler* (New York: Penguin Press, 2008), pp. 242–243.

118 *"measure their vulnerability"*: Richard Haass, "Sovereignty and Globalization," *Project Syndicate*, Council on Foreign Relations Op-Ed, February 17, 2006; see http://othr.ws/haass-states.

119 *"little republics in their own way"*: Indra Nooyi, CEO of PepsiCo, expressed her concept of corporate responsibility in a talk to the Boston Consulting Group, which is available on its website. See http://othr.ws/nooyi-responsibility.

Chapter 18: Management Across Borders

121 *world's funniest joke*: I would like to acknowledge Professor Richard Wiseman's generosity in giving me permission to quote some of the "world's funniest jokes." The complete list is available on the website at http://othr.ws/laflab.

123 *Dutch East India Company:* Frances Gouda, *Dutch Culture Overseas: Colonial Practice in the Netherlands Indies 1900–1942* (Singapore: Equinox Publishing, 2008), p. 41.

123 *Geert Hofstede:* Hofstede's work is considered a significant breakthrough in analyzing national cultures, and it has been validated through a number of studies. Dozens of books and articles have been written on Hofstede's theory of national cultures. His own books and website constitute perhaps the best overview of his theories and approaches. See http://othr.ws/geert-hofstede.

123 *four primary dimensions:* I have taken the liberty of slightly changing Hofstede's nomenclature in the interests of clarity and succinctness. The actual names of Hofstede's initial four dimensions are: Individualism, Power Distance, Uncertainty Avoidance, and Masculinity-Femininity. To these four dimensions, he later added Long-Term Orientation and Indulgence vs. Restraint. For more details, consult Geert Hofstede's website, http://othr.ws/geert-hofstede, or his book, *Cultures and Organizations: Software of the Mind* (New York: McGraw-Hill, 2010).

124 *Citibank:* This brief summary of the Citibank study, conducted by Stanford University researchers Michael Morris, Joel Podolny, and Sheira Ariel, merely touches the surface. The full study, "Culture, Norms, and Obligations: Cross-National Differences in Patterns of Interpersonal Norms and Felt Obligations Toward Coworkers," is available at http://othr.ws/citi-study.

124 *understanding other cultures:* Hofstede's theories have not been free of criticism. Some researchers believe that cultures are too complicated to be measured like weather trends. Others argue with the particular dimensions Hofstede identified. And, of course, some argue with his methodology. The International Business Center has a web page that lists the most prominent critiques, along with links to the original publications. See http://othr.ws/hofstede-critique.

126 *"the 'lens of culture'":* For a fuller explanation of Michael Morris's research on cultural lenses, see the report that Stanford University published, by Morris et al., "Cultural Lenses Change Business Focus," available at http://othr.ws/cultural-lens.

Chapter 19: Organizational Culture

129 *"what holds multinationals together":* This quote appears on Hofstede's website—http://othr.ws/geert-hofstede.

129 *Robert House:* For more on House's research, known as the GLOBE study, see R. J. House et al., *Culture, Leadership, and Organizations* (Thousand Oaks, CA: SAGE Publications, 2004). Or, for a briefer summary, visit http://othr.ws/globe-study.

130 *"society's instruments for change":* From House et al., *Culture, Leadership, and Organizations*, pp. 275–276.

131 *Global Mindset:* For more on the Global Mindset Inventory, see http://othr.ws/global-mind-set. Thunderbird School of Global Management charges for

use of the survey instrument, but will give corporations three free samples for evaluation.

132 *overseas experience has jumped:* The number of CEOs and other C-suite executives with international experience is from a study by Healthy Companies International, as cited in *U.S. News and World Report*, among other places. See http://othr.ws/usnews-international.

132 *read about the history:* Most travel guides include sections on local customs and traditions. There are even free iPhone apps like World Customs & Cultures (by Hooked In Motion, LLC), for foreign travelers. There are also many online resources, including Street Peeper (streetpeeper.com), eDiplomat (www.ediplomat.com), and Kwintessential (www.kwintessential.co.uk). For a more specialized printed overview, consider Michael Goodman's *Work with Anyone Anywhere,* which is an excellent guide to working with people in other countries (Belmont, CA: Professional Publications, 2006).

132 *World Affairs Councils:* To learn more about the World Affairs Councils of America (WACA) and to locate a nearby chapter, see http://othr.ws/world-affairs-councils.

Chapter 20: We Are What We Speak

133 *administrator once remarked:* From S. Bradford, "Over the River and into the Language Course," *Foreign Service Journal* (2006), pp. 24–25.

134 *Canadian researchers:* See K. England and B. Steill, "They Think You're as Stupid as Your English Is: Constructing Foreign Domestic Workers in Toronto," *Environment and Planning Annual,* 29, (1997), pp. 195–215, available at http://othr.ws/stupid-as-your-english.

134 *distrustful of people with accents:* The *Journal of Experimental Psychology* study was detailed in Pamela Paul, "A Failure to Communicate," *New York Times,* August 27, 2010; available at http://othr.ws/nyt-accents.

135 *personal web page:* See http://othr.ws/boroditsky-homepage.

135 *"do indeed think differently":* Lera Boroditsky summarized much of her research in the online publication *Edge.org.* See "How Does Our Language Shape the Way We Think?" June 12, 2009, available at http://othr.ws/boroditsky.

135 New York Times: A *New York Times* editorial published on February 9, 1984, misquoted linguist Benjamin Whorf as claiming Eskimos have 100 words for snow. See http://othr.ws/nyt-eskimo. Whorf actually claimed, in a 1940 article, that some Inuit had seven words for different kinds of snow. The number was further exaggerated over the years since Eskimo frequently combine adjectives with nouns to form new terms. In fact, Eskimos have about a dozen nouns for snow, about the same number as in English.

136 *eyewitness testimony:* See C. Fausey and L. Boroditsky, "Who Dunnit? Cross-Linguistic Differences in Eye-Witness Memory," *Psychonomic Bulletin and Review* (November 17, 2010). See http://othr.ws/who-dunnit.

136 *English and Spanish speakers:* Many linguists have noted the differences in

expressions of agency between English and Spanish. See, for example, A. Dorfman, "Footnotes to a Double Life," in Wendy Lesser, ed., *The Genius of Language* (New York: Random House, 2004), pp. 206–217, or D. I. Slobin and A. Bocaz, "Learning to Talk About Movement Through Time and Space: The Development of Narrative Abilities in Spanish and English," *Lenguas Modernas* 15 (1988), pp. 5–24.

137 *verbal gymnastics:* In French, *achievement* is translated as *réalisation* or *accomplissement*. Both French words indicate that something has been completed, but does not connote a sense of success or victory. Similarly, in Japanese, *decision making* is translated as *ishi kettei,* which is literally "to will a decision" or "to intend a decision." Both concepts indicate purpose, but fall short in describing the full mental process of selecting a course of action among many options.

138 *"when you're learning a new language":* From Boroditsky, "How Does Our Language Shape the Way We Think?" http://othr.ws/boroditsky.

139 *"encourage different kinds of cognitive expertise":* Boroditsky made these assertions in a "debate" on the *Economist*'s website, which is available at http://othr.ws/economist-debate.

139 *"shape the way we think":* L. Boroditsky, "Linguistic Relativity," in L. Nadel, ed., *Encyclopedia of Cognitive Science* (London: MacMillan, 2003) pp. 917–921.

Chapter 21: Horizontal Empathy

141 *Novartis Institutes for BioMedical Research:* For more information on Novartis R&D, see http://othr.ws/novartis-bmr.

144 *Afinitor:* Michael Nawrath, an analyst at Zuercher Kantonalbank, predicts that the Novartis cancer drug Afinitor will generate as much as $3 billion in annual sales across all indications. He expects Novartis will be able to broaden the use of the medicine, benefiting from the fact that it already has a good grasp of the therapy's mechanism and its side effects. See http://othr.ws/wsj-afinitor.

Chapter 22: Practical Empathy

148 *senior management and frontline workers:* The Economic Policy Institute has been tracking CEO compensation for several years using information from the *Wall Street Journal* and executive compensation experts such as Mercer Management and Hay Group. In 2011, it reported that the average CEO's compensation was 242 times greater than the average production worker's. That was down from 277 in pre-recession 2007. The peak was 298.5 in 2000, up from 24.2 in 1965. See http://othr.ws/epi-compensation.

149 *"most startling turnarounds in tech":* Peter Burrows and Matthew Campbell, "Alcatel-Lucent Chops Away at Years of Failure," *Bloomberg Businessweek,* April 28, 2011; see http://othr.ws/buswk-al.

149 Businessweek *called him "one of the best managers"*: Jennifer Schenker, "Good-bye to BT's Steady Hand, Ben Verwaayen," *Bloomberg Businessweek,* April 8, 2008; see http://othr.ws/buswk-bt.

Chapter 23: Me, Us, and Them

153 *"culture been so fragmented"*: Daniel Boorstin, *America and the Image of Europe* (New York: Meridian Books, 1960), p. 14.

153 *negative view of the federal government*: According to a 2011 Gallup survey, 63 percent of Americans have a negative view of the federal government, the lowest rating since the survey was begun in 2003 and on a par with attitudes toward the oil industry. See Frank Newport, "Americans Rate Computer Industry Best, Federal Government Worst," Gallup news release, August 29, 2011, http://othr.ws/gallup-fed.

153 *cultural distance between people*: Sociologists Claude Fischer and Greggor Matson express skepticism that America is more fragmented today than it was in the past. However, they believe the widening gap between Americans by income and education is substantial and serious. See "Is America Frag-menting?" *Annual Review of Sociology* 35 (August 2009), at http://othr.ws/america-fragmenting.

154 *"divided mankind into parties"*: From James Madison, "Federalist No. 10," November 22, 1787. See http://othr.ws/fed-papers. Madison's treatise on "fac-tions" is arguably the most famous and celebrated of *The Federalist Papers*.

155 *ideological divergence in Congress is the highest*: See Nolan McCarthy, Keith Poole, and Howard Rosenthal, *Polarized America* (Cambridge, MA: MIT Press, 2006). An abstract, with charts, is available at http://othr.ws/congress-polarization.

155 *"don't have to appeal to the center to win"*: From Lee Hamilton, "Why Is Con-gress So Partisan?" The Center on Congress at Indiana University (blog); see http://othr.ws/congress-partisan.

156 *"now than thirty years ago"*: Andrew Gelman, "Economic Divisions and Political Polarization in Red and Blue America," *Pathways* (Summer 2011); see http://othr.ws/gelman-polarization.

156 *can actually affect how the public interprets and learns*: Robert Shapiro and Yaeli Bloch-Elkon, "Political Polarization and the Rational Public," paper pre-pared for presentation at the Annual Conference of the American Association for Public Opinion Research, Montreal, Quebec, Canada, May 18–21, 2006; see http://othr.ws/polarization-public.

157 *"folly of crowds"*: Cass Sunstein, a legal scholar at the University of Chicago, has collaborated with behavioral economists to figure out how the law affects peo-ple's actual behavior and, conversely, how a real-world understanding of human dynamics should influence the writing and administration of laws. Sunstein was coauthor with Edward Glaeser of a paper for the Harvard Law School Pub-lic Law Research project that surveyed many of the recent studies on group

polarization. See Paper No. 08-14, which is available for download at http://othr.
ws/behavior-econ.

158 *"habitually step back and think"*: David Brooks, "A Case of Mental Courage,"
New York Times, August 23, 2010; see http://othr.ws/nyt-brooks.

160 *acquired unconsciously:* For example, see John Bargh and Ezequiel Morsella,
"The Unconscious Mind," *Perspectives on Psychological Science* (January
2008), pp. 73–79.

Chapter 24: Sisyphus Had It Easy

162 *Snopes tracked eighty-seven rumors:* Writer and blogger J. L. Bell counted and
categorized presidential rumors on Snopes.com. His analysis is available at
http://othr.ws/internet-rumors.

162 *issue of Obama's religion:* Pew's report was published in August 2010, based on
interviews taken between July 21 and August 5, 2010. For the full report, see
http://othr.ws/pew-obama.

164 *allowed the attacks of 9/11:* Zogby International released a poll conducted on
behalf of 911truth.org on September 7, 2007. For the full results and a demographic breakdown, see http://othr.ws/bush-cheney-911.

164 *"we do not first see, and then define"*: Walter Lippmann, *Public Opinion* (1922;
repr., New York: Penguin, 1946), p. 54.

164 *Misinformation is almost impossible to kill:* The persistence of political misperceptions is vividly described by Brendan Nyhan of the University of Michigan
and Jason Reifler of Georgia State University in their paper, "When Correc-
tions Fail," *Political Behavior* 32 (2010), published online March 30, 2010; see
http://othr.ws/nyhan-corr.

165 *Duelfer Report:* The Duelfer Report was commissioned by the Iraq Study
Group charged by the multinational force in Iraq to establish the facts about
Saddam Hussein's possession of weapons of mass destruction. See http://othr.
ws/duelfer-report.

166 *tested two political smears:* See S. Kosloff et al., "Smearing the Opposition:
Implicit and Explicit Stigmatization of the 2008 U.S. Presidential Candidates
and the Current U.S. President," *Journal of Experimental Psychology* 139, no. 3
(August 2010), http://othr.ws/race-salience.

166 *"amplified belief that Obama is a socialist"*: See Kosloff et al., "Smearing the
Opposition," available at http://othr.ws/race-salience.

167 *"interviewing respondents to the study"*: Brendan Nyhan made these comments in an interview with Brooke Gladstone, cohost of "On the Media," on
August 27, 2010. For a complete "Debunk This!" transcript, see http://othr.ws/
onthemedia-nyhan.

Chapter 25: Lost in a Loop

169 *Texting is the feature they use the most:* According to Pew Research, fully
72 percent of all teens use text-messaging, a sharp rise from 51 percent in
2006. Among teens, texting has now overtaken every other form of interac-

tion with their friends, including talking face-to-face. See Amanda Lenhart, "Teens, Cell Phones, and Texting," Pew Internet and American Life Project news release and summary findings, April 20, 2010; http://othr.ws/pew-texting.

169 *"there but not there."*: Sherry Turkle, *Alone Together* (New York: Basic Books, 2011). Turkle argues that people are increasingly functioning without face-to-face contact. For example, she describes a Skype conversation between a girl and her grandmother (p. 14) and notes that the girl is answering e-mails during the conversation. "Her grandmother was talking to someone who was not really there," Turkle observes.

169 *watching network broadcast news*: It's widely known that the viewership of broadcast television news has been in decline for more than a decade. The growing partisanship of cable TV news audiences has received less attention. See "Partisanship and Cable News Audiences," Pew Research Center for the People and the Press news release, October 30, 2009; http://othr.ws/pew-news.

170 *trusts the cable news outlets*: In a CBS *60 Minutes*/*Vanity Fair* poll in mid-2010, CNN was selected as the most trusted news outlet by 32 percent of respondents, followed by Fox News at 29 percent. Around 50 percent of those who chose Fox were Republicans and 46 percent of those who chose CNN were Democrats. The big three networks were selected by only 13 percent. For more, see http://othr.ws/news-trust.

170 *news consumption is changing*: For more on the changes in news consumption, see "A New Phase in Our Digital Lives," Pew Research Center's Project for Excellence in Journalism, September 12, 2010, available at http://othr.ws/pew-news-consumption. The Pew Research Center's 2011 report on the state of the news media indicated for the first time that more people get their news from the Internet than from newspapers. In fact, the Web is second only to television as a source for news and the trend line shows that even that gap is closing. See http://othr.ws/state-of-news-2010. Pew also released a 2011 study indicating that social media users tend to connect largely with people who are already within their network of friends and acquaintances. For example, social media users had met 93 percent of the people in their network prior to "friending" them and the largest block of social network friends were people they met in high school. The diversity of online social networks is about the same as for Internet users overall, as is their ability to consider multiple points of view, though MySpace users appear to be more empathetic, and Facebook users appeared to be more trusting. The complete Pew Internet and American Life Project study, "Social Networking Sites and Our Lives," is available at http://othr.ws/pew-social-media. Finally, a Harvard Medical School study found that while Facebook users typically have more than 100 "friends," only about six were real friends. The rest were, at best, acquaintances. See Paul Massari, "Connecting with Freshmen," *Harvard Gazette*, August 29, 2011, available at http://othr.ws/harvard-social-media.

171 *agree with their point of view*: See Silvia Knobloch-Westerwick and Jingbo Meng, "Looking the Other Way: Selective Exposure to Attitude-Consistent and Counter Attitudinal Political Information," *Communication Research* (June 2009). For a popular summary, see http://othr.ws/cr-reading.

172 *the public's trust*: John Gerzema and Edward Lebar, *The Brand Bubble: The Looming Crisis in Brand Value and How to Avoid It* (San Francisco: Jossey-Bass, 2008), p. 26.

172 *"American politics has often been an arena for angry minds"*: Richard Hofstadter, "The Paranoid Style in American Politics," *Harper's* (November 1964). The complete article is available at http://othr.ws/paranoid-politics.

Chapter 26: Voting with Your Feet

177 *"to another in a single year"*: From Bill Bishop, *The Big Sort* (New York: Houghton Mifflin, 2008), p. 8.

177 *county election returns in presidential elections*: According to Bishop, in 2004, 48.3 percent of voters lived in counties where the winner had a margin of at least 20 points; in 2008, 47.6 percent did. See *The Big Sort*, p. 305.

178 *"because that's the way we've made it"*: Bill Bishop, "Like with Like," Room for Debate (blog), *New York Times*, January 10, 2010; see http://othr.ws/nyt-bishop.

178 *Yahoo Research suggests*: Sharad Goel, Winter Mason, and Duncan J. Watts, "Real and Perceived Attitude Agreement in Social Networks," *Journal of Personality and Social Psychology* 99, no. 4 (October 2010), pp. 611–621. This Yahoo Research paper is available online at http://othr.ws/friend-sense.

179 *"pictures in our heads"*: Walter Lippmann, *Public Opinion* (1922; repr., New York: Penguin, 1946), p. 20.

179 *"stereotypes"*: Stereotypes are neither positive nor negative in themselves, but may support attitudes that are. For example, someone who associates Hispanics with illegal immigrants and dislikes undocumented aliens would probably feel negatively toward Hispanics. The Social Psychology Network has a good overview of stereotyping within the context of prejudice. See http://othr.ws/psychology-stereotypes.

179 *"Public Opinion with capital letters"*: Lippmann, *Public Opinion*, p. 20.

180 *"the feelings attached to those opinions"*: Lippmann, *Public Opinion*, p. 154.

Chapter 27: Free-Floating Anger

182 *in only three institutions*: The Gallup 2010 Confidence in Institutions poll was released on July 22, 2010. Results were based on telephone interviews conducted July 8–11, 2010, with a random sample of 1,020 adults, aged 18 and older, living in the continental United States. The margin of sampling error was ±4 percentage points. For more, go to http://othr.ws/gallup-trust.

183 *"more likely than minorities"*: Ronald Brownstein, "The Democrats' White Flight," *Atlantic*, January 7, 2011; see http://othr.ws/brownstein-minorities.

183 *Peggy Noonan:* Peggy Noonan, "America Is at Risk of Boiling Over," *Wall Street Journal*, August 7, 2010; see http://othr.ws/wsj-noonan.

183 *"intergenerational mobility":* A report on "Intergenerational Mobility in Europe and North America," from which this quote and data are taken, was published in April 2005 by the Centre for Economic Performance, London School of Economics. For the full report, see http://othr.ws/gen-mobility. For more data and background information, see the Economic Mobility Project, an initiative of the Pew Charitable Trust, at http://othr.ws/social-mobility.

183 *As Brownstein puts it:* Ronald Brownstein, "Corrosive Collapse in Confidence," *National Journal*, August 14, 2010 .

Chapter 28: Mind the Gap

186 *"a debunking discipline":* Claude Fischer, "Social Science and the Public After Mumford," lecture delivered at the Lewis Mumford Center for Comparative Urban and Regional Research, State University of New York at Albany, March 26, 2001. See http://othr.ws/fischer-debunk.

186 *"like snowball fights":* Claude Fischer, "Compared to What?" *Contexts* (Fall 2010), publication of the American Sociological Association; see http://othr.ws/fischer-context.

187 *"adopted new positions first":* Claude Fischer and Michael Hout, *Century of Difference: How America Changed in the Last One Hundred Years* (New York: Russell Sage Foundation, 2006), p. 223. Fischer's data also showed that public opinion doesn't always move in one direction. On the issue of abortion, for example, Americans' opinions have cycled back and forth from easing constraints to tightening them. Similarly, support for the death penalty rose from the 1930s to the 1960s, then dropped until 1990, when it started rising again.

188 *General Social Survey:* The GSS of the National Opinion Research Center (NORC) is a veritable cornucopia of information on people's attitudes on a wide range of issues over long periods of time. For more, see http://othr.ws/gss-sum. For more on attitudes toward pre-marital sex, go to http://othr.ws/gss-subject. Select "S," "Sex," "Pre-marital."

188 *"quarter of the [twentieth] century":* Fischer and Hout, *Century of Difference*, p. 245.

188 *"but a reality of much longer ago":* *Century of Difference*, p. 225.

188 *unemployment rate for black men:* The Bureau of Labor Statistics seasonally adjusted unemployment data for August 2011 is available at http://othr.ws/bls-unemployment. The jobless rate for African Americans has held steady at twice the rate for white Americans since the 1940s. And most distressingly, African Americans with the *same* education as white Americans have higher unemployment levels. Unemployment rates for college-educated African Americans is closer to that of white Americans with only a high school education. See Algernon Austin, "Unemployment in Black and White," Economic Policy Institute, March 26, 2010, http://othr.ws/austin-black-unemployment.

188 *poverty rate:* Poverty rates for black and white Americans are from a Septem-

ber 2011 report by the U.S. Census Bureau available at http://othr.ws/census-poverty. In November 2011, the Census Bureau issued a "supplemental report," intended to better reflect the costs of basic living expenses as well as the resources people have to pay them. Under these new measures, the total poverty rate increased to 16 percent from 15.2 percent. The poverty rate for African Americans decreased slightly to 25.4 percent while the rate for Hispanic Americans increased to 28.2 percent. Both rates were still significantly higher than the revised poverty rate for white Americans at 11.1 percent. For the supplemental poverty report, see http://othr.ws/census-supp.

188 *intermarriage:* According to Pew Research, about 15 percent of marriages in 2010 were between people of different races or ethnicity, including 9 percent of whites, 17 percent of blacks, 26 percent of Hispanics, and 28 percent of Asians. Because of high immigration levels over the past decades, intermarriage rates for Hispanics and Asians have not changed much since 1980. However, the intermarriage rates for whites are double what they were in 1980, and the rates for blacks are nearly three times greater. Still, white–black couples accounted for only about 12 percent of all interracial marriages. For more, see Paul Taylor et al., "The Rising Rate of Intermarriage," Pew Research Center, February 16, 2012, available at http://othr.ws/pew-intermarriage-rise.

188 *immigrants are also people of color:* See Algernon Austin, "Blacks Have Highest Unemployment Rates Among Foreign-Born Workers," Economic Policy Institute, August 3, 2011, http://othr.ws/austin-foreign-unemployment. The unemployment rate among Asian immigrants (7.3 percent) is comparable to that of white foreign-born workers because they tend to be better educated, on average, and a higher proportion work in technical fields or in jobs with strong ethnic or family ties. For example, 47 percent of Asian Americans work in managerial positions compared to 35 percent of white Americans. And while Asian Americans account for only 5 percent of U.S. workers, they make up a disproportionate share of software engineers (29 percent), computer programmers (20 percent), and system analysts (16 percent). On the other hand, when Asian Americans lose their jobs, they tend to stay unemployed longer than other ethnic groups. For additional background, see Haya El Nasser, "Cultural Factors Help Limit Recession's Impact," *USA Today* (November 16, 2009), at http://othr.ws/recession-culture.

189 *"of American slaves and the rest":* Fischer is an engaging and provocative contributor to the Berkeley Blog, where this quote originally appeared. See "A Fragmenting America? Parts 1 and 2" at http://othr.ws/fischer-big-split.

189 *Education is the biggest contributor:* Dalton Conley, *Social Class: How Does It Work?* (New York: Russell Sage Foundation, 2008).

189 *are more likely to get married:* Fewer than half (48 percent) of people with only a high school diploma marry versus about two-thirds (64 percent) of those with a college degree. And nearly half (44 percent) of births to women with only a high school diploma were to unwed mothers. See W. Bradford Wilcox, ed., *The State of Our Unions,* National Marriage Project, University of Virginia, 2010. See http://othr.ws/state-of-union.

190   *college degree has nearly tripled:* Information from General Social Survey, http://
othr.ws/gss-subject, Select "S," "Education," "Highest degree R have earned."

190   *cost of higher education is well beyond:* See, for example, Annalyn Censky,
"Surging College Costs Price Out Middle Class, CNN/Money, June 13, 2011,
available at http://othr.ws/college-cost.

190   *predictor of earning a college degree:* Dalton Conley, *Social Class: How Does It
Work?* (New York: Russell Sage Foundation, 2008).

Chapter 29: The Chicken Soup of Social Life

191   *"Trust is the chicken soup of social life":* Eric Uslaner, *The Moral Foundations
of Trust* (Cambridge, U.K.: Cambridge University Press, 2002), p. 1; see http://
othr.ws/uslaner-trust-foundation.

192   *"most people can be trusted":* See General Social Survey, at http://othr.ws/gss-
subject. Select "S," "Trust," and "People can be trusted."

192   *"was more egalitarian":* Robert Putnam, *Bowling Alone* (New York: Simon &
Schuster, 2000), p. 359. Furthermore, two medical epidemiologists have
separately concluded that, in addition to lower levels of social trust, income
inequality also results in higher rates of mental illness and drug use, shorter
life expectancies, greater levels of obesity, lower educational outcomes, more
births to teenage girls, and more violence and higher rates of imprisonment.
See Richard Wilkinson and Kate Pickett, *The Spirit Level: Why Equal Societies
Almost Always Do Better* (New York: Penguin Books 2009).

192   *"the strongest determinant of trust":* Eric Uslaner, *Moral Foundations of Trust*,
http://othr.ws/uslaner-trust-foundation.

193   *income equality:* The Gini Index is a common measurement of income equality. If everyone in a country had the same income, it would have a Gini Index
of 0; if all a country's income was in the hands of one person, its Gini Index
would be "100." In the 1960s, the U.S. Gini Index was about 39; in 2009 it was
about 47, an increase of about 20 percent. U.S. Census Bureau provided this
data. To explore this issue further, see http://othr.ws/census-inequality.

193   *Equality leads to greater optimism:* Eric Uslaner, *Moral Foundations of Trust*,
pp. 6–18; see http://othr.ws/uslaner-trust-foundation.

193   *Fourteenth Congressional District of New York:* This and other comparisons are
graphically and powerfully portrayed in *The Measure of America, 2010–2011*,
written by Kristen Lewis and Sarah Burd-Sharps for the American Human
Development Project (New York: NYU Press, 2010).

193   *hasn't been this wide since the 1920s:* See "Striking It Richer: The Evolution of
Top Incomes in the United States," published July 17, 2010, and available at
http://othr.ws/saez-income-gap.

194   *"the lower upper class":* Matt Miller, "Goldman Sachs and the Revolt of the Lower
Upper Class, *Washington Post,* April 21, 2010; see http://othr.ws/wp-miller.

194   *unemployment:* The Center for Labor Market Studies at Northeastern University in Boston divided American households into ten groups based on annual
household income. It then analyzed labor conditions in each of the groups dur-

ing the fourth quarter of 2009. The highest group, with household incomes of $150,000 or more, had an unemployment rate during that quarter of 3.2 percent. The next highest, with incomes of $100,000 to $149,999, had an unemployment rate of 4 percent. For the full report, see http://othr.ws/northeastern-university.

194 *lived paycheck to paycheck:* This figure comes from a September 16, 2009, survey commissioned by CareerBuilder.com; see http://othr.ws/careerbuilder-survey.

194 *personal bankruptcy:* The 1.5 million figure comes from the Administrative Office of U.S. Courts, November 8, 2010. For the latest data, see http://othr.ws/bankruptcy-stats.

194 *Americans are on food stamps:* U.S. Department of Agriculture, April 29, 2011. For the latest data, see http://othr.ws/americans-on-foodstamps.

195 *private communities:* Community Associations Institute statistics. See http://othr.ws/gated-communities.

Chapter 30: People Are Crazy

197 *"The reductive appeal to self-interest":* Barry Schwartz, "Addicted to Incentives," a presentation to the Third Annual Conference on Law and Mind Sciences, Harvard Law School, March 2009. See http://othr.ws/schwartz-incentives.

197 *can have perverse consequences:* The nuclear waste site and day-care examples were cited by Bruno Frey and Reto Jegen in their working paper, "Motivation Crowding Theory: A Study of Empirical Evidence," January 2000. See http://othr.ws/daycare-nuclear-waste.

198 *or money on the table:* See Eugene Caruso, Dobromir Rahnev, and Mahzarin Banaji, "Using Conjoint Analysis to Detect Discrimination: Revealing Covert Preferences from Overt Choices," *Social Cognition* 27, no. 1 (2009), pp. 128–137; available at http://othr.ws/trivia-game.

199 *our capacity to reason:* Cognitive scientists Hugo Mercier and Dan Sperber created quite a stir when they wrote that human reasoning skills are designed not to acquire new knowledge, but rather to "devise and evaluate arguments intended to persuade." See "Why Do Humans Reason? Arguments for an Argumentative Theory," *Behavioral and Brain Sciences* (June 26, 2010), pp. 57–74. Their "argumentative theory of reasoning" is online at http://othr.ws/why-reason.

199 *better decisions:* For a summary of recent research on decision making, see Sharon Begley, "I Can't Think," *Newsweek,* February 27, 2011, http://othr.ws/making-decisions. A more thorough analysis is presented by Nobel Prize–winning psychologist Daniel Kahneman in *Thinking Fast and Slow* (New York: Farrar, Strauss and Giroux, 2011).

199 *phone booth:* See Paula F. Levin and Alice M. Isen, "Further Studies on the Effect of Feeling Good on Helping," *Sociometry,* vol. 38, No. 1 (March 1975), pp. 141–147, at http://othr.ws/phone-booth.

199 *bakery:* See Kwame Anthony Appiah, *Experiments in Ethics* (Cambridge, MA: Harvard University Press, 2010), pp. 41–42.

199 *read words:* Cited by Paul Bloom, "First Person Plural." *Atlantic*, November 2008. See http://othr.ws/reading-words.

199 *to do terrible things:* In a classic series of experiments conducted by Stanley Milgram in the 1960s, participants were instructed to inflict electrical shocks on someone they could not see, but could certainly hear. The results were always the same—a majority of the participants continued inflicting the shocks at higher and higher voltages, even when the unseen subject was screaming in agony. "Stark authority was pitted against the subjects' strongest moral imperatives against hurting others," Milgram wrote, "and, with the subjects' ears ringing with the screams of the victims, authority won more often than not." See Stanley Milgram, "Behavioral Study of Obedience," *Journal of Abnormal and Social Psychology* 67, no. 4 (October 1963), pp. 371–378.

199 *humans bunch together in groups:* See K. Carsten et al., "The Neuropeptide Oxytocin Regulates Parochial Altruism in Intergroup Conflict Among Humans," *Science* (June 2010), pp. 1408–1411.

199 *teenage boys to different groups:* H. Tajfel et al., "Social Categorization and Intergroup Behavior," *European Journal of Social Psychology* 1, no. 2 (1971), pp. 149–178.

201 *"in order to know ourselves":* Miroslav Volf, "Living with the Other," *Journal of Ecumenical Studies* 39, no. 1–2 (Winter–Spring 2002), p. 8.

201 *"to other people's conceptions of you":* Cordelia Fine, *Delusions of Gender* (New York: W. W. Norton, 2010), p. 10.

202 *"the needs and feelings of others":* Jonah Lehrer made these comments on his blog, "The Frontal Cortex," which is an always provocative source of scientific information on what makes us who we are. See, for example, http://othr.ws/ lehrer-power. More recent research suggests that one's social class can also affect one's ability to empathize with others. According to one study, people in a lower social class are "more empathically accurate in judging the emotions of other people." See Michael Kraus et al. "Social Class, Contextualism, and Empathic Accuracy," Psychological Science OnlineFirst, October 25, 2010, http://othr.ws/social-class-empathy.

202 *Crockett calls "heading to the 'hood'":* Roger Crockett is an occasional contributor to the "Conversation" column of the Harvard Business School's blog. These quotes are from an entry he wrote on July 27, 2010, "White Executives Should Head to the 'Hood." See http://othr.ws/hbr-crockett.

Chapter 31: Fluent Listening

204 *Jack Rowe:* For more on story of Aetna's turnaround and Rowe's role in it, see Jon Katzenbach and Zia Khan, *Leading Outside the Lines* (San Francisco: Jossey-Bass, 2010), pp. 157–164.

Chapter 32: Presence

209 *"probably moonlight as a model":* This observation, and the last quote in the chapter, which comes from Bob Selander himself, are from a profile of

Selander, "Mastermind of MasterCard," by Stephen Sawicki, *Greenwich* magazine, April 2007.

210   *"because he wants to do it"*: Eisenhower was quoted in *The Federal Career Service: A Look Ahead* (Washington, DC: Society for Personnel Administration, 1954).

Chapter 33: Congruence

215   *Joseph Volpe*: Volpe cataloged his complaints in his 2006 autobiography, *The Toughest Show on Earth: My Rise and Reign at The Metropolitan Opera* (New York: Knopf, 2006), especially pp. 241–245. The subtitle's royalist allusion belies the book's brash and everyman tone. His problems with Lincoln Center's redevelopment plans—and especially with its redeveloper—are largely confined to Chapter 17 (out of the book's twenty-one chapters).

215   *decidedly mixed reaction*: See Nicolai Ouroussoff, "The Greening of Lincoln Center," *New York Times*, May 20, 2010, at http://othr.ws/nyt-critic.

216   *Anthony Tommasini*: See Anthony Tommasini, "A Citadel of Culture Shows a Friendlier Face," *New York Times*, December 31, 2010, available at http://othr.ws/nyt-tommasini.

Conclusion: How to Be OtherWise

218   *"the priorities of truck drivers"*: See Charles Murray, *Coming Apart* (New York: Crown Forum, 2012), page 101. For a briefer explanation of Murray's view that American society is cleaving into two classes, see his article, "Belmont and Fishtown," in *The New Criterion*, January 2012, available at http://othr.ws/nc-murray.

219   *Adam Smith observed*: See Adam Smith, *The Wealth of Nations*, Book 3 (New York: Collier and Sons, 1911), p. 180. A public domain copy is available at http://othr.ws/wealth-of-nations.

219   *"benign indifference to difference"*: Trudy D. Conway, "From Tolerance to Hospitality: Problematic Limits of a Negative Virtue," a speech delivered at the annual meeting of the Society for Philosophy in the Contemporary World, June 2004; see http://othr.ws/conway-difference.

220   *"to feel good about others"*: Adam D. Galinsky and Gillian Ku, "The Effects of Perspective-Taking on Prejudice: The Moderating Role of Self-Evaluation," *Personality and Social Psychology Bulletin* 30, no. 5 (May 2004), pp. 594–604. The authors also concluded that perspective-taking by people with low self-esteem leads to no reduction in stereotyping or prejudice. And they further speculate that perspective-taking may be less successful in reducing prejudice in "collectivist" societies, where self-esteem is less relevant and intergroup conflict more common. See http://othr.ws/perspective-taking-self-esteem.

220   *"a fusion of horizons"*: Hans-Georg Gadamer, *Truth and Method,* 2nd rev. ed., trans. J. Weinsheimer and D. G. Marshall (New York: Continuum, 2004), p. 305.

222   other-directed: David Riesman defined this term in his book *The Lonely Crowd,* rev. ed. (New Haven, CT: Yale University Press, 2001), pp. 17–22.

Index

ABC News, 229*n*, 237*n*
abortion, 83, 188
  American opinions, 258*n*
  Roberts ruling on clinics, 165
accountability, x
ad campaign, of MasterCard, 211
Adams, John, 154
adaptability, 106
Addicks, Mark, 31–32, 34–35
adoption of new ideas, 187
adoptions, transnational, 220–221
Advertising Age, 26
advertising techniques, 31
Aetna, 159, 204–207
Afinitor, 144, 253*n*
Africa, General Electric in, 59
African Americans, 5, 188
  assimilation, 233*n*
  beauty products purchases, 35
  earnings, skin color and, 43–44
  generational divisions, 30
  legacy of past racism, 45
  shadowed while shopping, 237*n*
agnostics, in U.S., 80
agreement, changing levels on graph,
  186–188
AIG, 111
Alabama, immigration laws, 13
Albanese, Matteo, 249*n*
Alcatel-Lucent, 149
alienation, 183
Alone Together (Turkle), 169
American Demographics (Francese), 26–27
American Dream, 72, 183, 195
American economy, and human behavior, 197
American exceptionalism, 19
American Idea, 19–20
American Institute of Architects, 216
American Muslims, 72
Americans, lack of world knowledge, 217
analysis, inside-out and outside-in, 116–117
ancestors, primordial, 1
anger, 181–184
Anglican Communion, 64
anti-immigration groups, 232*n*
anti-Semitism, 4

anti-white bias, 48
antisocial behavior, 92
anxiety, 54, 238*n*
Arab awakening, 74
Arizona
  immigration laws, 12, 229*n*
  violent crime rate in, 230*n*
arrest rates, of recently arrived immigrants,
  13
Asian-American community
  gender pattern in marriage, 240*n*
  newspapers, 233–234*n*
Asian Americans
  employment, 259*n*
  skin color bias, 44
Asians, exclusion from immigration, 44
assimilation, 18, 21–23, 233*n*
assumptions, unconscious, 49
AT&T
  foreign markets, 109
  in Singapore, 126
  women in management, viii
atheists, in U.S., 80
attentiveness, 210
  demonstrating while listening, 207
authority, respect for, 85
Ayoob, Mohammed, 74

baby boomers, 28, 234*n*
bad biology, 97
Banaji, Mahzarin, 238*n*
Beck, Glenn, 72
Beckwith, Mark, 63–66
behavior, 220
  and American economy, 197
  cooperative, 85
  influence of external events, 199
beliefs, 220
  facts and preexisting, 166
  impact of contradictions, 157
Benedict XVI (pope), 76, 245*n*
Betty Crocker, 32
Beyond the Melting Pot (Glazer), 20–21
bias, implicit, 237*n*
Bible, 241*n*
The Big Sort (Bishop), 177

bilingual Americans, 24
births
    in Hispanic populations, 232*n*
    to unmarried women, 30
Bishop, Bill, 176
    The Big Sort, 177
Black Americans, 21, *see also* African
    Americans
black culture, urban, 46
black/white divide, 188
Blair, Tony, 71
blindness, to commonalities, 5
Block, Ed, 178
blogs, 157
Bloom, Paul, 86
Bloomberg Businessweek, 149
Bohr, Niels, 65
bonding, 53
Boorstin, Daniel J., 153
Boroditsky, Lera, 134–135, 137–138
Bowling Alone (Putnam), 52–53
BP, 182
Brazil, 134
Brokeback Mountain, 67
Brooks, David, 158
Brown, DeNeen, 43
Brownstein, Ron, 183
Bruni, Frank, 66
Buchanan, Pat, 54, 239*n*
The Bureaucratic Entrepreneur (Haass), 115
Bush, George W., 161–162, 164
    and Eid stamp, 163
business community, decline in reputation,
    119
businesspeople, learning from politicians,
    115–120
buying power, 28

cable news program, 169, 256*n*
Cameron, David, 25, 234*n*
Campbell, David, 80
Canada, 131–132
Cargill, 111
Carter, Graydon, 242*n*
Carter, Jimmy, 82
Caruso, Eugene, 198
categorical thinking, 2–3, 228*n*
categorization, 164
Cedar Rapids, Iowa, Islamic Center, 75–76
Celan, Paul, "Death Fugue," 69
Center for Labor Market Studies, 260*n*

Century of Difference (Fischer), 186
CEOs, 119
    compensation, 148, 253*n*
    international experience, 252*n*
    Verwaayen on responsibilities, 147
certainty, faith and, 65
cetnik (Serbian fighters), 70
CFR (Council on Foreign Relations), 114,
    116
change, in world demography, 3
Cheney, Dick, 114, 164
China
    leadership profile in, 129–130
    P&G consumer market study, 105
Christianity
    church attendance, 79
    church membership, 81
    and homosexuals, 62
    hostility to Islam, 76
    intersection with Islam, 75
church and state separation, 81
Churchill, Winston, 165–166
Citibank, 251*n*
    employee cooperation, 124
civil rights movement, 21
class distinction, and college education,
    189–190
climate change, 118
Clinton, Bill, 34
CNN, 169, 256*n*
collaborative work of scientists, 143
collective culture, vs. individualism, 123
college education
    and class distinction, 189–190
    opinions on prevalence, 27
college students, self-reported empathy, 97
colorblindness, 47, 57, 240*n*
colorism, 43–45
commonalities
    blindness to, 5
    vs. differences as emphasis, 76
communication, emotion and, 91
Communication Research, 171
communications technologies, 168
    in-language media, 233*n*
community, 161
companies
    defining self-interest, 174
    multinational, 102, 133, 249*n*
company size, 128
competition

evolutionary, 97
free-market, 98
competitive breeding, 17, 232n
concepts, language and description of, 137
confirmation bias, 165
conflict, in American society, 11–12, 228n
conflict resolution, ix
congruence, 212–216
conservatives, 86, 218
containerization, 102, 249n
cooperative behavior, 85
corporate identity, and diversity management, 56
corporate social responsibility, 118
Cosby, Bill, 37
cost of diversity, 52–60
Coulter, Ann, 167
Council on American-Islamic Relations, 245n
Council on Foreign Relations (CFR), 114, 116
countries, variation between, 78–83
county election returns, in presidential elections, 177
Crain Communications, 26
creativity, 159
credibility, of NGOs, 111
Crest toothpaste, 103
crimes, 230n
immigrants and, 13
violent, in Arizona, 230n
Croatia, 69–70
Crockett, Roger, 202
cross-border issues, organization participation in, 117
cross-cultural marketing, 40
cross-functional teams, 144
crowds, folly of, 157
cultural exchanges, 24
cultural lenses, 251n
cultural sensitivity, 38
culture, 39
fragmentation, 153–160
framework based on respective values, 123–124
Hofstede theories, 251n
influence of, 126
marketing and, 34–41
organizational, 128–132
organizational vs. national, 127, 129
culture war, 86
in U.S., 84, 87

customers, salespeople's understanding of, 210

Darwin, Charles, 89
The Expression of the Emotions in Man and Animals, 247n
de Lauretis, Teresa, 241n
de Waal, Frans, 97–98, 249n
"Death Fugue" (Celan), 69
death penalty, 44
decision making, crowds and, 158
Democracy in America (Tocqueville), 19
Democratic party, 156, 184
religious belief and, 82
demography of world, change, 3
designer multilateralism, 117
Diamond, Jared, 235–236n
differences, vii
vs. commonalities as emphasis, 76
manager awareness of, 140
reconciliation of, 213
stressing, 200
disgust, 86
diversity, 3
cost of, 52–60
needed in science disciplines, 142
Putnam research on, 239n
in workplace, 56
divisions, Madison on, 154
dockakuka (Japan), 104
doctors, implicit bias, 239n
dot.com bubble, 198
drug charges, 236n
DuBois, W. E. B., 189
Duelfer Report (2004), 164, 255n
Dutch East India Company, 123
Dychtwald, Ken, 234n

e-mail, volume of reckless, 161
economic classes, transitioning between, 194–195
economic conditions, 185
economic growth, 193
migration patterns and, 177
Economic Policy Institute, 253n
economic risks, 116
economics, and psychology, 197
Edelman, Annual Trust Barometer, 110, 250n
eDiplomat, 252n
education
and class distinction, 189–190
and marriage, 259n

Egypt, public opinion on U.S. foreign policy goal, 242–243*n*
Eisenhower, Dwight, 210
Ekman, Paul, 247*n*
Elam, Deb, 58
electrical shocks experiment, 262*n*
emotion
    communication and, 91
    educating, 97
    and morality, 85
    primary, 90, 247*n*
    and reason, 97
    vs. reason, 165–166
    in workplace, 89–91
emotional filters, for viewing world, 164
emotional intelligence, 89, 247*n*
emotional mechanisms, commonalities, 85
empathy, 1, 93–94, 95, 209, 218
    animals and, 98
    decline, 96–97
    fairness and, 202
    horizontal, 141–145
    practical, 146–149
    self-reported by college students, 97
    and social class, 262*n*
employee affinity groups, 58–60, 240*n*
employees
    regaining confidence, 206
    Verwaayen communication with, 149
employers, 238*n*
end-of-life counseling, 171
English language, 24
    international business and, 133
Environmental Defense Fund, 112, 250*n*
Episcopal Church in the U.S., 63–64
Equal Employment Opportunity Commission, 240*n*
equality, optimism and, 193
Ernst & Young, 202
ethnic groups
    generational differences, 30
    and population growth, 34
ethnicity, celebrating, 57
ethnocentrism, 22
Europe, 24–25
    Muslims in, 73
    view of American religiosity, 83
European Union, 15
    Muslims in, 243*n*
evolutionary competition, 97
excluders, and excluded, 5

exclusion, 248*n*
    violence and, 92
executives
    ability to relate, 202
    attitudes about, 182
    see also CEOs
experience, and trust, 192
The Expression of the Emotions in Man and Animals (Darwin), 247*n*
external events, influence on behavior, 199
extreme position, viewing opinion, 158
eyewitness testimony, language variations, 136–137

Facebook, 256*n*
Facial Action Coding System (FACS), 247–248*n*
facial expressions, 90, 205
facts, and preexisting beliefs, 166
FAIR (Federation for American Immigration Reform), 232*n*
fairness, 1, 202
faith, 70, 75
    Beckwith on, 65
Faith Matters survey, 246*n*
families, single-parent, 30
fear, from inequality, 193
federal government
    Americans' view of, 153
    negative views of, 254*n*
Federation for American Immigration Reform (FAIR), 232*n*
FedEx, 112
feeling, 6
feeling thermometer, minorities and, 244–245*n*
femininity, in culture, 124
Fetzer, Joel, 15
Fine, Cordelia, 201
Fischer, Claude, 23, 188, 189, 254*n*
    Century of Difference, 186
fluent listening, 204–208
Food and Drug Administration, 143
food stamps, 194
Ford, Richard Thompson, 45–46, 237*n*
foreign aid, NGOs and, 111
foreign-born populations, 15, *see also* immigration
foreign currency, trading, 102
foreign language, *see* language
foreign markets, companies' learning about from NGOs, 110

foreign trade, 102
Founding Fathers, 158
Fox News, 169, 232*n*, 256*n*
fragmentation, 185
fragmentation of culture, 153–160
Francese, Peter, 31, 40
  American Demographics, 26–27
  on Hispanic families, 36
free-market competition, 98
French language, 137
friends
  diversity of opinions, 178–179
  political views and, 178
Frito-Lay, 36
Frost, Peter, 43
functional MRI (fMRI) research, 199, 239*n*
functional myopia, 144
fund-raising campaigns, of Lincoln Center, 215
fusion of horizons, 220

Gadamer, Hans-Georg, 220
Gallup organization, 182, 254*n*
  2010 Confidence in Institutions poll, 257*n*
  on same-sex marriage, 241–242*n*
  on prejudice toward Muslims, 244*n*
game theory, 52
gated communities, 195–196
gay marriage, *see* same-sex marriage
Gelman, Andrew, 156
gender, 4, 62
  of nouns, 137–138
gender bias, 4
gender identity, 4
gender pronouns, preferred, 62, 241*n*
gender stereotypes, 47
General Electric, 58–59, 112
General Mills, 31–32
  Para Su Familia, 36
  Qué Rica Vida, 32
General Social Survey, 186, 188, 258*n*
  on homosexuality, 241*n*
generalizations, 38–39
Generation X, 28
Generation Y, 28
generations, characteristics and values, 234*n*
genetic differences, race and, 42
German language, 137
gerrymandering, 177
Gibson, John, 232*n*
Gilfeather, John, 181–182

Gingrich, Newt, 72, 243*n*
Gini Index, 260*n*
Glazer, Nathan, 233*n*
  Beyond the Melting Pot, 20–21
Global Attitudes report, 246*n*
global businesses, environment of, 117
Global Industry Analysts, 237*n*
Global Mindset, 251*n*
  of manager, 131
global outlook, Americans and, 131
globalization, 14, 102, 108, 118, 249*n*
  simultaneous with localization, 104
  U.S. company efforts, 103
GLOBE study, 251*n*
glocalization, 104, 250*n*
goals, of Congress members, 155
God, 79
Golden Rule, 75
Goleman, Daniel, 247*n*
Google, 171
gossiping, 161
Graham, Franklin, 72, 243*n*, 245*n*
grandparents, 30
Great Recession, 89, 119, 189
  and unemployment, 194
greed, 98
Greenberg, Hank, 111
Greenwald, Anthony, 238*n*
gross domestic product (GDP), in U.S., 102
group identity, 220
groups
  anti-immigration, 232*n*
  behavior in, 199
  personal identity and membership in, 200
gut values, 84–88

Haass, Richard, 114–118
  The Bureaucratic Entrepreneur, 115
Haidt, Jonathan, 83, 84–88, 246–247*n*
Hamilton, Lee, 155
Hanson, Jon, 50
Harris Interactive, 237*n*
Harvard Business Review, 89, 101–102
hate crimes, 241*n*
Hayes, Randall, 112, 250*n*
heads of household, women as, 30
health insurance policies, 205–206
height, and leadership quality, 49
heterosexist language, 62
hierarchies, Verwaayen on, 147–148
Himmelfarb, Gertrude, 219

Hispanic-Americans, 5
  cultural briefing on, 38
  families, 35
  newspapers, TV and radio stations,
    233–234n
  population, 34, 234–235n
  second generation and mainstream culture,
    37
  women's view of mother's role, 31
  women's views of breakfast, 35
Hispanic immigrants, 44
Hofstadter, Richard
  "The Paranoid Style in American Politics,"
    172–173
  Social Darwinism in American Life, 249n
Hofstede, Geert, 123–125, 128–129, 136, 251n
Holzer, Harry, 230n
Homo sapiens, adaptations, 11
homogeneity, perspective on culture,
    124–125
homophily principle, 178
homophobic language, 62
homosexuals, 61–68
  religious views and, 83
horizons, fusion of, 220
horizontal empathy, 141–145
hospitality, 219–220
House, Robert, 129
housing market
  bubble, 198
  normalcy, 199
Hout, Michael, 186
human behavior, and American economy, 197
human nature, oversimplification of, 97
Human Resource Executive Online, 56, 240n
humor, 121–122, 251n
Huntington, Samuel, 71, 242n

IBM, 123
ignorance, 3
illegal immigrants, 12, 229n
Immelt, Jeff, 59
immigration, 11–13
  Americans' opinion of, 230n
  Arizona laws, 12, 229n
  efforts to restrict, 15
  Hispanic, 44
  hostility and, 15
  impact in U.S., 17
  name changes, 233n
  prejudice against, 188–189

  value to U.S., 25
Immigration and Nationality Act of 1965, 17, 21
immigration tsunami, 229n
implicit bias, 237n
Implicit Bias Test, 239n
implicit social cognition, 49–50, 238n
in-language media, 233–234n
income equality, 260n
income gap, senior management vs. line
    workers, 148
income inequality, 194, 260n
  and trust, 192
income, of women, 4
independent voters, 185
India, income and significance of religion, 79
individualism, 39, 179
  vs. collective culture, 123
Indonesia
  language, 138–139
  public opinion on U.S. foreign policy goal,
    242–243n
inequality, impact of, 193
Inglehart, Ron, 78
inside-out analysis, 116–117
institutions, trust in, 191–192
intellectual capital, and overseas assignment,
    131
interdisciplinary education programs, 143
intergenerational mobility, 183
intermarriage, religious, 81–82
international business, American companies
    and, 115
International Fund for Animal Welfare, 112
international migrants, 15
International Rescue Committee, 108, 109, 212
International Telecommunications Union, 117
Internet, 164
  isolation and, 168
  as news platform, 171
interracial and interethnic marriage, 23, 55,
    234n, 259n
investor psychology, 198
iPhone apps, on local customs, 252n
Iraq, weapons of mass destruction, 164
irony, 242n
Islam, 72
  intersection with Christianity, 75
  see also Muslims
ITT, 146

James, Harold, 249n

James, William, 1
Japan, *dockakuka*, 104
Javidan, Mansour, 130–132, 144
Jefferson, Thomas, 154
Johnson & Johnson, 182
Johnson, Lyndon, 17
jokes, 121–122, 251*n*
Journal of Experimental Psychology, 134
Justice Department, 13

Kagame, Paul, 110
Kang, Jeffrey, 238*n*
Keys, John, 109
knowledge of self, 201
Koreans, 5
Kosloff, Spee, 166
Kraft, 182
Krippner, Stanley, on humanity, 6
Kull, Steven, 243*n*
Kwintessential, 252*n*

labeling, 2
language, 41, 108, 252–253*n*
   acquisition of second, 133
   attitudes and, 134
   concept description and, 137
   reason to learn second, 134
   time markers in, 139
Laurie, Marilyn, vii–xii
leadership, 129–130, 210
   for cross-functional teams, 145
   height and, 49
   minorities in senior ranks, 240*n*
Lehrer, Jonah, 202
Leonard, Thomas, 249*n*
lesbian, gay, bisexual, and transgender
   (LGBT), 61–68
Lesser, Elizabeth, 96, 248*n*
Levitt, Ted, 31, 101–102
Levy, Reynold, 107–111, 212–216
liberals, 86, 218
limbic system, 91
Lincoln Center for the Performing Arts, 108,
   212–216, 263*n*
Lippman, Walter, 164, 179
listening, fluent, 204–207
literacy, of females, 118
local customs, respect for, 104
localization, simultaneous with globalization,
   104
localized products, vs. standardized, 102

logistic function, 186–187
Lopez, Ian Haney, 235*n*
loyalty, 85

Madison, James, 153–154
mainstream America, mythology of, 27
Malaysia, 79
Mallaby, Sebastian, 112
managers, 209
   awareness of differences, 140
   Global Mindset, 131
   income gap with line workers, 148
market research, 181
marketing
   culture and, 34–41
   multiculturalism and, 35, 39–40
   need for change, 31
   to older consumers, 29
marriage
   and education, 259*n*
   interracial and interethnic, 23, 55, 234*n*,
      259*n*
   interreligious, 81–82
   miscegenation laws, 218
   same-sex, 64, 67, 87–88, 218
Martin, Michel, 239*n*
masculinity, culture view of, 124
MasterCard, ad campaign, 211
Matson, Greggor, 254*n*
McDonald's, 39–40, 104, 112, 235*n*
McIntosh, Peggy, 48
McKinsey Global Institute, 249*n*
media campaigns
   of NGOs, 112
   and trust decline, 172
melting pot, 20, 232*n*
   myth of U.S. as, 18
Merck, 112
metacognition, 158
Mexico, 13
   importance of religion, 79
middle class, 233*n*
   new, 228*n*
   resentment of, 94
middlescence, 234*n*
migrants, *see* immigration
migration patterns, in U.S., 176–180
Milgram, Stanley, 262*n*
Miller, Matt, 194
minorities
   feeling thermometer and, 244–245*n*

minorities (*continued*)
    population growth, 228*n*, 234*n*
miscegenation laws, 218
misinformation, 164, 255*n*
    efforts to correct, 167
mobility, intergenerational, 183
Moltmann, Jürgen, 70
money, movement across borders, 14
monkeys, suspicion, 238*n*
Montagu, Ashley, 235*n*
Moore, Michael, 167
Moral Foundations Theory, 246–247*n*
moral values, 84–88
moralistic trust, 192, 193
morality, 246*n*
    different systems of, 219
Morocco, public opinion on U.S. foreign
    policy goal, 242–243*n*
Morris, Michael, 126–127
motivation to help, reciprocity and, 124
Moynihan, Daniel Patrick, 18, 20, 180
MSNBC, 169–170
MTV, in Europe, 103–104
multicultural communities, purchasing
    power, 34, 235*n*
multicultural marketing, 35, 36
multiculturalism, 21, 25, 27, 233*n*
    marketers and, 39–40
multigenerational country, 28
multilateralism, designer, 117
multinational companies, 102, 249*n*
    communication in English, 133
multiracial population, 23
Murray, Charles, 218
muscular liberalism, 234*n*
Muslim American Public Opinion Survey,
    243*n*
Muslims, 4–5, 72
    American, 72
    anger toward U.S., 243*n*
    basic values in Western societies, 73
    discrimination against, 244–245*n*
    in European Union, 243*n*
    prejudice against, 74, 77, 244*n*
myopia, functional, 144
MySpace, 256*n*

names, of immigrants, 233*n*
National Journal, 183
National Opinion Research Center (NORC),
    258*n*

National Security Agency, 250*n*
National Survey of Family Growth, 27
natural selection, 1
Nawrath, Michael, 253*n*
NBA basketball games, 239*n*
negative attitudes, research on, 181–182
negative stereotypes, 38
new ideas, adoption of, 187
new middle class, 228*n*
New York City
    Congressional districts contrast, 193
    ethnic groups, 20
    foreign-born populations, 233*n*
New York Times, 135, 213, 252*n*
    on Lincoln Center, 215–216
news sources, 169–171, 256*n*
    Internet as, 171
newspapers, 170
niche market, 27
9/11 Commission, 155, *see also* September 11,
    2001, attacks
nongovernmental organizations (NGOs),
    109–113, 116, 117–118
    growth in influence, 250*n*
    media campaigns, 112
Noonan, Peggy, 183
Nooyi, Indra, 119–120, 250*n*
the norm, 11
Northwestern University, 220
Novak, Esther, 36, 37–38, 110
Novartis Institutes for BioMedical Research,
    142, 143–144, 253*n*
Nyhan, Brendan, 164

Obama, Barack, 93–94
    rumors about, 162–163
    on working-class culture, 248*n*
Occupiers, 173
OECD Factbook 2010, 15
One Nation, After All (Wolfe), 21–22, 233*n*
online dating, race and, 240*n*
opinions
    diversity of friends', 178–179
    false information and, 164–165
    on news media, 170
optimism, equality and, 193
organizational culture, 128–132
Ortega y Gasset, José, 201
orthogonal thinking, xi
ostracism, 248*n*
Other, x, 200–201

fear of, 54
including, 201
interaction with, 203
meeting with one considered, 96
who is, 3–6
other-directed, 222
OtherWise, xii
fusion of horizons and, 220
how to be, 217–222
learning to control predispositions, 180
race and color and, 48
respect for individuals, 221
seeing through the Other's eyes, 92–98
Ouroussoff, Nicolai, 215–216
outside-in analysis, 116–117
outsiders, identifying, 50
overseas assignment, preparation for,
    130–131

Pakistan, public opinion on U.S. foreign
    policy goal, 242–243n
Palin, Sarah, 171
"The Paranoid Style in American Politics"
    (Hofstadter), 172–173
partisanship, and perceptions of reality, 156
partnership, with NGOs, 112
Patient Protection and Affordable Health
    Care Act of 2010, 171
peace, 70
people, movement across borders, 15
PepsiCo, 119–120
personal identity, 57, 214
group membership and, 200
perspective taking, 95
pessimism in U.S., 183
Pew Research Center
on American Muslims, 72, 74, 243n
on Arizona immigration laws, 230n
on conflict in U.S., 11, 228n
on cultural threats, 24
on "four freedoms," 246n
on immigration, 15, 229n, 231n
on news media, 170
on perceptions of Obama's religion, 162
on population growth, 228n, 234n
on race and marriage, 55, 240n, 259n
on social media, 256n
on teen texting, 255–256n
on values in U.S., 80, 84
Phelps, Fred, 62–63, 241n
point of view, considering another's, 95

polarization, 185, 254–255n
and public opinion, 156
political divisions, 185
political donations, 174
political factions, 154–155
political parties, religious belief and, 82
political points of view, exposure to alterna-
    tive, 157
political risks, 116
political segregation, 177
political spears, 166
political views, friends and, 178
politicians, 172
businesspeople learning from, 115–120
and cost for misinformation, 167
Poole, Keith T., 155
poor neighborhoods, in U.S., 195
population growth, 228n
shift in, 108
Portes, Alejandro, 22
poverty rate, 188, 258–259n
power distribution, 123
practical empathy, 146–149
preferred gender pronouns (PGPs), 62, 241n
prejudice, 43, 180
accumulation of, 160
babies' signs of, 1
against immigration, 188–189
against Muslims, 74, 77, 244n
reducing, 95
of specialists, 144
prejudicial thinking, 50
premarital sex, change in opinions, 188
presence, 209–211
presidential elections, county election returns
    in, 177
pride of employees, 206–207
Prio-Odio, Marian, 36–37, 38
privileges, 48
Procter & Gamble, 35, 36, 103
in China, 125–126
Chinese consumer market study, 105
goal in new markets, 105–106
products, standardized vs. localized, 102
psychic numbing, 98
psychological capital, and overseas assign-
    ment, 131
Psychological Review, 238n
psychology
and economics, 197
investor, 198

public confidence, 182–183
public officials, 238–239n
Public Opinion, 164
public opinion, 179–180
    analysis, 186
    and polarization, 156
    trends in U.S., 246n
purity, 85
Putnam, Robert, 54, 80, 192, 239n, 246n
    Bowling Alone, 52–53, 239n, 260n
    on religion, 55

quality of life, vs. survival, 78–83
Queer theory, 61–62, 241n
queerness, 61–68
quotas for immigrants, 16, 17
Quran, 74–75, 77

race, 42–51
    and marriage, 55
    Montagu on, 235n
    white vs. black perceptions of equality,
        47–48
race relations, in U.S., 45
racial profiling, 47
racist views, 17–18
rationality, 197–203
reading, decline, 97
Reagan, Ronald, 82
reason, and emotion, 97, 165–166
reasoning, 261n
    perspective taking as, 95
reciprocity, as motivator, 124
reconciliation, 69
Reifler, Jason, 164
relationships, vii
    college education and, 190
    social, xi
religion, 78
    conflicts from differences, 71
    and homosexuality, 63
    of Obama, 162–163
    tolerance, 81
religiosity, declining, 79
religious affiliations, 55
religious intermarriage, 81–82
religious right, 82–83
Republican party, 156, 184
    religious belief and, 82
research, functional MRI (fMRI), 199
research teams, diversity, 143

resentment, from inequality, 193
respect, 222
    for authority, 85
    for individuals, 221
    for local customs, 104
Revlon, 36
Riesman, David, 222
risks, political and economic, 116
river blindness, 112, 250n
Roberts, John, 164–165
Robertson, Roland, 104
Robinson, Michael, 246n
Roosevelt, Franklin, "four freedoms," 246n
Ross, Brian, 229n
Rowe, Jack, 159, 204
rumors, 161
Russell, Bill, 66
Rwanda, 109–110

S curve, 186–187
Saez, Emmanuel, 193
salespeople, understanding of customers, 210
Salins, Peter, 19–20, 232–233n
same-sex marriage, 64, 67, 87–88, 188, 218
    Gallup organization on, 241–242n
sanctity, 85
Scandinavian Political Journal, 239n
Schwartz, Barry, 197
scientific training, disciplinary boundaries,
        142–143
scientists, language and, 141
Selander, Bob, 134, 209–211
self
    knowledge of, 201
    sense of, 2
self-awareness, 90–91, 221
self-concept, 201
self-esteem, 220
self-expression, 246n
self-interest, 97–98, 197–198, 249n
self-isolation, 178
self-priming, 127
self-regulation, 90–91
self-righteousness, 87–88
Selig Center for Economic Growth, 34, 235n
senior citizens, baby boomers as, 29
separation of church and state, 81
September 11, 2001, attacks, 69, 72, 242n
    commission, 155
    opinions on, 164
sexual orientation, 67

sharing horizons, 220
"She-conomy," 235*n*
Shepard, Matthew, 63
Silver-Parker, Esther, 47
Singapore, AT&T in, 126
single-parent families, 30
Sinistra Proletaria, 249*n*
skin color, 42–43, 235–236*n*
slavery, 45
smartphones, 169
Smith, Adam, *The Wealth of Nations*, 219
Snopes.com, 161–162, 255*n*
social acceptance, barriers to, 22
social activists, 116
social capital, 52–53
    and overseas assignment, 131
social class, and empathy, 262*n*
social cognition, implicit, 49–50, 238*n*
social conflict, 228*n*
social context, emotional responses and, 97
Social Darwinism, 249*n*
Social Darwinism in American Life (Hof-
    stadter), 249*n*
social diversity, and expression of indepen-
    dent views, 58
social isolation, 53, 97
social lines, ability to redraw, 55
social media, 149, 161, 256*n*
social networks, 170–171
Social Psychology Network, 257*n*
social relationships, xi
    college education and, 190
social responsibility, 118
social science, data for, 78
society, fault lines in, 186
sociology, 186
Socrates, 168
South China University of Technology, 125
Southern Poverty Law Center, 232*n*
specialists, prejudices of, 144
Spencer, Herbert, 249*n*
standardized products, vs. localized, 102
state budget, 229*n*
Stein, Dan, 232*n*
stereotypes, 160, 179, 257*n*
    of Asians, 44–45
    gender, 47
    getting acquainted with one from group,
        96
    negative, 38
strangers, 2

perspective of issues, xi
strategic trust, 191
Street Peeper, 252*n*
suicide bombings, 72, 73
Sun Yat-sen University, 125
Sunstein, Cass, 254–255*n*
super-rich, views of success, 194
survival, vs. quality of life, 78–83
suspicion, 2, 50, 228*n*
    of immigrants, 231*n*
    from inequality, 193

Tadmor, Brigitta, 140, 145
Tajfel, Henri, 199–200
talk radio hosts, and cost for misinformation,
    167
Target, 174
Tatum, Beverly Daniel, 53–54, 57
Tea Party, 173, 184
teams, cross-functional, 144
television news, 256*n*
testosterone, and skin color, 43
texting, 169, 255–256*n*
Thatcher, Margaret, 16
theory of mind, 1
thinking
    categorical, 2–3
    language and, 134–139
    setting aside time for, 159–160
threat, 2
Time magazine, 232*n*
time markers, in language, 139
Tocqueville, Alexis de, 81
    Democracy in America, 19
tolerance, ix, 3–4, 68, 219
    religious, 81
Tommasini, Anthony, 216
traditional values, in U.S., 80–81
transnational adoptions, 220–221
Tribalat, Michèle, 73
trickle-down theorists, 98
trust, 191–196
    in cable news, 256*n*
    decline, 53
    media campaigns and decline, 172
Trust Barameter, 110
Turkle, Sherry, 256*n*
    Alone Together, 169

Ullmann, Berenike, 105
uncertainty, culture handling of, 123–124

understanding, 220
unemployed, 194
unemployment rate, 188, 258*n*, 259*n*,
    260–261*n*
Unilever, 38
uniqueness, 179
United Kingdom, Crest toothpaste in, 103
United Nations, 15, 69, 110
    World Food Programme, 111
United States
    change in, 3
    companies' globalization efforts, 103
    culture, 18, 24
    economy and quality of life, 80
    emotion vs. reason, 165–166
    gross domestic product (GDP), 102
    households, 27
    immigrants as threat, 16
    migration patterns, 176–180
    Muslims' anger toward, 242–243*n*
    poor neighborhoods in, 195
    prejudice against Muslims, 74
    stereotypes, 179
U.S. Bureau of Labor Statistics, unemploy-
    ment data, 258*n*
U.S. Census Bureau, 15
    New Immigrant Survey, 236*n*
    poverty rate, 258–259*n*
U.S. Congress
    members' goals, 155
    partisanship in, 155, 254*n*
U.S. Congressional Budget Office, 12
    on unauthorized immigrants, 229–230*n*
U.S. Immigration and Naturalization Service,
    232*n*
U.S. Postal Service, Eid stamp, 163
U.S. Supreme Court, Roberts nomination,
    164–165
unmarried women, births to, 30
UPS, 112
upward mobility, barriers to, 22
urban black culture, 46
us and them, 4
Uslaner, Eric, 191, 195

values, economic development and, 80
Verwaayen, Ben, 146–149
violence
    crime rate in Arizona, 230*n*

exclusion and, 92
Volf, Miroslav, 69–71, 75, 76, 172
    and identity, 201
Volpe, Joseph, 215, 263*n*

Wall Street Journal, 183
Walmart, 112
way of life, protecting, 24
The Wealth of Nations (Smith), 219
weapons of mass destruction, 164
websites, personalized content, 171
Welzel, Christian, 78
white privilege, 48–49, 238*n*
Williams, Kip, 248*n*
wisdom, 6
Wiseman, Richard, 121
Wolfe, Alan, *One Nation, After All*, 21–22,
    233*n*
Wolfensohn, James, 112
women, 4
    as heads of household, 30
    literacy, 118
    in management, viii
    Muslim treatment, 74
    Muslims in U.S., 72
workforce
    immigrant participation in, 12–13
    multigenerational, 29
    prime-age, 234*n*
working-class white Americans, resentment
    of, 94
workplace, emotion in, 89–91
world
    Americans' lack of knowledge on, 217
    emotional filters for viewing, 164
World Health Organization, 112
world values, 78–83
World Values Survey, 78, 79, 80, 246*n*
    trust in, 192
World Wildlife Fund, 112

Yahoo News, 171–172
Yang, Jeff, 106
Yo-Yo Ma, 22
Yugoslavia, 70–71

Zakaria, Fareed, 74
Zangwill, Israel, 232*n*
Zhou, Min, 22